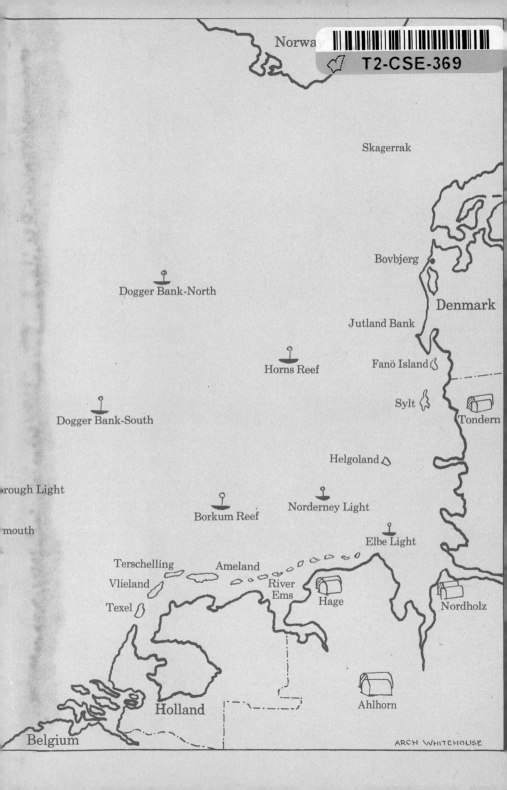

THE ZEPPELIN FIGHTERS

To Pete
Happy Reading
June 1968
With Love
Marian, Tony and Children

BOOKS BY ARCH WHITEHOUSE

Wings of Adventure
Hell in the Heavens
Hell in Helmets
Crime on a Convoy Carrier
The Real Book of Airplanes
Fighters in the Sky
The Years of the Sky Kings
Tank
The Years of the War Birds
Bombers in the Sky
Combat in the Sky
Squadrons of the Sea
Billy Mitchell
Action in the Sky
Legion of the Lafayette
Amphibious Operations
Subs and Submariners
Adventure in the Sky
Decisive Battles of the First World War
John J. Pershing
Heroes and Legends of World War I
Espionage and Counterespionage
Squadron 44
The Fledgling
The Early Birds
Heroic Pigeons
Spies With Wings
The Famous Fighting Ships
The Zeppelin Fighters
Fighting Wings
Frank Luke

Arch Whitehouse

The
Zeppelin
Fighters

DOUBLEDAY & COMPANY, INC.
GARDEN CITY, NEW YORK, 1966

Library of Congress Catalog Card Number 66–20955
Copyright © 1966 by Arch Whitehouse
All Rights Reserved
Printed in the United States of America
First Edition

Dedicated to
Captain Sir William S. Stephenson, M.C., D.F.C.
Royal Flying Corps

Received this book as
50th birthday present from
Tony & Marian Ciriscioli
1968

H. T. Chambliss Sr.

CONTENTS

INTRODUCTION

We who are well aware of the impact of atomic bombs, the power of nuclear fission, the high arcs of ballistic missiles and the devastation wrought by supersonic bombers, may look with contempt or amusement at the suggestion that German dirigibles of World War I could possibly cause widespread panic, destruction, or present a menace that could threaten a whole nation; or that flying an aircraft against such a vulnerable raider could, by any stretch of the imagination, be considered a risky assignment. After all, weren't those Zeppelins merely elongated variations of the old country-fair balloons, powered by a couple of modified automobile engines that fanned them through the sky at a most leisurely speed? And weren't those old airships inflated with hydrogen, a particularly flammable gas that would explode at the mere suggestion of a flame or spark? All an airman had to do was to take off, find the inflated raider—that usually was conveniently mounted on a tripod of searchlight beams—and fire a few short bursts of incendiary bullets.

It must have been as simple as that.

Zeppelin raids? What possible damage could those unwieldy gasbags do to a modern city? What kind of bombs were available, and how many could they carry? Who could take those Zeppelins seriously? You don't mean to say those old dirigibles could create widespread panic or paralyze a civilian population's will to resist such a hazardous method of attack? Besides, wasn't bombing from the air illegal?

The approach of a dirigible airship today would be looked upon with only casual interest, and from recent news reports there is a possibility that the Zeppelin-type airship may be restored to the air-transport lanes. Inflated with helium, a nonexplosive gas, the dirigible may resume commercial flights, particularly in the field of carrying freight.

But in the early months of World War I, as the writer can testify, raiding Zeppelins were quite capable of driving a certain portion of London's population to near panic. The damage they inflicted, perhaps minor compared to Hitler's bombings of 1940, was still considerable, and especially effective when we remember that no such attack had been made before on an unfortified city.

The early raids were terrifying, for they set up the threat of an enemy invasion—a dread that had been first aroused when Louis Blériot flew across the English Channel on July 25, 1909—and the declaration that Britain no longer was a secluded island was scrawled in blood spilled by the low-yield bombs dropped from Zeppelins. We must also remember that all military engagements are relative. Drake's scattering of the Spanish Armada, Nelson's victory at Trafalgar, or Admiral Dewey's triumphant move on Manila are little more than half-remembered panoramas put on at national exhibitions, compared to the Battle of Jutland or the savage naval engagements that spread death and destruction across the wide Pacific less than a quarter of a century later. But men died, grand ships went to the bottom and proud governments fell just as conclusively in Drake's, Nelson's, or Dewey's time. Bombs dropped by the Zeppelins of 1915–18 had exactly the same impact on the minds and bodies of Londoners as did those dropped by German Junkers, Dorniers, and Focke-Wulfs twenty-five years later. The difference was in the amount of bombs, the number of raids, and the type of explosive delivered. We might add that the fire-storm attack that leveled Hamburg was nothing more than a routine air raid when compared with the atomic attack on Hiroshima—and these disasters occurred about only two years apart.

Between 1915–18 German Zeppelins made 208 raids on Great Britain; a total of 5907 bombs were dropped, 528 people were killed, and 1156 wounded. These figures may not be impressive when set against the raids of 1939–45, but more than two hundred night raids had to be endured by a people who had enjoyed their island security for more than three hundred years. The more than five hundred people who were killed in these raids died just as dead as their descendants who perished in the rubble of London during the Great Blitz.

But what was worse, this proud people had to realize and then admit that in 1915 they had no reliable defense against the Zeppelin raiders. Meteorological conditions were usually in favor of the airship, and winds amicable to the Germans allowed the dirigible crews to rise to an easterly current that would carry them in silence over the British Isles. Since their engines were switched off, the explosive-laden airships would be over or near their targets long before the coast watchers had detected them, and on the release of their bomb loads, would then rise to even greater heights and make a safe return. The aeroplane pilots of that day were completely frustrated as it was unrealistic for them to take off until the Zeppelins had been spotted, and under such conditions it was impossible to gain sufficient height to engage them.

There were no weapons in the artillery inventory that could be sufficiently elevated to fire at the raiders, and few were capable of hurling an explosive shell to the level at which the dirigibles were flying. Thus it can be seen that we are not dealing solely with the threat of a new military weapon, the evasive airship, the unfamiliar thunder of engines overhead, the crash of explosive totally new to civilians, or the horror of seeing one's home sliced through its cross-section to display its inner intimacy to all who might stop and gaze. We are dealing with the reactions of a particular race of human beings who had long dreaded such indignities. It might be well at this point to ask the reader how he thinks he and his family would react under the same conditions. The civilian population of the Western Hemisphere has never endured such bombardments or suffered the indescribable terror of a nighttime air raid.

To repeat: we are dealing with the morale of people in a totally unfamiliar situation. Airmen who had only just mastered the primary rudiments of flying—few of them with any military background—were asked to perform what was almost impossible; take a very unmilitary machine to altitudes few of them had ever dared or experienced to engage a dreadnought of the skies—at night! Only a handful of British pilots of that day had been off the ground after darkness fell, and those who had risked the hazard had performed the feat in an aircraft that was hardly equipped for night flying. There were no reliable night-flying instruments, and those that were available did not have radium-illuminated dials or indicator needles. Cockpit lighting was in a very primary stage as not many designers had considered the possibility of their machines being called on to fly after dark.

There were no provisions for lighting the landing strips, and wireless, as it was then known, worked reasonably well from fixed ground stations or from ships at sea, but the equipment was bulky, heavy, and generally unsuited for the 1914–15 aeroplane. Thus, the airman ordered aloft to challenge a Zeppelin had no contact with the ground, once he had taken off to engage. He had to make the most of that all-important instrument, the Mark-I eyeball, and trust that the ground force might aid him by pointing out his target with searchlight beams. But, as was to be expected, there were dozens of searchlight beams flashing in all directions on Zepp nights.

Against all this we must accept the fact that Count Ferdinand von Zeppelin's marvel was an almost perfect flying machine for it had reached a high point of development with several years of successful air-transport history. The dirigible had been in the hands of skilled engineers for many years, and by 1914 hundreds of efficient crewmen had been trained on long flights made under the most propitious circumstances. It was an ideal craft for naval reconnaissance, most stable and comfortable in the air, and it could fly at a very respectable speed or hover for hours in any selected area. But a more important argument in its favor was that it could carry a reliable radio set and maintain communication with weather stations and signal its observations to the Commander-in-Chief.

So popular was the dirigible airship in Germany that for a time prior to the outbreak of war the heavier-than-air machine was almost completely ignored. Both the Army and Navy persisted in developing a standard of dirigible operations so that when the bugles rang out both services had trained ground crews and a number of lighter-than-air craft ready.

It can be seen, therefore, that with the exception of its flammable lifting gas, the Zeppelin had a tremendous edge on the London or Paris defenses, and this edge was enjoyed until an aeroplane could be produced that was capable of carrying light bombs and incendiary ammunition to the dirigible's working altitude. But the courage, determination, and service pride necessary to provide the competition required months of preparation. And, as we have learned about all military weapons, the new device is only as good as the hand that guides it.

The first Royal Naval Air Service airmen assigned to this frustrating work unquestionably were a breed apart. For one thing, they had to stand by in England, sitting out the weary months while their flying-school companions were across the Channel engaging the enemy. Over there was action, promotion, honors, and awards, but most of all the satisfaction of day-by-day accomplishment. Not so with the men of the Home Defense Establishment. They remained at home to suffer the taunts of the public, the frustrations of a hopeless job, and the tortures of the damned while they waited for their great chance.

But one day their chance came, and they responded in the Great Tradition. The undefended cities were boldly guarded, the darkness was no longer a quaking dread. Gradually, the scales were tilted, the tide turned, and with that the enemy had to, and did, put on a display of courage and heroic sacrifice that must be listed in the same column with that of their British adversaries. A campaign such as this we shall never see again.

Here, then, is the seldom-told story of these engagements, the details of these fantastic air raids—the first in the history of mankind—but above all it offers the bold stands made by the young men of Britain who never faltered in the gallant defense of their homeland.

AUTHOR'S NOTE

Any book that attempts to present years of technical history, varied personalities, and memorable battles, demands tireless research, volumes of accurate data, the experience of correlating such material and placing it where it will reflect its importance or interest in the main stream of the story.

Although I flew with the Royal Flying Corps from March 1917 to the end of the war, my duties did not reward me with any active participation in the Zeppelin menace. My only association with these dirigible raiders was when I was caught in air raids while spending leave in London. However, I had developed a keen interest in that phase of World War I history, and on several occasions in other books have attempted short features on the lives and experiences of several Zeppelin fighters. All this led to an inspiration to write a more complete history of this particular phase of aerial warfare.

I had collected much information and many books on the general subject, but lacked the important technical material. Then, by rare good fortune, I was introduced to Dr. Douglas H. Robinson of Pennington, New Jersey, who had spent several years gathering reliable data and photographs on the history of the German Naval Airship Service. To this end he had taken the time to learn the German language before probing through the available files, and then finding and interviewing survivors of those thrilling days. In fact, he had written a very valuable history titled *The Zeppelins in Combat* that had been published in a very limited edition in England. Unquestionably, this is still the finest work presenting the German side of the conflict that has ever been published. Unfortunately, it is now out of print.

Dr. Robinson became interested in my project, and invited me to his home to look at his library, and his files of other memorabilia relating to the military history of the Zeppelins. I was fascinated with his collections and his wide knowledge of the subject, and as a reward for my appreciation of his efforts, he handed me a copy of *The Zeppelin in Combat,* gave me permission to draw on the information therein, and to use it as a source book. He also provided many of the Zeppelin photographs presented in this book. I can only hope my work fulfills his kind expectations, or that it in some small way reflects my appreciation of his professional generosity.

I am indebted to Captain Sir William S. Stephenson, now a resident of Bermuda, who furnished me with the anecdotes relating to William Leefe Robinson. Sir William, formerly a member of Number 73 Squadron, Royal Flying Corps, and the victor over twenty-one enemy aircraft, was himself shot down late in July 1918, and because of his determined efforts to escape was quickly clapped in the infamous Holzminden POW camp where he met W. Leefe Robinson. The two became good friends and made several attempts to escape, but only Captain Stephenson was successful.

The Curator of Photographs, Imperial War Museum, in London, kindly provided several photographs and valuable information on the histories of the British airmen who were engaged in combating the enemy airships.

Arch Whitehouse,
MONTVALE, NEW JERSEY.
DECEMBER 11, 1965

Comparable ranks in the German services used in this book:

ARMY

U.S.	GERMAN
Major	Major
Captain	Hauptmann
1st Lieutenant	Oberleutnant
2nd Lieutenant	Leutnant

NAVY

U.S.	GERMAN
Commodore	Commodore
Captain	Kapitan zur See
Commander	Fregattenkapitän
Lieutenant Commander	Korvettenkapitän
Lieutenant	Kapitänleutnant
Lieutenant (jg)	Oberleutnant zur See
Ensign	Leutnant zur See

THE ZEPPELIN FIGHTERS

I

THE OPPOSITION

The Zeppelin airship, many will agree, was designed expressly for the destruction of England. Although the dirigible had to prove itself on the world's first network of commercial airlines, developed and supported by large funds willingly contributed by the German public, it eventually inspired the Imperial Staff with its possibilities as a long-range military weapon. Count Ferdinand von Zeppelin, himself, had no such intent once his airship had reached its peak, though during its early development he had toyed with the idea of providing the Fatherland with a weapon that would afford a military supremacy, and, in particular, nullify the strength of the British Royal Navy.

By 1914 the Count was an old man, and he must have regarded the organizing of the Army and Navy Airship services with as much regret as that of many idealistic inventors who lived to see their work channeled into the destruction of the civilization the invention had been designed to inspire and enrich. As a war weapon, the Zeppelin was actually armed and militarized by two subordinates of the Count, Commander Peter Strasser and Dr. Hugo Eckener.

The airship which still bears the Count's name has furnished a fascinating story, and how this German aristocrat became involved with lighter-than-air development is equally interesting. We first meet him when he was acting as a German Army military observer, together with a number of President Lincoln's Staff officers, during the Civil War. He was twenty-four years old at the time and became intrigued with balloons when he watched the noted Professor C. T. S. Lowe go aloft in a captive balloon and direct artillery fire on the Confederate lines. Count Zeppelin was a trained observer and unquestionably a valued military agent who had made the most of his friendly associations in France, Great Britain, Belgium, and Denmark. He was particularly interested in the defenses around Antwerp and the British military programs at Aldershot.

After his Civil War trip young Von Zeppelin made a balloon ascent at St. Paul, Minnesota—an experience that was to play a lead role in his life—and when he returned to Germany he began to consider a practical dirigible, an airship that could be guided about the skies just as an ocean liner is steered about the seas.

He, however, did not build the first engine-powered airship. That honor went to Paul Haenlein, a young German experimenter who had spent some time in England, and, in fact, was a member of Britain's Royal Aeronautical Society. Haenlein took out a patent in 1865 for the "Earliest Known Airship with a Semi-rigid Frame," which he later constructed in Germany. This machine was actually equipped with a gas-burning engine, the same coal gas with which the envelope was inflated. As fast as the engine consumed gas from the envelope, it was replaced with air pumped back in. By 1875 Haenlein had improved his machine to the point where it carried a car below the framework, an accommodation in which the crew, engine, and extras were carried, thus initiating a standard practice in the building of later dirigibles.

Another German who contributed much to the development of the dirigible, although receiving little credit for his efforts, was an East Prussian law student, Hermann Ganswindt, whose parents hoped he would become a learned judge, but their son proved to be a mechanical genius. During his long, hectic life, Hermann tinkered with fire engines, bicycles, engine-powered vehicles, motorboats, and airships. According to the well-known Willy Ley, he also planned a spaceship.

Born in 1856, Ganswindt became interested in the airship after he learned of the efforts of Stanislaus-Charles Henri-Laurent Dupuy de Lôme and Henri Giffard of France. In 1852 Giffard had built an elongated gasbag from which hung a metal tube that in turn bore a small control platform and a three-horsepower engine which drove a three-bladed propeller. Giffard had flown aboard this machine from the Paris Hippodrome and landed safely at Trappes. All very interesting and worth-while, but Ganswindt came to the conclusion that airships should be much larger than anything the inventors had devised so far, and putting his ideas on paper he eventually obtained a patent for a true dirigible, one capable of flying at a speed of fifty miles per hour. Anything less, Hermann argued, would, on encountering a normal wind, be turned into a free balloon.

We know now that Ganswindt had the right idea, but he did not have a suitable engine, nor could he gain the interest and financial backing of the German War Ministry.

In 1879 a banker, poet, and scientist, Dr. Edmund Clarence Stedman of New York, proposed a rigid airship that offered many similarities of the wartime Zeppelin. He borrowed his design from fish, and because aluminum was too costly at that time his framework was to be built of steel, brass or copper tubing. In one version he placed a tractor propeller in the bow of the framework, but later placed an engine with two screws below the main framework. No such airship was ever completed and flown, but Dr. Stedman was well ahead of Count Zeppelin in the concept of a dirigible airship.

However, full credit goes to the German nobleman, for on July 2, 1900, he made his first flight with a rigid airship when he soared over Lake Constance, establishing a new era of aerial navigation. The machine, which had been built in a floating shed, was 420 feet long and 38 feet wide with a full-rigid framework of aluminum trussing covered with linen and silk that was treated with pegamoid, a trade name for a waterproof formula. Inside the hull were seventeen compartments, many of which carried ballonets to hold the hydrogen gas. Two gondola cars were swung below the hull framework, and each accommodated a 16-horsepower naphtha engine. The engines drove a pair of four-bladed propellers. The airship was steered by vertical rudders and maintained equilibrium by means of a three-hundred-pound weight that was slid back and forth to raise or lower the nose.

The first flight of LZ.1 (*Luftschiff Zeppelin*) as she was known, was far from a rousing success, but she did remain in the air for about eighteen minutes while carrying five people. The effort ended when the weight control broke, causing the main framework to buckle, and the rudder controls fouled. Later, it was reported that LZ.1 had reached a height of 1300 feet, but because one of her propellers had refused to twirl she could do no better than eight miles an hour.

Three months later, in October 1900, LZ.1 had been overhauled, several improvements had been added, and her structural weaknesses corrected. Once more the sixty-two-year-old former lieutenant general of cavalry, Count Zeppelin, took her aloft, and this time she flew for more than eighty-five minutes, and might have remained in the air longer, but a mechanic had mistakenly poured distilled water into one of the fuel tanks. However, during this flight she made several sweeping turns over Lake Constance and attained a speed of twenty miles per hour. Sightseers who thronged the shore near Manzell gave her a rousing reception when Count Zeppelin brought her back to her hangar without the slightest mishap.

A third flight was made a week later, on October 24, and again misfortune marred the effort. The framework proved to be structurally unsound, and the Count could keep her in the air for only twenty-three minutes. And with that the old soldier accepted defeat, broke up the airship, sold the aluminum for scrap, put the engines and hangar up for sale, and decided to liquidate his company. The news of his capitulation brought sorrow to many Germans, and the then King of Württemberg, a state in the southwest angle of Germany, feeling smpathetic toward the aging aeronaut, set up a state lottery that netted 124,000 marks, and this fund was handed over to the Count to continue his work.

With this money and other generous donations from various sources, Zeppelin built another dirigible, *LZ.2*, that had the same dimensions as the previous airship, but was much stronger and had two engines that produced five times more propulsive power. The sliding weight device was replaced in this model by horizontal rudders.

The history of *LZ.2* offers several conflicting features, but she probably was test-flown on November 30, 1905. This was a pleasant, sunny autumn day at Manzell but a trifle gusty for airship handling. Dr. Hugo Eckener, a native of Flensburg who was living nearby while writing a book on economics, had been asked by the editor of the *Frankfurter Zeitung* to prepare an article about Count Zeppelin and his airship operations.

Eckener, who was striving to acquire a lectureship, was somewhat bored with the assignment. By this time the old Count was considered by many people to be something of a crank, a queer character who was wasting family funds with this hopeless, almost childish folly of building airships. There were many amusing stories going the rounds.

With his mind full of figures and problems of economy, Hugo Eckener no doubt felt he was wasting his time on this ridiculous quest for an improbable means of transportation, but the article would bring in a few marks, so he wandered down to the lake and, instead of presenting himself at the hangar, stood out on a small peninsula to watch the proceedings as the airship was being walked out of its floating shed. He was not totally ignorant of Count Zeppelin's efforts for he had seen one of the flights of *LZ.1* several years before and he had some general knowledge of the structural details of the new airship. But to his orderly mind this business of aerial navigation was not much more than a circus-like carnival to entertain sightseers.

He watched the airship rise and take off, but after she had gained a little height it was seen that the forward propeller ceased to turn, but the aft airscrew kept churning. Then the stern of the framework started to drop until it touched the water, and with that the steering rudders were snapped off. Someone switched off the rear engine and the airship leveled again. Then as everyone began to breathe with relief the wind increased and the airship was driven toward the mountainous shore on the Swiss side of the lake. The throng of spectators gasped, fully expecting to see the great airship become a total wreck.

At this point a mob scene occurred, somewhat akin to the comic movies of that time. As the battered airship promised a dizzy climax, rescue and salvation came from an unexpected source. A dock worker jumped into a fast motorboat, roared off and caught up with the drifting *LZ.2*. A line was dropped from the gondola, taken by the motorboat skipper, and the big dirigible was towed back to its dock.

Half amused, half contemptuous, Dr. Eckener returned home and wrote a short article which plainly indicated he felt there was no rewarding future in lighter-than-air navigation.

The *LZ.2* was returned to its shed and the mechanics went through the labors of checking the engines and giving them a complete overhaul. By January 17, 1906, she was ready for her second trial. Again Dr. Eckener was asked to cover the flight, and as he walked out to the lake front he noticed that though the weather was still good with lots of sunshine, a few clouds high above were moving across the sky at a good pace. He wondered whether the dirigible really had the power to buck that kind of opposition, or whether the Zeppelin would become a free balloon.

The *LZ.2* was once more walked out to her float and when the engines were started she cast off and seemed to rise rapidly. Eckener figured that she had reached an altitude of about 1700 feet. The propellers twirled and flashed in the sun, and from the ground it appeared she was racing across the lake at a speed well over thirty miles per hour. Eckener agreed that she would have to produce such speed to compete with any reasonable head wind.

The crowd along the lake shore roared its approval, and all were certain Count Zeppelin was at last on the air trail to success. Then, suddenly it was seen that the propellers were no longer turning, and looking through a telescope Dr. Eckener could see the crew in the forward gondola working desperately to get the engines going again.

There have been many varied accounts of what happened next, but evidently the strong south wind was too much for the helmsman. *LZ.2* began to drift back toward the lake shore. Because there was no slipstream to afford leverage, the rudder was of no use, and, completely helpless, the dirigible was twisted and turned until she was taking the full force of the wind along her length. Under these conditions *LZ.2* continued to drift until she disappeared from view.

A few hours later the news reached Friedrichshafen that the Count's *LZ.2* had crashed at Kisslegg. When the dirigible came down the stern section was fouled in a large tree. The only real damage occurred in that section, but with the hours the wind increased and the great framework was slammed back and forth, breaking several circular ribs. This grounded the ninety-ton airship for good, and it had to be dismantled with axes, saws, and cutting torches. Dr. Eckener, who had hurried to the scene of the crash, watched this demolition, and then wrote another article for the *Frankfurter Zeitung*.

He commented that although the airship had taken off smartly, she had not behaved well under comparatively high speed. Then, when she lost her power, she appeared to be helpless under the stress of the forces of weather, and he suggested that some framework buckling could have resulted. If so, it may have fouled the long, rigid transmission-control systems running from the gondola to the engines. This stress could also have buckled the propeller shafts. In his closing statement Eckener pointed out that the form of Count Zeppelin's airship was ill-adapted for high-speed propulsion through the air. It was an interesting comment, for Dr. Eckener was more than a student of economics; he was a splendid yachtsman, and a better than amateur engineer.

A few weeks later an aristocratic gentleman, clad in smart morning clothes and radiating a military bearing, arrived at Dr. Eckener's home. A housemaid darted into the doctor's studio and announced breathlessly that a gentleman who was outside wished to speak to the *Herr Doktor*.

Eckener frowned for he was seldom interrupted at this hour of the morning.

"Did he give his name?"

"*Graf* Zeppelin, *Herr Doktor*." (*Graf* is the German word for count.)

This announcement set up a general scramble as the doctor's wife rushed their children's playthings into the nursery, and Eckener tried to find the reason for this unusual visit.

"Show the *Graf* into the drawing room and tell him I'll be with him immediately."

Dr. Eckener had seen Count Zeppelin in ordinary business clothes on the street and in workman's coveralls at the scene of the crash at Kisslegg, but was somewhat surprised, on entering his drawing room, to find an aristocratic gentleman in formal clothes, looking the accepted picture of a retired cavalry officer.

There are again several versions of what transpired during this meeting, but Thor Nielsen, in his fine work *The Zeppelin Story*, seems to have presented a reliable report from which the conversation along the following lines might be reconstructed.

The peppery visitor wasted little time with formalities.

He took a copy of the *Frankfurter Zeitung* from a pocket, and flourished it as a matador would his cape.

"I take it you write for this newspaper."

"A part-time association, sir."

"You are an engineer, *Herr Doktor?*" the Count snapped.

"Not exactly. I am an economist."

"An economist."

"But I am also a sailor. I was brought up in Flensburg, so I know something about wind pressures . . ."

"Which, of course, makes you an aeronautical engineer," the Count replied, but his eyes twinkled and he said, "Never mind, my boy, this is a remarkable article. Very interesting."

"If I made any mistakes, I hope you will correct me."

"You drew some inaccurate conclusions, but you were not far wrong."

"After all, I was not aboard, sir."

The Count became very amiable. "Perhaps next time. But there was no frame distortion . . . not enough to affect the power transmission, but you have a good point. The real cause was failure of the carburetors. They have not been modified for aeronautical purposes."

Hugo Eckener listened to further details, but his mind dwelt on the reason for this visit. Why had the Count taken the trouble to call and present a lecture on internal combustion engines?

"Carburetors can always be fixed with a set of small tools," the Count added.

"Of course."

"However, as I said, you have a keen mind," the Count went on. "I should explain that we do have one real problem, and I'm glad that you noted it and made a sound comment. It is difficult to keep a rigid airship on course . . . for it tends to be unsteady on its longitudinal axis, but all that will be corrected in the next one I build."

"You are going to build another?" Eckener said with some surprise.

Count Zeppelin ignored the question. "It has come to my

attention, through one of my collaborators, that the French have built small steering surfaces into their balloons; they call them *empanage*. They act like feathers on an arrow. I intend to build such small rigid steering surfaces into the stern of my next airship. Now what do you think of that, *Herr Doktor?*"

But Eckener had no response, except to remark that he hoped such a feature would work.

All smiles, the Count rose from his chair and held out his hand.

"I must be going. You are perhaps very busy?"

"It has been very interesting."

"Good! If in the future you should need more information about my airship for another article, please come and see me. I shall be delighted to see you," and with that the old Count pulled on his yellow gloves, tapped on his top hat and marched out smartly swinging his cane. Eckener accompanied him to the garden gate still pondering on the meaning of the visit.

At lunch an hour or so later, Mrs. Eckener made a natural inquiry. "Well, what did your important visitor want?"

"Oh, nothing much. He was telling me a few details about his last flight."

"Tell me, does the *Graf* talk or act as silly as many people intimate?"

Hugo came back from a short reverie. "Far from it. Not at all. But still—one can't be sure. Amazingly enough, however, after several failures he still plans to build another."

Mrs. Eckener who was blessed with or burdened with women's intuition said, "You'd better get on with your book. That's more important than airships."

Three days later Dr. Eckener received a formal note from Count Zeppelin. It was an invitation for dinner at the *Deutsches Haus* later that week. Hugo lit a cigar and considered the letter: "What now?" he said to his wife. "I told him clearly that I am an economist, and only a part-time journalist. What can he want of me now? He can't possibly believe that anyone will pour more money into his expensive hobby. The man is a stubborn optimist, and in practical matters as guileless as a child."

But Dr. Eckener could not turn down the invitation; there was the matter of social politeness, but if he accepted, he intended to make it fully clear that he was a busy man and had no extra time to devote to the economics of aeronautics or the publicizing of airships. At best it was a harebrained venture.

So Dr. Eckener accepted and on the night in question was warmly greeted at the hotel by the Count who was most friendly, and whose courtly manners were charming. The old gentleman had two rooms in the hotel, although his home was in Stuttgart.

There was good food, unobstrusive service, and the best of wine. The Count spoke of his past, and explained that he had retired as a lieutenant general of cavalry at age fifty-two. He had faced many years of idleness until he took up a science that had attracted him many years before when he was a military observer during America's Civil War. He had also been intrigued with the story of Léon Gambetta who, on October 8, 1870, during the Franco-Prussian War, had escaped from besieged Paris and landed in Tours by using a balloon.

"But they were simply spherical balloons, borne by the prevailing winds," chided Hugo Eckener.

"Of course, but we shall someday build a dirigible that will fly great distances, carrying passengers and freight. We may even build and fly military dirigibles. There could be a great future for Germany in such a machine."

The two men exchanged knowing glances.

"It is amazing that you have been able to get people with money interested in your venture."

"It wasn't easy, and yet I had the example of the French who had achieved some results with powered balloons, so I first tried to interest the German Army—from the military point of view—but they ignored me. By good fortune I became acquainted with a young engineer, Theodor Kober, and it was he who drew my first blueprints and produced the basic principles of construction—a series of transverse rings or frames joined together by longitudinal members. I took out a patent on this in 1895."

For the rest of their evening together the Count fascinated Eckener with the motley history of the dirigible airship; his problems, his trials, his ill fortune. The younger man was proud of the intense loyalty Von Zeppelin had for his Fatherland. The Count was completely convinced that the dirigible airship would one day place Germany at the pinnacle of world power.

"To the Fatherland," the *Graf* said when another bottle of wine had been brought in.

Their glasses clinked and when they sat down, Hugo said, "My dear *Graf*, could I be of any help?"

The old gentleman simply smiled. He must have known his cause had won.

Hugo went on, "I know little, or nothing about airships, but I am a writer and there is power in the pen. I was once a student of psychology and that combined with the written word . . ."

"Please go on."

"As I see it, one of your problems is to sell government officials and technical experts on the practical value of the airship. But a second problem, perhaps more important, is to convince the man on the street. Once you get the public behind you, you will have a strong influence to turn on the experts."

"I have become interested in the military value of the dirigible," Count Zeppelin countered, "and I am not sure the man on the street would be interested in supporting a new weapon of war."

"Let us concentrate on the dirigible as a means of transportation. Remember how enthusiastic the crowds were when you last flew out over the lake? I am positive I can bring the general value of the airship to the German people."

"We must talk more," the Count decided.

As a result of that dinner and the personal appeal of the old Count, Eckener gave considerable attention to publicizing the military and commercial value of the dirigible. So well was this labor of friendship carried out in so many newspapers and technical magazines, a nationwide response was enjoyed. Over the following year Count Zeppelin, with money donated by various associations and another lottery, financed and built a third Zeppelin, LZ.3, which in its first two trial flights covered more than sixty miles on each run. Dr. Eckener made the most of these accomplishments through a number of articles, and in response the Airship Committee of the German War Ministry contributed half a million marks to the development of the Zeppelin.

Up to this time the government had been placing its hopes in a powered balloon constructed by Major August von Parseval who at the command of Emperor Wilhelm had produced an elongated bag fitted with a rudder and elevators from which hung a small gondola carrying an engine that twirled a large four-bladed propeller.

At this point several of Eckener's articles on economics had also attracted some attention in that field, and as a result he was offered the editorship of the *Flensburger Nachrichten,* a first-rate bourgeois newspaper owned by Friedrich Maass, his brother-in-law. The salary was good and the work of some importance, but if he accepted it meant that the Eckeners would have to leave their Friedrichshafen home and return to Flensburg. It also meant that Hugo would have to forsake his nearly finished book and miss the opportunity for a lectureship—all his plans for the future. It also meant he would be deserting Count Zeppelin and the great plan to perfect the dirigible airship.

After some lengthy consideration, and following his first flight aboard the LZ.3, Eckener decided that as the editor of a good newspaper he would be linked closely with the main current of events of the whole nation. He would, generally speaking, have his finger on the public pulse, and while at Flensburg he might have a chance of a lectureship at the University of Hamburg. Considering all this, he took the plunge, forsook Friedrichshafen and returned to his home town of Flensburg.

His new job proved to be a bleak disappointment for he was greeted with cold disdain by the other employees who naturally felt that a touch of nepotism had cropped up, and that other, worthier men had been ignored. Hugo also soon discovered that a provincial newspaper was no place for a man who hoped to write and publish the kind of articles he had planned. After weeks and months of disappointment and frustration, Eckener was offered early in 1908 the post of Industrial Editor of the *Hamburger Fremdenblatt*.

This was a trifle better for in this post Hugo was again able to take some interest in the development of the dirigible airship. By August 1908 Count Zeppelin had built a fourth dirigible, *LZ.4*, with which he planned to attempt a twenty-four-hour endurance flight. On hearing of this Eckener hurried down to Friedrichshafen to cover the event, for he had learned that if this endurance test was successful, the government might buy one, and perhaps two, dirigibles for military service.

When he arrived at the Lake Constance dock he was also told some of the detailed requirements concerning the test. The airship would not only have to stay in the air for a full day but would have to cover a distance of 440 miles in that time and then return safely to its hangar. Eckener saw the importance of this test. If it was successful Germany would buy the *LZ.3* as well as the newly completed *LZ.4* for which the Count would receive 2,500,000 marks. If the attempt failed the old Count would be left with only his memories, the two airships and the hangar, but no future.

Dr. Eckener tried to see the bright side of the picture. The summer before the Count had flown *LZ.3* for twelve hours, an effort that marked his sixty-ninth birthday. Hugo saw *LZ.4* off with Count Zeppelin at the controls, and then waited for reports to come in. The whole of Germany halted with bated breath for news on the progress of the flight.

The plotted cruise ran from Basle over Strassburg and Speyer to Worms. *LZ.4* was reported moving with majesty over Worms and heading for Mainz. Then a number of telephone calls failed to keep track of the dirigible, but there was a good weather report. Finally, a telephone rang, and Count Zeppelin's voice came through. "That you, Eckener? We are down. Oh, we landed safely, but the forward engine broke down again. We have the mechanics working on it, and I trust we can soon take off once more."

"Can we do anything from here?"

"No. I am just concerned about the gas cooling off which makes us a little heavy. If we do manage to get off, I may have to leave two or three of the crew here and some of the equipment." With that Count Zeppelin hung up, and Dr. Eckener had to sit and worry over the next few anxious hours.

The people of Friedrichshafen were already decorating the town for the *Graf's* return. Still, no further news from Zeppelin, nor had anyone in Mainz seen anything of a dirigible airship. Then at midnight someone in the Mainz police department called Eckener and shouted over the telephone, "Your airship has just flown over the town. Then it turned and headed southward."

Eckener gasped. "The *Graf* is making a night flight!"

Everyone at the airship dock tried to snatch a little sleep. The early newspapers came out with the reports that the Zeppelin had reached Mainz, but after that there was no more news, good or bad. Six more hours ticked away, and then from Stuttgart came a message that the forward engine had burned out a shaft bearing while approaching Mannheim. The *Graf* had decided to fly to Stuttgart, land there and hope that Daimler's factory could send out men and equipment to make necessary repairs. It was learned later that the dirigible had actually landed near the village of Echterdingen with no damage of any kind.

Eckener was sad, but cheered by the fact that the dirigible could be landed safely under such conditions. Two safe landings in open country ought to convince Berlin that the

Graf had a reliable machine. Who would want more evidence of the dirigible's reliability?

Then, later that afternoon another telephone call came through from Stuttgart, and Dr. Eckener fully expected to hear that *LZ.4* had been repaired and had taken off again. Instead, he heard, "This is Daimler's in Stuttgart. The Zeppelin caught fire . . . it is burned . . ."

A sudden storm had come up and had snatched the airship out of the hands of a force of soldiers who had been marched in to act as a ground crew. The high wind that tore the big dirigible from the men who held the guy ropes, raised it high and then smashed it to earth. The airship caught fire, and its blackened and gaunt skeleton lay across the open field in sharp contrast against the lingering sunset.

It was a portent of disasters to come.

As Dr. Eckener went to the railroad station, hoping to get a train for Stuttgart, he caught a new surge of public enthusiasm. The stationmaster explained it.

"The *Graf* will be able to build again! Contributions are pouring in from all over Germany. A manufacturer in Ludwigsburg started it with a donation of 50,000 marks. The factories and banks are joining in."

On the train the talk was of nothing but Count Zeppelin. "He'll have more money in no time. The whole nation is behind the *Graf.*"

By the time Hugo had caught up with Count Zeppelin in Friedrichshafen he was sitting before a pile of telegrams. More than 100,000 marks had been donated for him to build again. Before many days had passed the sum had reached 6,000,000 marks!

Some Germans believed that *Graf* Zeppelin could become a second Bismarck.

A few days later Dr. Eckener was sent for again, and once more he left his cozy study in Hamburg and traveled to Friedrichshafen where he was met by thirty-five-year-old Alfred Colsman who was a member of a firm that had supplied the Count with the aluminum used in the dirigible framework. A short time before the Echterdingen disaster Herr Colsman had offered to assist in organizing a new Zeppelin company, and by now had actually taken up the program. This generalization was talked over in the Count's office, and then Colsman and Eckener repaired to the dining room of a nearby hotel, and over wine and cigars Colsman explained that because of the *Graf's* rising popularity; the large amount of money being contributed for further development; and official Berlin's interest in the dirigible as a new means of transportation, it had been decided that a Zeppelin Foundation—a trust organization that would act as the parent company of the Zeppelin Airship Company—would have to be organized. Colsman outlined the plan and named the men who were to have the important executive positions. Eckener was offered a post as a public relations man, and after lengthy talks, refusals, pleadings, consideration, and guile, Dr. Eckener became something of an economic adviser, publicity man, and legal mind.

The Zeppelin Airship Company, Ltd. was finally organized toward the close of 1908, and the Eckeners headed back to Friedrichshafen. A few weeks later the Kaiser made a personal visit to the Lake Constance dock and there decorated Count Zeppelin with the Order of the Black Eagle, calling him the "greatest German of the century."

Dr. Eckener who had wished to write books, lecture on economics, and pursue the life of a university professor, was caught up in the world's newest industry—aerial navigation.

By reading between the lines of the books written about the Zeppelin Airship Company, Ltd. it can be seen that by now Dr. Eckener saw the dirigible only as a weapon of war. When asked who he thought was going to buy their airships, he said, "Why, the German Airship Battalion, of course."

Alfred Colsman was a remarkable organizer, and shortly after the new company had been set up, he concluded an arrangement with Karl Maybach in which they jointly founded the Aircraft Engine Construction Company, Ltd. in Bissingen. Later, about 1912, the factory was moved to Friedrichshafen where it became the Maybach Engine Construction Company.

All this took place at about the same time. An aircraft engine plant was going up, while the new Zeppelin company was moving its offices into its new accommodations. The future of the dirigible was very bright. No longer were airships built in a floating hangar on the lake. Now they were being constructed in a modern factory on a broad, flat field. Nearby internal combustion engines, designed for aerial propulsion, were being turned out by teams of experts. Had the engines matched the airframes, there is no telling how the story might have ended.

When Dr. Eckener was shown his new office he learned that the company had delivered the old *LZ.3* to the German Airship Battalion in Metz, but only after the dirigible had been lengthened about fifteen feet. This airship was to be known as Army Airship *Z.1*. The *LZ.5*, then being built in the old lake hangar, was to be delivered to the Army base at Cologne, and was to be known as Army Airship *Z.2*. The first Zeppelin to be built in the new plant, listed as *LZ.6*, was being constructed on speculation as it had not as yet been ordered by any government department. Count Zeppelin had great hopes that the German Navy would take *LZ.6*, but there was no assurance that such a sale would be made.

Colsman had other plans. It was he who first conceived the idea of a practical air line, using dirigibles, but strangely enough, the Count now frowned on this for he felt that putting his beloved airships into transportation service was nothing more than cheap commercialization of his invention. Eckener saw the merit of Colsman's plan, but thought that he was being somewhat hasty as the Count's airships had not really proved themselves. His chief argument was that up to date the Maybach engines had failed to perform to expectations, particularly in the transmission of power from the engines to the propellers.

But Colsman had his way, and at Frankfurt-am-Main the German Airship Transport Company was founded in November 1909. He arranged an International Airship Exhibition and invited all German mayors to examine the plans, bid for airline connections and possibly invest in the company. The Count was won over, and personally landed the LZ.5 at the exhibition while making its delivery to the Army at Cologne. The mayors of four large cities were ready to advance a sum of three million marks to get the German Airship Transport Company into the air.

One day while a dirigible was being displayed to a group of potential investors, a new type of aircraft arrived and landed on the Frankfurt field. This machine had wings—not gas cells—and it was propelled through the air by a tractor airscrew. The crew of the Zeppelin looked at this queer machine in mild amusement. The pilot came forward and introduced himself.

"Good afternoon. I am August Euler."

Dr. Eckener bowed and shook hands. "That is quite a hedge-hopper you have there." Everyone, including the aeroplane pilot, laughed. Euler was taken aboard the dirigible, and was amazed to see the comfort and convenience of the passenger cabin.

"It will be a long time before aeroplanes will be able to take such loads into the air," he admitted. "By the way, do airship pilots require licenses?"

"Of course," Eckener explained. "I myself hold Number 10."

"Ah." Euler smiled. "I have you beat in this. I am Germany's Number 1 aeroplane pilot."

Dr. Eckener was a trifle flustered at that, but laughed, enjoying the joke on himself. He could not know that one day, not too far off, this hedge-hopper type of aircraft would take its place in a war and eventually drive the gas-filled dirigible out of the skies.

II

THE PLANS FOR ARMAGEDDON

But the rest of the world was not standing by while Dr. Eckener continued his formidable build-up of Count Zeppelin and the giant dirigibles. A United States Army officer, Lieutenant Frank P. Lahm of the 6th Cavalry, won the World's First Balloon Cup race when he was awarded the James Gordon Bennett Aeronautic Cup in 1906. With Major Henry B. Hersey, one of Teddy Roosevelt's Rough Riders, Lieutenant Lahm piloted the spherical balloon *United States* from Paris, across France, crossing the English Channel at night, and landing at Whitby, Yorkshire, covering the 410 miles in twenty-two hours, seventeen minutes. An Italian was second, and a Frenchman third.

The Brazilian coffee tycoon, Alberto Santos-Dumont, made the first heavier-than-air flight in Europe in 1906. The Wright brothers had first flown a powered plane three years before, but the aeroplane was making slow progress. In 1907 a French dirigible *La Patrie*, the third such airship built by the Lebaudy brothers, French sugar refiners, flew with considerable success for the French Army. It was piloted by an aeronaut named Juchmes. But in November 1907 she was torn from an insecure anchorage and swept across France, England, and Ireland to disappear over the Atlantic. The Lebaudy ships were semirigids, that is to say they were stiffened with a curved central rib to which the bag was attached and the power gondola hung.

Great Britain took up the lighter-than-air machine in 1907 when Colonel J. S. Cooper and Samuel F. Cody, an American airman, built and flew a semirigid airship for the Royal Engineers. This machine, named *Nulli Secundus*, was destroyed during a heavy rainstorm, but she encouraged further research in that field of aerial navigation.

The United States saw some country-fair exhibitions by Captain Thomas S. Baldwin, Captain Horace B. Wild, Lincoln Beachy, and Roy Knabenshue who devoted much time to the development of these primitive, cigar-shaped balloons that carried bamboo catwalks and low-powered engines.

The Farman brothers in France gave huge impetus to the development of heavier-than-air craft when Henri broke all kinds of records with his Voisin-type biplanes, and further interest was created when the *Scientific American* magazine offered a large trophy to be competed for by heavier-than-air machines.

But the balloon and dirigible were still high in the public's mind, and in 1907 a Major Von Gross of the German Army who commanded the Balloon Battalion at the aeronautic base at Tegel, a suburb of Berlin, designed the Gross Auto Balloons, a succession of which were built under his supervision for maneuvers with German troops in military war games. Kaiser Wilhelm financed Gross, and the Kaiser's brother, Prince Henry, and the German Crown Prince flew as passengers on numerous occasions. As a result of this a very friendly rivalry developed between Major Von Gross and Major August von Parseval of the Bavarian Army whose motor balloons were also used in maneuvers. In fact, in 1913 Great Britain ordered a Parseval type for the Royal Navy and it was flown over Brooklands and London by a German officer, August Stelling, and three mechanics. The only Britisher aboard was the then Captain Murray F. Sueter, first Director of the Naval Wing of the Flying Corps.

During the year 1908 when Count Zeppelin was enduring

his trials, a number of Americans were concentrating on the development of the aeroplane. The Wrights had reached a point where they could fly twenty-five or thirty miles in a complete circle. Wilbur Wright had taken one of their biplanes to France where he was giving amazing exhibitions, while Orville Wright remained in the United States where he hoped to sell a biplane to the United States Army for reconnaissance work. Glenn Curtiss was developing aero engines and building a series of *June Bug* biplanes. America suffered its first airship accident in 1908 when a 450-foot-long Morrell airship, carrying fifteen people and her inventor J. A. Morrell of San Francisco, exploded and burned shortly after taking off. All aboard were seriously injured, but none was killed.

In that same year a semirigid airship, designed, built, and flown by Captain Thomas S. Baldwin, was purchased by the United States Army for $10,000 as a "practicable military means of dirigible aerial navigation." Nothing much came of that venture. Also in 1908, the French government's third semirigid airship, the *Republic*, made several very successful flights, but in September 1909 she broke a propeller, the flying blade gashed the envelope, and she collapsed. Her crew of four was killed in the resultant crash.

The Wrights and Curtiss continued to improve their machines and eventually were engaged in a long, tedious legal fight over the right to the aileron control that they were using on their biplanes. The litigation was finally settled at the outbreak of World War I when the United States government took a hand. Other designers in Europe were also contributing to the development of the aeroplane, chiefly through public exhibitions, air races, and aviation meets that often turned into tragic Roman holidays.

In the meantime, with the coming of the heavier-than-air craft, dirigible airship enthusiasts began to take a new viewpoint concerning the value of the Zeppelin and semirigid airships. It was obvious to the men who were investing in lighter-than-air activity that the dirigible had a great future in the commercial, passenger-carrying field, rather than as a military reconnaissance machine. Up to this time few men had openly predicted that dirigibles could, or might be used as aerial bombers. Back in 1899 the Hague Conference prohibited military aircraft from discharging projectiles or explosives, but it was agreed they could be used for reconnaissance and other purposes. This agreement was accepted by all major powers, but, interestingly enough, by the next year the first Zeppelin dirigible had been completed and flown, and, as a result, the military aircraft clauses considered at the 1907 Hague Conference were suddenly found by many important powers to be unacceptable. Naturally, expediency and available resources of certain belligerents would eventually decide how wartime air power would be used.

By 1909 there was considerable talk about passenger and freight-carrying air lines, and in that year the French Compagnie Transaevienne that had been organized in March displayed an airship called the *Ville de Nancy* at the Nancy Exposition. This company had planned an air line to connect Paris and Bordeaux, and their semirigid airship, built by the Astra Company of Paris, was to become popular as the first French-built passenger airship. Another passenger-carrying semirigid was *La Belgique*, built by Louis Godard, of the famous French aeronautical family, and Robert Goldschmidt at an airship dock in Brussels. That same year Louis Blériot made his epic flight across the English Channel from France to England, an adventure that proved Britain was no longer an island, and geographical boundaries could be passed with immunity.

On August 29, 1909, more than one hundred thousand Berliners gathered at Tempelhof field, and more than two million more crowded the rooftops to greet the *Graf* and his mighty Zeppelin as she nosed in from the south. National emotions reached a high pitch as church bells pealed, but few of the spectators would have dared predict that twenty years later these German dirigibles would have been developed into great passenger carriers, and in fact circumnavigate the globe.

However, that Sunday in August was the Count's and Dr. Eckener's greatest triumph, for on this occasion the former theorist, economist, lecturer, researcher, and author was in command of LZ.3. The arrival had been beautifully stage-managed, and the reception was held without a hitch. Kaiser Wilhelm was on hand, attended by his entire retinue. Count Zeppelin was carried off in the Kaiser's car to spend the rest of the day at the Royal Palace, while Dr. Eckener, resplendent in full military regalia, and wearing a spade beard, remained on board, taking full charge during the time the Count spent with his Emperor.

How did Hugo Eckener become an airship captain? Simple. Realizing that the Count would not continue forever, Alfred Colsman looked around for a new commander. There were a few Army airship men available, men who had trained on the Parseval ships, but none of them had administrative ability. Eckener had sailed yachts, knew something about navigation, and had made one or two flights aboard LZ.3 where he learned about distributing water ballast, but more important he had the courage to make decisions, and so he was a natural choice to become commodore of the *Deutsche Luftschiffarts A.G.*, which became known as Delag from its initials.

Eckener's giant step from a public relations man to airship captain was as easy as that, a promotion we like to think can happen only in America, but in this case the background was Germany.

By midnight LZ.3 was reprovisioned, refueled, and again rose for the return to Friedrichshafen, a trip that required almost a week as the airship was beset with mishaps and delays, but the German Imperial Navy, nevertheless, ordered four large Zeppelins—for reconnaissance missions.

The Count did not relinquish his command immediately. Almost a year later, June 22, 1910, he took the helm on the first commercial airship flight and guided *Deutschland* (*LZ.7*) on its maiden voyage from Friedrichshafen to Düsseldorf, a journey of three hundred miles, carrying twenty passengers—including ten women—who had paid about fifty dollars each for the experience. After a pleasant voyage of about nine hours, they landed safely at Düsseldorf, and the next day sailed on to Dortmund where they picked up twelve more passengers and returned to Düsseldorf.

Five days later *Deutschland* was wrecked in a violent storm and crashed in Teutoburger Forest. Her crew and passengers were saved although the luxurious aluminum cabin was completely wrecked, but by now Delag was flush with funds, having been capitalized for $750,000, and a huge fleet of Zeppelins was to be built that would connect various German cities. In fact, over the next four years—up to the outbreak of World War I—two of these airliners, *Schwagen* and *Victoria Louise*—covered 21,700 air miles and carried 5577 passengers.

By now virtually all of Germany was vitally interested in Zeppelin dirigibles, chiefly as a basis of investment, for everyone was intrigued with the new mode of transportation, and as far as the public in Germany was concerned, the aeroplane need never have been invented. Dirigibles did get into trouble and on occasion were wrecked on landing, but seemingly suffered few casualties. They were repaired quickly, or replaced, and to the general public this was the ideal form of long-distance transportation.

These giant airships were as well known by name as the transatlantic liners of that period. The rest of the world tried to keep pace with this lighter-than-air progress, but no one outside of Germany seemed to have the touch, the know-how, or technical ability to construct a commercially sound dirigible. Also, the Count was not permitted to sell his airships to foreign countries, and frustrated in this field, outsiders naturally turned to heavier-than-air craft. France, Russia, Great Britain, and the United States did make considerable strides in this sphere, but their machines were of no commercial value. They were flown in city-to-city air races. They put on aerobatic displays at state and county fairs, and only in a few instances were specially designed for what was called "military purposes," meaning air reconnaissance (cavalry of the clouds), aerial photography, and when there were newspaper photographers around they were dressed up with machine guns or wireless sets. In this there was some mild fanfare to the effect that the aeroplane was fast becoming a military weapon, but in all truth there was no such aircraft until World War I had been raging for several months.

The seething political cauldron in Europe could not be ignored, and while the rest of the world was making the most of the spruce and linen aeroplane, bombastic men in Germany continued to build battleships to compete with the growth of Royal Navy and Britain's far-flung mercantile fleet. At the same time German naval authorities were convincing themselves that the Zeppelin could play an important role in future naval operations. Then, too, France's continued interest in the aeroplane was disturbing, and Russia's ability to build and fly large multi-place aircraft seemed to be directed at Berlin. British fliers were appearing all over the world, winning many highly publicized races, and making a special show of their seaplanes in impressive demonstrations with the Grand Fleet.

All this outside activity finally needled Berlin to act, and in 1912 a German pilot named Fischer, won the world's first seaplane meet while flying a French Farman fitted with floats. With that success a few military minds in Germany finally turned to the development of worth-while heavier-than-air craft.

During these anxious years, concerned with the continued growth of the British Navy which he believed to be the real obstacle to German world expansion, Kaiser Wilhelm poured public funds into his naval dockyards. This was a personal phobia, as he intended to build his sea force up to the same strength and level of efficiency as that of the German Army. The military had purchased Count Zeppelin's *LZ.1* dirigible and ordered a second, the *LZ.4*, that was destroyed by fire in 1908. But this did not deter the airship men or the public, for, as explained, more money poured into the Friedrichshafen enterprise. Zeppelin LZ.2 was also bought by the Army, but was quickly wrecked, and another went up in flames a few months later.

These mishaps were actually due to badly trained crews and careless handling, but these early operations created an airship tradition. Hundreds of men were to become skilled in the handling of these aerial giants, and hangers and docks were being built everywhere to accommodate the dirigibles.

When war broke out in August 1914 Hugo Eckener left his Hamburg-Delag desk and reported to the Chief of the Dockyard Section of the new Naval Airship Division at Kiel, and volunteered his services as an airship commander with the German Navy. He was warmly greeted, but, as was to be expected, was told he was too important to risk on military operations, and that he could better serve the Fatherland training airship commanders, and drawing up the instruction schedules of crews and mechanics. He was immediately sent to the Hamburg-Fuhlsbüttel headquarters of the Naval Airship Division where he was enthusiastically received by Fregattenkapitän Peter Strasser, who had been a former gunnery officer and had been trained by Eckener as an airship pilot. By now Strasser was Führer der Luftschiffe, and a very ambitious young officer. He startled Eckener with his advanced views of how big dirigibles should be used in modern warfare. Strasser did not concentrate on aerial observation or long-range reconnaissance, rather he predicted that he soon would have an armada of aerial dreadnoughts with which he could carry the war deep into the British countryside, and in his regular lectures proudly claimed he could strike terror into the people just by flying over the country at night and making the populace listen to the beat of Zeppelin propellers. Calmer heads, however, saw Zeppelins only as reconnaissance machines.

By this time the German Army had nine operational dirigibles that included three commercial airships that had been hurriedly commandeered for war purposes, but the

Navy, with about half that number, was far ahead in aeronautical thinking. Furthermore, naval personnel seemed to take to airship training and flight maneuvers more readily than Army men. They had a more instinctive approach to the art of long-distance airship flying, and were quite at home above the broad blue sea, whereas military men were expected to co-operate with cavalry, infantry, and artillery only a few hundred feet above the mud and slots of the trenches.

However, the Army and Navy staffs felt that they had been burdened with a military weapon for which they had no particular use. There was no precedent on which to base any positive tactics, and though these beautiful airships had proved themselves in civilian transportation, the military had little, or no idea, how to use them in battle planning.

The public that had supported Count Zeppelin and his dirigibles, now expected the same airships to bring war to Belgium and Britain. How much Dr. Eckener's airship publicity had contributed to this is difficult to define, but by the time World War I started other propagandists had made the most of the Zeppelin as a military machine. They had built up Prussian military supremacy, German genius, and Teutonic thoroughness to such an extent that not only Germany but much of the rest of the world accepted the miracle of the dirigible and fully expected it would have a leading role in blasting Britain out of the conflict.

The Zeppelins did not attack London the first night of the war, but many Englishmen expected they would. Great Britain had been the target of German propaganda for several years. The penny-a-liners had drenched the popular press with frightening articles that presaged these dreaded attacks on cities and towns. Hack writers had loaded the bookstalls with melodramatic volumes devoted to airship attacks from across the North Sea. The "penny-dreadful" press turned out volume after volume, based on the exploits of the James Bond of that day whose regular assignments always focused on the next airship raid on some important military complex. In fact, the enduring, or fore-stalling, of airship raids on London were standard features of all the "thriller" magazines. Is it any wonder that Germany's Zeppelins had planted a deep-rooted dread in the minds and breasts of many Britons long before the beat of airship propellers was heard over Albion?

After the first danger signal had been raised when Louis Blériot flew a bamboo and linen monoplane over the English Channel, a committee was formed to examine the dangers produced by the "potentialities of airships," the finding of which stated that such dangers could only be exposed by building aircraft in return. This clause was to have a lasting effect on the development of an aircraft industry in Great Britain.

The Royal Navy, in turn, became concerned for the safety of vital naval bases. The Army was consulted, and the problem was eventually dropped in the lap of the Home Ports Committee. This august body did its best, but with no previous air attack to guide them, there was little that could be done. In 1910 there was no Royal Flying Corps. The Royal Engineers had been experimenting with a few kites, an observation balloon or two, and some effort had been made along the line of the semirigid airship, but none of this seemed promising as far as raiding Zeppelins were concerned. It was obvious that no form of passive defense by means of fixed armaments or overhead cover, or of mobile defense by means of guns mounted on automobiles, could be regarded as sufficient in all circumstances. Another clause in the committee's finding stated that the most effective form of meeting aerial attack was by means of dirigible airships or aeroplanes, and in order for these to be free to assume an active role, fixed defenses of a special nature (searchlights and coastal observation) would have to be provided.

There was vague talk of underground shelters, suitable cover for magazines and the dispersal of important munitions plants, but most important, it was agreed that experiments should be conducted at an early date with a view to acquiring more information regarding various considerations affecting aerial attack and the best type of ordnance to harass enemy aircraft.

Amazingly, no one seemed to remember that Zeppelins were inflated with hydrogen gas, a vapor that could be ignited with some sort of incendiary bullet. Not even when a few science-fiction hacks of the day wrote about a new "secret vapor" they called "dioxygenous gas" that not only would give the airship triple lifting capacity but could not be ignited by spark or flame, did anyone concentrate on an artillery projectile that might put the torch to these cigar-shaped gasbags.

But it should be remembered that many complacent people in Great Britain believed in the humane restrictions of the Hague Convention; it was unthinkable that any military power would adopt aerial bombing. They also refused to believe that a potential enemy would use poison gas, employ flame throwers, or sink unarmed passenger ships. It can be seen, therefore, that the happy-go-lucky, contented, Victorian era was brought to an end by Prussian determination for military supremacy.

Gradually, the British mind was impregnated with many grim possibilities. A few months before the First World War began there were persistent rumors of ghostlike dirigibles prowling about the North Sea, presumably to spy on the British coastline. These reports usually insisted that spectral, cigar-shaped forms were speeding silently far above the range of any known gun or aeroplane. Probing searchlights only added to the phantasm as night after night they illuminated streaks of clouds, convincing imaginative watchers that whole fleets of Zeppelins were moving on England.

Then on November 1, 1911, one year after Britain's Home Ports Committee had made its report, a bomb was dropped from an aeroplane. This illegal act occurred during the Italian-Turkish War that ended with the annexation of Libya by Italy. An Italian military aviator, a Lieutenant Gavotti, had a strong desire to see what would happen if an aerial bomb could be dropped on a concentration of human beings. Piloting an Etrich monoplane that was powered with a 130-horsepower Austro-Daimler engine, he flew over the Turkish lines near Tripoli. He carried four bombs in a leather bag, and from a height of 600 feet dropped one on a Turkish encampment, and was so pleased with the "disastrous results" he flew back and dropped the rest.

No one connected with the Hague Convention made the slightest protest, and, ignoring the widespread report of this terrorism, the British Master-General of Ordnance, who acted as aeronautics chief at the War Office, stated, "We are not convinced that either aeroplanes or airships will be of any utility in war."

Officialdom moves slowly, and it was not until 1912 that Great Britain was finally goaded into forming the Royal Flying Corps, and that same year the Royal Aircraft Factory at Farnborough turned out its tenth operational aeroplane. However, Winston Churchill, then First Lord of the Admiralty, was making plans for a Royal Naval Air Service. By this time, too, the Germans were coming to appreciate the potential of the heavier-than-air machine, and the astounding sum, approximating $20,000,000, had been offered as prize money, and to finance the building of aircraft and engines, but it was not until 1911 that a design satisfactory to German officials was produced by Igo Etrich, an Austrian. Etrich had tried to sell his first models to his own government, but with no success. A German Secret Service operator got in touch with Etrich, with the result that his *Taube* (dove) design was purchased outright by the Rumpler factory at Berlin-Lichtenberg. The government ordered the Rumpler factory to turn out twenty Taubes at once. Fortunately, the heavier-than-air school of thought persuaded the German authorities that aeroplanes would be of more use to a modern army than all of the Count's gasbags. But that is another story.

And fortunately for Great Britain, Germany was far from

ready to launch mass attacks on her enemy by Zeppelin, for the Airship Service began operations with a number of disasters that delayed their basic plans for several months.

The first dirigible that was delivered to the German Navy crashed over Helgoland one year after it was put into service. In 1913 the Imperial Navy accepted another Zeppelin that exploded during its delivery flight, killing everyone aboard. A third, LZ.3, was the only dirigible in service when Dr. Eckener joined Captain Strasser. This airship was 490 feet long and had a gas capacity of 795,000 feet. It was powered by three engines, furnishing 630 horsepower, and giving it a speed of forty-seven miles an hour. It lifted a maximum load of eight and one-half tons, and had an operations' ceiling of 6000 feet.

Captain Strasser soon made his demands and opinions known, and future Zeppelins ordered for naval operations were to be fitted with machine guns and bomb compartments. They were also to be powered with more efficient engines that would enable their commanders to operate day or night in any reasonable weather. Dr. Eckener contributed an aviation weather service that was quickly adopted and widely extended. Strasser then had his dirigibles equipped with first-class wireless sets, and with the months, as London finally developed its air defenses, it was essential that dirigibiles sent against England should be able to fly at greater altitudes.

Within a few weeks after war was declared, Strasser and Eckener had become powerful figures in this new German air arm. Count Zeppelin no longer had a role, for he was now an old man nearing eighty who could understand little of this modern conflict. Strasser and Eckener became the aerial war lords, a point quickly forgotten in the postwar years, particularly when Dr. Eckener, in charge of all Zeppelin operations, was wildly acclaimed the world over. From most accounts, Strasser and Eckener wished to make immediate raids on Britain, but the Kaiser opposed them, and it was not until January 1915 that he allowed the two to make raids on England.

The Kaiser did insist that no deliberate attacks be made on Buckingham Palace, St. Paul's Cathedral, Westminster Abbey, all museums, and government buildings. There were no restrictions on hospitals, schools, or the homes of non-combatant civilians.

But luck was not immediate with the German airship services. Three Army dirigibles were lost on operational flights during the first months of the war. The Naval Airship Service fared little better, for after the two Zeppelin disasters in 1913 that had taken most of its experienced officers—and left Peter Strasser in charge—the organization was on the point of being disbanded. Only the timely delivery of a new LZ.3 from the Zeppelin factory at Friedrichshafen in May 1914 kept the Naval Airship Service in existence.

War was the last thing anyone in England wanted in that memorable year of 1914. A balmy summer had come unusually early, bringing a sense of serenity, adding to the tranquil mood of all Britishers. Week by week, a kindly warmth put everyone in a holiday mood, and cloudless skies encouraged thoughts of pleasant rambles across the countryside, or relaxation at the seashore. The tone of the times was tuned to felicity.

Social Reform had been adopted and a program of Old Age Pensions and Insurance schemes had seemingly freed the lower classes from some of their cares. The long strikes and lockouts that had run riot two years previously had come to a close and the wealthy classes were grateful to the Liberal Party to which this progress could be credited. Those out of work could apply to the Labor Exchange for guidance. Only across the Irish Sea was there any evidence of unrest.

By 1914 the automobile was an accepted vehicle of transportation. There was the wonder and efficiency of Guglielmo Marconi's wireless telegraph. A few men had had the pleasure of flying in what was called an aeroplane. The opera and the ballet blossomed, Feodor Chaliapin had just made his first English appearance, and the then thirty-five-year-old Thomas Beecham, backed by a fortune made in a patent medicine called Beecham's Pills, had brought classical music and the dances of Stravinsky, Karsavina, Fokine, Diaghliev, and Nijinsky to the masses. Dame Nellie Melba had opened the opera season at Covent Garden singing Mimi in *La Bohème*.

If you were titillated by the world of fashion you might have been intrigued by the list of new names across the Channel—Doucet, Boué, Soeurs, Worth, Poiret, and Paquin. Remember the Watteau hat, that gay confection of straw, ribbon, and tea roses? That was practically regulation. The new hobble skirt provided many a vicarious thrill.

The middle class had discovered the joys of reading and for six shillings were devouring the latest best sellers—novels, biographies, or even bulky histories. Romance was as popular as ever, and most everyone was reading Charles Garvice's *The Woman's Way*, W. J. Locke's *The Fortunate Youth*, Marie Corelli's *The Innocent*, Baroness Orczy's *Unto Caesar*, and, of course, Ethel M. Dell's *The Swindler*. New works were available from the pens of Arnold Bennett, John Galsworthy, and *Strand Magazine* was presenting the latest Sherlock Holmes. James Joyce, who had had great difficulty in getting his *Dubliners* published, was now slaving at something he was to call *Ulysses*. But most interesting, H. G. Wells who dealt in scientific plots had just published an imaginative work titled *The World Set Free*, in which he presented a fanastic "and improbable" bomb which released the power of the atom!

The British theatre scintillated. Bernard Shaw's *Pygmalion* had just opened at His Majesty's Theatre with Mrs. Patrick Campbell as Eliza Doolittle and Sir Herbert Burbohm Tree as Professor Henry Higgins. This was the play in which the shocking word "bloody" was heard for the first time from the lips of a lady, a thrill that set London agog for months. Those who reviewed the play could not know that half a century later *Pygmalion* would be converted into a musical, have its title revised "for the masses" and presented on stage and screen as *My Fair Lady*.

On the musical comedy stage and at the music halls Raymond Hitchcock, George Robey, Little Tich, Elsie Janis, Nelson Keyes, and Violet Loraine were performing nightly. An American act, known as *Potash and Perlmutter* was competing with *Kismet, When Knights Were Bold,* and *The Belle of New York.* A new Bioscope film, *Harry Lauder Among the Mormons,* had a queue lined up along the Kingsway, and an Anglo-American Exposition at Ranelagh presented *Wonders of the Panama Canal, The Grand Canyon,* and *America's Sky Scrapers.*

There was every evidence that August would provide a first-class Bank Holiday.

But on June 28 the Austrian Archduke Franz Ferdinand and his commoner wife Sophie were assassinated by an anarchist in the Serbian township of Sarajevo. Austria delivered an ultimatum to Serbia, threatening to annex that country by force. This meant that Russia would take up Serbia's cause, and Germany would side with Austria. That would put Russia at Germany's throat, and France, having made an alliance with Russia, would get a chance for revenge for her defeat at the hands of the Germans in 1870. It was as simple as that—on paper—but through the quiet halls of European diplomacy it was realized that an assassin's bullet in Sarajevo had afforded Berlin an excuse to run riot; that here at last was an outlet for her vast military force.

Serbia did her best to placate Austria, and in fact accepted the ultimatum within two hours of the deadline, and then asked that the case be brought before the Hague Conference. None of this was satisfactory, and the Austro-Hungarian Empire—that heterogenous relic of the Middle Ages ruled by the aging Emperor Franz Josef—declared war on Serbia, exactly one month after the assassination. The next day Russia ordered mobilization in districts bordering on Austria, and with that Germany declared that any further Russian mobilization would bring her into the field on Austria's side, so Austria-Hungary set up a general mobilization, supported, if not impelled, by Germany.

But despite this belligerent posturing, there was a faint hope that war could be averted. Sir Edward Grey of Great Britain did his best, although hampered somewhat by the Tories. He would not assure the French that Britain would intervene, but he was determined to uphold the neutrality of Belgium, which had been guaranteed for seventy-five years by the five powers now involved.

While this European diplomatic situation seethed, few people in England believed Great Britain would become involved. She had no binding commitment to fight with any European power. Her most serious problem at the time was the Home Rule controversy and the danger of civil war if an attempt were made to force Ulster under a Parliament sitting in Dublin.

The British Cabinet, meeting on August 1, now permitted Grey to warn the German Ambassador that violation of Belgian neutrality might mean war, and when this was made public, practically the whole of Great Britain arose to object, arguing that this effort was nothing more than a move to "maintain the balance of power." They could see no reason why Britain should take the side of Russia against Germany, and pointed out that if Russia won it would only set up an ever greater disturbance of the balance of power. If, on the other hand, Germany won, it would in effect be a victory for the principle of the balance of power. In the face of all this the Tories were still willing to take up the sword.

On Sunday, August 2, German troops occupied the Grand Duchy of Luxembourg. That same evening an ultimatum was delivered to Belgium demanding free passage through her territory. Earlier that eventful day Grey had obtained from the Cabinet authorization to inform the French Ambassador that if the German fleet moved to attack the French coast, the Royal Navy would oppose it. This was some comfort to France, as she had concentrated the bulk of her fleet in the Mediterranean. When the news of German troops marching across the Belgian border was flashed that night, Prime Minister Herbert Asquith declared that the British Army should be mobilized the next day. The First Lord of the Admiralty, Winston Churchill, already had the fleet at a most strategic position.

By Monday morning the Belgian government had rejected the Berlin ultimatum, a gesture that electrified all the members of the British Cabinet. Grey instructed the British Ambassador in Berlin, Sir William Goschen, to present an ultimatum, and, in default of a satisfactory reply before midnight, to ask for his passport. No formal answer was forthcoming.

By August 2, Germany had formally declared war on Russia, and the next day declared war on France. And with that, to Germany's amazement, Great Britain declared war "for a scrap of paper," her word to defend Belgium's neutrality.

No one in Berlin mentioned *Der Schlieffenplan*, a battle plan that had been in the archives of the German War Ministry since 1891. Its most important feature was the invasion of Belgium, the keystone of German strategy, and the password to victory. And for this Great Britain went to war, hoping to maintain the balance of power in Europe, a balance that had produced two generations of peace.

III

STRATEGIC AVIATION

To the general perplexity of the British public no Zeppelin raids were made against their homeland; in fact no enemy aircraft of any type were sent against British cities during the first months of the war. The question was put time and time again, but officialdom had no answer.

On August 26, London newspapers, using panic-type headlines, reported that Zeppelins had made a bombing attack on the Belgian city of Antwerp. In the text matter it was stated that six "shrapnel bombs" had been dropped from an airship at night and twelve civilians had been killed and a hospital damaged. There was further comment to the effect that King Albert had been involved in the danger, and there was a touch of indignation in the explanation that the hospital was unquestionably flying the flag of the Geneva Convention.

"The bombs exploded with terrific force," a Reuter's message stated.

Gradually, the news revealed that a Zeppelin had had a major part in the German attack on the forts at Liége. The world read of General Mathieu Leman's heroic defense of Belgium's last stronghold, and how "brave little Belgium" had only been overwhelmed by broad ranks of German artillery. It was learned that one of the strongest cupolas of the fortress had been destroyed by a bomb dropped from a Zeppelin, and the most was made of that account. It was explained that with that destruction the rest of the forts were swept away "like sand castles on the seashore before the relentless waves of the oncoming tide."

But the dreaded raiders failed to appear over Britain, and the civilians enjoyed repeated nights of rest and peace. Each day brought new theories or explanations for this puzzling situation. The wishful thinkers thought that a flight from the German coastline to Britain was either too far or too risky; the Zepp captains might be fearful of British weather, a point adopted by some meteorological experts who explained that there were decided turbulences, eddies, and violent updrafts spiraling from seaside cliffs, or were set up within the man-made canyons of London that would make it difficult for airships to risk flights over England. The military mind assumed that all of Count Zeppelin's dirigibles must be working with the German Army in France— or perhaps cruising about over the broad North Sea looking for the British Grand Fleet.

A whole month passed without Zepp raids, but the public which had predicted these aerial invasions, developed a new attitude. The early confidence began to seep away, and there was a persistent rumor, whispered in the pubs and fish shops, that a Zeppelin was hidden in the hills of the Lake District—just outside Grasmere, to be exact. This tall tale was soon elaborated, and it was stated that this skulking dirigible took off every night and carried out reconnaissance flights over Bristol, London, and even the Portsmouth dockyards.

This widespread report was not discounted until Lieutenant B. C. Hucks of the Royal Flying Corps was sent out to scout this specter of Grasmere. Lieutenant Hucks, who was a noted racing airman of that period, took a Blériot-11, and made a complete search, probably enjoying the scenery, but found nothing. Not only was there no Zeppelin to be seen, but there was nothing that looked like a possible landing area. But these rumors and alarms triggered new defensive measures, and by early September the Commissioner of the Metropolitan Police of London drew up the first ordinance that led to the early restrictions on street lighting.

Much was expected from this early form of dimout, and it was hoped that raiding Zeppelins would have difficulty in finding the city; only a few people appreciated the fact that the glistening Thames would provide an almost perfect guide to every section of the metropolis. But more important at the time, the blackout precautions sobered the British public. The prospects of living in a ghostly semidarkness nurtured new apprehensions, and many felt that this restriction presaged an immediate breakdown in modern civilization. There were those who feared that complete social chaos would result if London's night illumination was in any degree lessened. The thoughtful ones realized that this war against the Hun, as he was called, was in no way comparable to the faraway Crimea, the Boer War, or the Irish Uprising.

A few days after Lieutenant Hucks had had his day over Grasmere, a Royal Naval Air Service seaplane, patrolling out of Felixstowe on the East Coast, spotted a Zeppelin about sixty miles away. The dirigible made no move to approach Britain, and finally disappeared in the mist.

That was enough!

The lighting restrictions were put into force immediately. All householders were ordered to lower their window shades before lighting oil lamps, gaslights, or electric bulbs. The headlights of buses and tramcars were filtered down, a great number of street lights were switched off, and the smaller ones were partly painted over to prevent any upward gleam. To the general public all this reduced the city to a mammoth cave, and once more fears and imagination ran wild; all kinds of dire results were predicted, but as the weeks dragged on with no air-raid warnings, with no searchlights dividing the sky into sharp segments, the community spirit rose, and all the old jokes about Jerry's gasbags were revived.

And to add to this resurgence of spirit, it was learned that the German Army had lost three Zeppelins on their first war missions. Their *L.6* had flown from an airship base at Cologne to support the attack on the garrison town of Lutetia outside Paris. She carried a heavy bomb load, and because of low clouds had to approach her target at a low altitude. She was badly damaged by artillery and infantry fire and had to withdraw. On her return *L.6* eventually crashed near Bonn.

Another Army Zeppelin, *L.7*, flew from her base at Baden-Oos and headed toward the Vosges with the intention of bombing a French military camp. Again, weather conditions forced a low-altitude approach. *L.7* also came under terrific artillery and infantry small-arms fire, and the 520-foot-long dirigible had to limp away. After losing much gas she crashed near Saint-Quirin in Lorraine.

The third disaster must have tickled the funny-bone of the British public. The Army *L.8*, flying out of Trèves, was fired on by German troops who had not been instructed in airship recognition. Turning away from that unexpected reception, the Zeppelin unhappily found itself over a French force that immediately opened fire with rifles and machine guns. The steering gear was seriously damaged, and many of the gas cells punctured. *L.8* floated about over what might be considered no-man's land, and then wrecked herself in Badonviller Forest. The crew did its best to set fire to her, so as to destroy her, but nothing they tried would ignite what hydrogen gas was left. While they chopped at the engine and control car a troop of French cavalry charged into the scene, hacking away with their sabres, whereupon the German airmen made a game show with their infantry rifles, and most of them escaped into their own lines.

At this point Captain Strasser and Dr. Eckener, holding the honorary rank of lieutenant commander, took the initiative. They first accelerated all Zeppelin construction, and more hangars and sheds were erected at the Friedrichshafen and Potsdam sites. They devised a revolving hangar at Nordholz, a sandy waste near Cuxhaven on the Elbe River. This hangar enabled the ground crew to walk-out the dirigibles, no matter in what direction the wind was blowing. Finally they took over the Delag two-ship hangar that had been built at Fuhlsbüttel, another at Hamburg, and the chain of meteorological stations that extended along the coast from Ostend to Königsberg.

Admiral Alfred von Tirpitz, then Secretary of State for the German Navy, dictated a memo from his headquarters on November 18, 1914: *"The English are now in terror of Zeppelins, perhaps not without reason. I contend here for the standpoint of an 'eye for an eye' but I am not in favor of 'frightfulness.' Also the indiscriminate dropping of bombs is wrong; they are repulsive when they hit and kill an old woman, and one gets used to them. If one could set fire to London in thirty places, then the repulsiveness would be lost sight of in the immensity of the effect."*

This was all the belligerent Peter Strasser needed. So far, he had not progressed in the Navy at the pace he had hoped, and he wished that his future might be found in his command of the Naval Airship Service. He had a point. By December 1914, Strasser who had gone to war with but one Zeppelin, now had a fleet of five, all fully manned, modified for military operations, and ready to strike. He tried to get the Army Airship Service to co-operate and combine their forces with his for a full-scale plan of action against England, but the military men, despondent over their disasters in August, declined to accept the naval commander's offer.

During this time, the Kaiser who could not face up to bombing London, vacillated and limited Strasser's airships to routine naval operations, but an Admiral Bachmann, then Chief of Staff of the Imperial Navy, presented the opinion that Germany should leave no measures untried to crush England, and that successful raids on London, in view of the already existing nervousness of the people, would prove a means to this end. It will be seen that Admiral Bachmann was a student of psychological warfare.

It may be well at this point to explain the prefixes to be used in identifying the airships assigned to the German Navy and Army Airship services. Previous to the outbreak of the war Zeppelin-built dirigibles were listed as *L.1, L.2, L.3,* etc. *L* stands for *Luftschiff* (airship). To keep this history clear Naval Airship Service ships will be designated with the prefix *LZ . . . LZ.10, LZ.11, LZ.12,* etc. and Army Airship Service dirigibles will be identified as *L.5, L.6, L.7,* etc. Schütte-Lanz airships will be presented as *SL.1, SL.2, SL.3,* etc., while those of the Parseval type will be noted as *PL.6, PL.19,* etc. This is done to clarify situations where airships of the same numeral might confuse the reader.

Official Britain, and particularly the Royal Naval Air Service, began to think in terms of strategic aviation. There was no such term or theory at the time, but no one will argue that what was about to transpire was not a first-class exhibition of that military science.

An offshoot of the Royal Flying Corps, the Royal Naval Air Service was something of a stepchild, having been hurriedly organized in 1912. The First Lord of the Admiralty, Winston Churchill, a firm believer in the aeroplane as a military weapon, had established a chain of seaplane stations along the east and south coasts of England. Some of these had been built as early as 1912, and at about the same time an old cruiser, HMS *Hermes,* was commissioned as a parent ship for the Royal Navy and fitted out to carry two seaplanes that could be launched on small trolleys from a short flying deck built out over the bows.

This improvisation soon established the fact that, for the time being at least, military aviation was moving in two directions. There had to be a military arm trained and equipped for the requirements of the Army in the field, and a naval arm designed to co-operate with the Grand Fleet. The two services could not be combined, for in each case the problems and responsibilities were far apart. From the start of the war the R.N.A.S. faced dozens of new problems as the service was not fully established until July 1, 1914, about a month before the start of hostilities.

When war seemed imminent it was also clear that the Army wing (Royal Flying Corps) would have to take the offensive role, while the Navy wing (Royal Naval Air Service) would be assigned to all problems of the defense of Britain. At the time, it was obvious, too, that all aeroplanes and airships available to the Naval wing could supplement or even take the place of the coastguard service. It was then that Churchill's coastal bases were most appreciated.

At the beginning of the war the R.N.A.S. possessed fifty-two seaplanes, of which only twenty-six were serviceable—but forty-six more were on order. Churchill had recommended three types of machines for this air Navy; one designed for overseas fighting (a seaplane) that could operate from a ship as a base; a scouting seaplane to work with the fleet at sea; and a home-service fighting aeroplane to repel enemy aircraft. The directive went into considerable detail concerning the method of attacking Zeppelins: "An aeroplane should attack these machines obliquely from above by dropping small bombs or strings of fire balls that would be drawn like a whiplash across the envelope."

It is interesting to relate that the first Zeppelin brought down by an aeroplane in the air, a victory scored by Flight Sub-Lieutenant Reginald A. J. Warneford, was caused by the use of Hale bombs in a method similar to Churchill's suggestion.

As can be appreciated, the principal task of the R.N.A.S. was to defend Great Britain's east coast from attack, and to safeguard shipping in the English Channel. By October 1914, *Hermes* had been further modified to carry three seaplanes, but before the month was out she was torpedoed in the Channel, upon which the Admiralty quickly converted three cross-Channel steamers, *Empress*, *Engadine*, and *Riviera*, to serve as seaplane carriers.

As soon as the Germans had established themselves in Belgium, the menace to Britain was apparent, and new flights of R.N.A.S. aircraft were moved to cover the area between the Thames and the Humber. These planes were also ordered to keep a sharp watch for Zeppelins. Although defensive work, it took a grim toll; a number of seaplanes were wrecked, several pilots were lost, and inevitably R.N.A.S. men yearned for a more aggressive role. They wished to raid Kiel and Wilhelmshaven, but there were no aircraft capable of such an attack.

Realizing the problems involved, and the importance of attacking German air bases and factories before their aircraft could begin raids on Britain, designers, engineers, and practical pilots were put to work to produce aeroplanes that would fill the varied requirements, and by early 1915 these teams had succeeded in building a 225-horsepower Short Tractor that was said could carry five hundred pounds of bombs over a distance of three hundred miles, and return. Then, in order to reduce these flying distances, it was decided to establish an R.N.A.S. base on the continent at Ostend, and a squadron that had been settled at Eastchurch on the east coast of England was shuttled across the Channel with a mixed bag of aeroplanes, and one small airship for patrol duties. Some of the R.N.A.S. personnel were immediately stalked and watched by two members of the Royal Marines who were under the impression that these men in mixed naval uniforms were German airmen. Such situations were typical of the times, for none of us had any idea what sort of uniform the Belgians might be wearing. We only knew of German soldiers in smart dress uniforms, but did not know for certain what they would wear on active service. It was much the same with the French. Some of their regiments began the campaign wearing walking-out uniforms, while others were hurriedly equipped with an azure-blue dress, a tone that did not contrast too greatly with the German field-gray.

After days of such problems, the lack of servicing equipment, and the fact that the front line was very fluid, the R.N.A.S. squadron was ordered back to Britain. During these proceedings it was halted temporarily at Dunkirk, and

Commander Charles Rumney Samson was ordered to operate against all enemy Zeppelins and other aircraft within one hundred miles of Dunkirk. To comply, Commander Samson was provided with several so-called armored cars as the aircraft available were far from suited to the task. Armed only with old Maxim guns, Commander Samson's armored cars stayed such wild forays, even ranging as far as Lille, chasing German staff officers off the roads and wrecking their glossy Mercedes, the Germans put a price of £50,000 on his head. These exploits with old cars, armored with sheets of boiler plate, became adventure classics that were widely read in the early months of the war.

At the same time, the available aircraft were flown on low-level intrusion missions, spotting for the armored cars, anticipating the days when observation planes would guide fleets of armored divisions in blitzkrieg tactics. But at the time Samson's exploits were soon forgotten and were never fully explored by wartime historians. However, while this R.N.A.S. squadron was still based at Dunkirk the first actual strike against Zeppelin bases was set up and carried out on September 22, and the following is taken from an official British abstract.

The original Eastchurch squadron had ten pilots and a weird collection of aircraft that included three B.E.2 biplanes, two Sopwith Tabloid biplanes, two Blériot monoplanes, one Henri Farman biplane, and one Short seaplane that had been converted to a landplane by substituting wheels for floats. The one airship, *Astra Torres*, was soon sent back to England.

A short time before, the Zeppelin *Hansa* had made a raid on Antwerp, an incident that revived the earlier idea of the Zeppelin menace, and plans were drawn to halt any raids before they started. It was agreed that airship sheds at Cologne and Düsseldorf should be bombed. The first raid was planned for September 12, and three aircraft that had been flown out to a flat stretch of beach were pegged down in the shelter of sand dunes while Squadron Commander

E. L. Gerrard called on Belgian military authorities for permission to use one of their airfields for the take-off. While negotiations were under way a sudden squall whipped along the beach, ripped out the holding-down pegs, and sent the aircraft cartwheeling over the sands. All three planes were completely wrecked.

Commander Samson then selected four planes for another try and a new base was set up outside Antwerp. Three 20-pound Hale bombs were fixed to the machines, and by September 22 all was ready for this historic attack. Two planes were detailed for the Cologne sheds and two for the Düsseldorf hangars. This was the first British raid on German territory.

The aircraft took off smartly, crossed the Roer and Rhine rivers, but then ran into an area of fog. There was no such thing as blind-flying navigation, so three of the planes turned back, but the fourth, piloted by Flight Lieutenant C. H. Collett, continued on and by good fortune came out of the murk at 6000 feet and found Düsseldorf spread out below. Gliding down to 600 feet to locate the aircraft sheds Lieutenant Collett cruised around for about five minutes, and finally found his target. He set a course to fly directly over the sheds, and then released his three bombs when the hangars came into his primitive bombsight. He made a sharp climbing turn to check his score. One of the bombs fell a few yards short and exploded, but apparently did no harm. The other two pierced the shed roof but did not explode, so no serious damage was incurred. With that, Collett turned home and arrived safely.

The German Army that was moving along the French coast now threatened Antwerp and most of the R.N.A.S. aircraft and pilots were ordered back to Hazebrouck, but one of the flights stayed on outside Antwerp and did its best to maintain the harassing schedule. Some of its machines did ground-strafing, using light bombs and rifle fire in the endeavor to delay the enemy's advance.

Meanwhile another raid was planned to be made on the Cologne and Düsseldorf sheds, and two planes were prepared—all that were available—one assigned to each target, but there was some concern that the enemy would reach Antwerp before the Sopwith Tabloids could take off. On the morning of October 8 the weather was considered too bad for flying and the raid was held up for a few hours. Later in the morning the flying field was under fire, so there was no choice. Squadron Commander Spenser D. A. Grey and Flight Lieutenant Reginald L. G. Marix took off in the face of enemy gunfire though the weather was still unfit for flying. The ground crew stayed on, standing by their armored cars.

Commander Grey set off for Cologne and Lieutenant Marix for Düsseldorf, both of them hoping for a break in the weather. The squadron commander found his target completely obscured, so he went down to 600 feet and cruised about under heavy rifle and artillery fire for about twelve minutes, but could not find the Zeppelin sheds. Not wishing to waste the effort, he turned and roared at the main railroad station and dumped his bombs, but with what result was never explained.

Lieutenant Marix had better luck, and certainly a more exciting time. In the first place he flew over the treetops for one hundred miles, eventually finding Düsseldorf and his target. Starting from a level of 600 feet he went into what may have been the world's first dive-bombing run and cleared his bombs over the hangars. At first, he thought that again the bombs had failed to explode, but as he circled the area he finally saw a shed roof cave in, and then a great column of flame and smoke that went skyward. He was certain there must have been a Zeppelin inside, for only a concentration of hydrogen could have sent up that five-hundred-foot tower of flame.

While circling the field, however, his plane was fired on by a battery of guns that had been set up after Collett's raid on September 22, and one burst probably punctured the fuel tank. Marix ran out of gas when he was within twenty miles of Antwerp and had to make a forced landing in a field. A Belgian peasant who was cycling along a road, stopped to gaze at this strange machine, and while under this spell, Marix (so the story goes) swapped the grounded aeroplane for the bicycle and pedaled to Antwerp where he was relieved to learn that the armored-car boys had driven off a force of attacking Germans, and the flying field was again available. Twenty-seven years later, as an Air Vice-Marshal of the R.A.F., Marix bombed and sank a German vessel in the Norwegian harbor of Aalesund.

It was learned later that Lieutenant Marix had destroyed LZ.9 that had just been delivered, and the resulting explosion had flattened the machine and erecting shop. Thus, the first score was made against the great dirigibles invented by Count Zeppelin.

By six o'clock that evening it was decided to evacuate Antwerp, and the ground staff serviced two of the remaining aircraft while under rifle fire from nearby woods, and Grey managed to get away, reaching Ostend by noon the following day. The fall of Antwerp nullified all plans for a British offensive in Belgium; instead they retreated by stages with the Royal Naval Air Service playing a gallant role all the way out.

Another effort to halt the Zeppelin menace was better planned, one with the features of an adventure story. This time, at the behest of the French, it was decided that the main Zeppelin factory at Friedrichshafen should be attended to, and for a time there was a dash of cloak-and-dagger activity to enliven the proceedings. In the first place, the mayor of the French town of Belfort had collected information concerning the target and the prevailing weather conditions, in and out. Then, Lieutenant N. Pemberton Billing, a well-known flying enthusiast and seaplane designer before the war, slipped aboard the transport *Manchester Importer* which immediately moved out of Southampton for an unannounced port. Aboard were four new Avro-504 biplanes that been transferred from a special train, and with the aircraft were two pilots, Squadron Commander E. F. Briggs and Flight Commander John T. Babington, both of whom wore civilian clothes. Before *Manchester Importer* moved from her wharf, eleven R.N.A.S. mechanics slipped aboard.

After a short conference with Briggs and Babington, Billing left the transport and went aboard the cross-Channel packet to Le Havre so as to be at the French port in time to arrange for a special train, and the unloading of their secret cargo for transfer by rail to its final destination.

On his arrival Lieutenant Billing had a train shunted to the dock at which the *Manchester Importer* would tie up, and as night fell the Avros were to be hoisted from the hold and lowered to the special railroad flatcars, but in the middle of this operation the Le Havre electric power plant broke down, and most of the heavy crates had to be hoisted from below by brute strength and off-loaded for the remainder of their journey.

They rumbled away from the French port by midnight, and early the next morning were being unloaded at Belfort on the Alsatian border from where, of course, they were to make a bombing attack on the Zeppelin plant at Friedrichshafen on Lake Constance. The aeroplanes were off-loaded at a disused factory siding, loaded on French Army trucks, and hauled to the Belfort aerodrome. Then the service staff of the R.N.A.S. went to work assembling the machines. The Avros, numbered 179, 873, 874, and 875, had to be assembled, the bomb-release gear tested, fuel and oil tanks filled, but because they were powered with secondhand 80-horsepower Gnome engines, it was felt there was no need for test flying. Each machine was to carry four 20-pound Hale bombs.

Speaking of bomb racks, it should be explained that there was no such thing as a standard bomb-dropping assembly, but the Avro Company had contrived a Rube Goldberg device that sometimes worked, and accommodated four 20-pound high-explosive bombs and four incendiaries. But for this raid only four high-explosive bombs were carried.

The secrecy was maintained to the last common denominator, and the conspirators could not wait to get away, but at that point it was suddenly realized that two other pilots, Squadron Commander Shepherd and Flight Lieutenant S. V. Sippe, who had been selected for the raid, had not reported in. A few telegrams back and forth from the Admiralty disclosed that Shepherd and Sippe "must be somewhere in France" but no one knew where. The tracing took in Le Havre, Dijon, and Jenvissy but no R.N.A.S. pilots could be flushed. Finally, the two missing men turned up at Dijon and plans were made to send them by automobile to Belfort. All well and good, but travel by road was not simple during those anxious days; sentries were stupid or arrogant, and Shepherd and Sippe did not arrive at Belfort until Sunday, November 15. Both men were tired out, and Shepherd was obviously ill, so the raid was canceled for a day to give the squadron commander a chance to recuperate.

The next day promised fine weather, but then it suddenly reversed and all aircraft were grounded. The barometer fell and a keen wind from the east brought an Alpine temperature that threatened engine trouble. Considering that they would have to fly a distance of over 250 miles, including climbing over the Vosges Mountains, this was a difficult task for the little Avros.

The inclement weather continued until Tuesday, the 17th, when they might have taken off, but Shepherd damaged his machine while attempting an engine test, so the raid was called off once more, and weather kept everything grounded until November 21. Throughout this time the planes were kept at readiness, except for the Castrol (a lubricant composed mostly of castor oil) that had to be heated in a shed because of the low temperature outdoors. The weather was checked from many sources, and the anxious hours and strain of waiting finally put the ailing Shepherd in bed, and his place was taken by Flight Sub-Lieutenant R. P. Cannon.

On the 21st conditions looked reasonably favorable. The sky was clear and the barometer steady. Meteorological checks indicated an easterly wind at 2000 feet blowing at twenty-five to thirty miles per hour, and above that it was moving due west at twenty-five miles per hour.

The pilots were briefed again, and Pemberton Billing's original plan gone over once more. A round-about course had had to be selected that would take them around the northern border of Switzerland to avoid infringing on Swiss neutrality. Could they have taken a direct course, they would have saved themselves many miles. As it was, they had to fly over the Black Forest mountains that towered to 3500 feet, and hope to avoid the seasonal mist that featured the Rhine Valley before they could take a straight course south between the two arms of Lake Constance to reach their target. They would have to fly a distance of 125 miles each way, which was close to the flight range of the Avros.

The four machines were hauled out shortly before nine o'clock in the morning, and with a final inspection sent off, one by one. Briggs, Sippe, and Babington had no trouble, but Cannon's plane could not develop enough power to get off the ground. The sub-lieutenant did his best, but only succeeded in breaking his tail skid. Pemberton Billing decided that Cannon would never make it, so he flagged the three off on their historic mission. Cannon's Avro was dismantled and repacked to be shipped back to England.

Briggs, Babington, and Sippe formed a three-ship wedge and followed the planned course, but gradually Briggs left the other two behind. They were over Basle on the Rhine by 10:20, and continued on down the Rhine Valley at 400 feet until Sippe and Babington became separted in a cloud area between Schaffhausen and Constance. From all accounts, Sippe was well ahead of Babington and following the extreme edge of the lake.

At this point Sippe went down low and skimmed over the lapping water to avoid detection, and at times was less than ten feet above the lake while heading for Friedrichshafen. Crossing the lake he stayed close to the north shore until he was about five miles from the target area. Then he started to climb, going up to 1200 feet from where he no-

1. A pre-war photograph of the *L.1* showing details of the open control car, an outboard radiator, and the ladder running up to the interior of the main frame.—FRIEDRICH MOCH PHOTO.

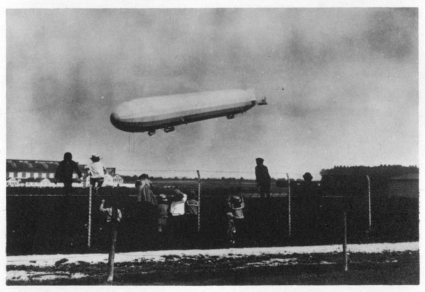

2. Schoolchildren of 1913 enjoyed a real thrill watching *L.2* coming in from a trial flight and preparing to land at Friedrichshafen.—LUFTSCHIFF-BAU ZEPPELIN PHOTO.

3. One of the early commercial Zeppelins. Here is *L.2* being walked out of her shed at Johannisthal. Note large headlight in front of control car. This airship was later destroyed in a severe storm.—FRIEDRICH MOCH PHOTO.

4. Count Zeppelin, in civilian cap seen aboard *LZ.6*, a training ship of the Naval Airship Division. Here, left to right are Hauptmann Kuno Manger, Dr. Hugo Eckener, Count Zeppelin, Hermann Kraushaar, and Rudolph Westphal.—FRIEDRICH MOCH PHOTO.

5. Getting down to business. A scene in the control car of *LZ.16*. Hans-Karl Gayer, commanding officer is seen checking his log. Erich Blew, head of training is next and the third officer is Kurt Dehn, Gayer's Executive Officer.—FRIEDRICH MOCH PHOTO.

6. This is the Morane Parasol flown by Sub-Flight Lieutenant Reginald Warneford when he shot down *LZ.37* over Belgium. The plane was powered with a 80-hp Le Rhone engine, carried no guns but was equipped with a primitive bomb rack.—IMPERIAL WAR MUSEUM PHOTO

7. Sub-Flight Lieutenant Warneford before he gained his fame. He is seen here before a Farman Shorthorn trainer. Warneford was killed a short time after his victory over *LZ.37*.
—IMPERIAL WAR MUSEUM PHOTO.

8. Lieutenant William Leefe Robinson, who was awarded the Victoria Cross for destroying *SL.11*, the first Zeppelin to be brought down over England. Robinson, later a Bristol Fighter pilot was shot down on the Western front and captured. He died shortly after the Armistice.
—WHITEHOUSE PHOTO.

ticed shrapnel bursts north of Friedrichshafen which he assumed were being fired at Briggs. From that height he could also spot the great Zeppelin sheds that gleamed like silver, but could see no trace of another Avro.

When Sippe was half a mile from the main sheds he went into an approach dive and leveled off at 700 feet. He released one bomb into a troop concentration area, mainly to put the gunners into a panic. He turned back and put two more into the factory and a hangar, but the fourth would not slip from the rack. He jerked his plane by all means available, but the bomb would not eject. During this time rifle and machine-gun fire came from all directions, and the Avro bounced about in the turbulence that surged up from the great buildings, so he turned north and raced away from the gunfire, annoyed that he still carried a bomb. He went back once more and tried to dislodge the recalcitrant missile, in fact, aiming it at the old waterside shed where Count Zeppelin had housed his first dirigible, but the bomb refused to slide out of the rack. To evade the heavy machine-gun fire, he dived again and raced over the glinting surface of Lake Constance, and set course for the long flight back to Belfort where he arrived almost four hours after take-off. As his Avro touched down one wheel collapsed causing the machine to skid across the turf.

A few minutes later Babington reported in by telephone, explaining that he had made a successful attack, but had had to force-land near Vesoul about thirty miles away. It was learned that Babington had followed Sippe all the way to the target and arrived there in time to see him racing away with shrapnel bursts following him. Making the most of that diversion Babington dared the opposition, and from 900 feet dropped two bombs over the big sheds. Heavy shrapnel fire burst all around him, so he nosed down almost vertically and released two more. As he pulled out, two bomb explosions, evidently his first two contributions, rammed him over on his back, but as he fought for control he saw the smoke of bomb explosions drifting over the sheds, and workmen running in all directions. Panic seemed to have seized them. After making a sharp turn inland, Babington then turned back over the lake again, heading very low through a curtain of machine-gun bullets from the waterside hangar. With that he set a course over the lake, flying directly into the sun and a short time later was going down the Rhine Valley and passing over Basle. Then he ran into a patch of mist and decided to land while he could see the ground.

The leader of the raid, Commander Briggs, was not so lucky. After getting rid of his bombs he was forced down in enemy territory when his fuel tank was riddled by machine-gun bullets. As he landed he was captured by a group of enraged German civilians, but was eventually rescued by German soldiers and taken to a hospital in a semiconscious condition. Another account, perhaps apocryphal, relates that Briggs later escaped in company with a very young Army lieutenant who was adept at female impersonation. Slight of build, with a clear complexion, he made an intriguing figure when he put on girls' clothing. So he acted the part of Briggs' sweetheart, and the two of them eventually got safely home, playing their roles to the best advantage.

It was established afterward that one new Zeppelin was completely destroyed during the bombardment, and the factory itself was severely damaged as nine bombs had hit and exploded at very vulnerable sections of the layout. But as far as the Allies were concerned there were further benefits. This widespread damage resulted in a frantic reorganization of the Zeppelin works. The defenses were tripled, strong nets were strung over the factory and sheds, trusting that nothing more hazardous than 20-pound bombs would be delivered. Heavier weapons were installed and many searchlights mounted, and as a final effort two gunboats were anchored offshore. All these expensive precautions were maintained until the end of the war, and though the sheds were not attacked again, many men and weapons were kept in idleness during the next four years.

Of some interest is Flight Lieutenant Sippe's patrol report

taken from the official records of the Royal Naval Air Service:

9:55 A.M. Left Belfort and shaped course for Basle, following numbers 873 (Briggs) and 875 (Babington).

10:25 A.M. Arrived Basle. Passed to the north. Observed No. 873 going away to the south.

Overtook No. 875. No. 873 several miles to starboard.

Followed Rhine at height of about 5000 feet, keeping north.

11:00 A.M. Above clouds in Rhine Valley. No. 873 passed across and took up position ahead and about a mile to port. Continued to Schaffhausen when suddenly lost sight of 873. No. 875 about two miles astern and about same height.

11:30 A.M. Arrived extreme end of lake and came down to within 10 feet of water. Continued at this height over lake, passing Constance at a very low altitude, as considered less likelihood of being seen. Crossed lake and hugged north shore until five miles from objective. Started climb and reached 1200 feet. Observed twelve or fourteen shrapnels bursting slightly north of Friedrichshafen. Presumed they were directed against No. 873.

11:55 A.M. When half a mile from Friedrichshafen put machine into a dive and came down to 700 feet.

Observed men lined up to right of shed. Number estimated 300 to 500.

Dropped one bomb in enclosure to put gunners off aim and, when in correct position, two into works and shed.

The fourth bomb failed to release. During this time very heavy fire, mitrailleuse and rifle, was kept up and shells were being very rapidly fired. Dived and flew north out of range of guns, then turned back to waterside shed to try and release fourth bomb. Bomb was not released. Was fired on by two machine guns (probably mitrailleuse).

Dived down to surface of lake and made good my escape.

1:50 P.M. Arrived Belfort.

Matters settled down for the next few weeks as far as anti-Zeppelin activity was concerned. The German Army Airship Service was hampered by the general war situation and had few dirigibles to risk on long, dangerous missions.

New crews had to be trained, weather stations set up, and all in all, there was plenty to do in carrying out required reconnaissance missions on both the Eastern and Western fronts.

Strasser and Eckener concentrated on building up the Naval Airship Service, determined that once they had sufficient aircraft, crews, and, most important, suitable ammunition to hurl against their British enemies, they would set up a round of savage raids against London that they hoped would soon bring Britain to her knees.

Shortly before Christmas, actually on the night of December 24, a German U-boat had encountered the Harwich Force that was escorting the seaplane carriers *Engadine*, *Riviera*, and *Empress* on a Fleet-Air mission aimed at the airship sheds at Nordholz about eight miles south of Cuxhaven. By dawn of December 25 this force, escorted by the cruisers HMS *Arethusa* and HMS *Undaunted* with a screen of destroyers and submarines appeared at a position twelve miles north of Helgoland. Each of the makeshift carriers bore three Short seaplanes that were to be put over the side and sent off to bomb the new airship shed. It was also hoped that the airmen could obtain some information on the class of ships lying at anchor at Wilhelmshaven in the Schillig Roads, or in the mouth of the Elbe.

When the more detailed alarm was received LZ.5 and LZ.6 were sent out from Nordholz with Kapitänleutnant Horst von Buttlar-Brandenfels commanding the first, and Kapitänleutnant Klaus Hirsch the second. They first made contact with the British Fleet just before dawn of Christmas Day, for they also had headed for the famous rock of Helgoland. The dawn had opened cold, but the sea was reasonably smooth when LZ.6 reached the island of Amrum. Buttlar, stationed well forward in the open control car heard his executive officer shout, "I believe I see three enemy ships ahead, sir."

Taking up his glasses the young airship commander studied the three strange vessels for several minutes, and realized they were auxiliary warships of some kind. He then showed he was not an experienced seaman by coming to the conclusion they were minelayers. But their appearance was enough for him.

"Prepare a code message for the *Seydlitz*," he ordered. "We must cut these intruders off at once." He did not know he was planning to trap three British seaplane carriers.

The *Seydlitz*, a battle cruiser, acting as a reconnaissance flagship, lay in Jade Bay about forty miles away. She should be able to trap these impudent Britishers.

The message was written, coded and signed, but shortly after the radioman began tapping out the warning, *LZ.6*'s set lost its power. There was a wild scramble to trace the failure and to check the whole antenna system, but nothing they did remedied the situation. Kapitänleutnant Buttlar realized that a glorious chance for promotion was slipping from his grasp.

Then, to his concern, a lookout reported a seaplane coming up from Helgoland, approaching their port side. It was not immediately identified, so Buttlar ordered his signalman to demand a recognition signal. The seaplane pilot fired a green signal flare, indicating it was a friendly aircraft, so Buttlar had his coded signal relayed to the seaplane by flash lamp and asked the pilot to forward it to the Senior Officer, Reconnaissance Ships, through the coastal radio station on Helgoland. In a short time they could hear over their own receiver the original warning being sent on to the *Seydlitz*.

Having carried out that duty, Buttlar moved to take a closer look at the mysterious vessels below, and then noticed that one seemed to be lagging behind. This was *Empress* which was hampered by condenser trouble. The German commander decided to act offensively, and getting rid of three tanks of fuel and much water ballast, he rose from 1600 feet to 5800 feet and took cover in scattered clouds. He had three 100-pound bombs tied to the catwalk below the Zeppelin's hull that were fastened with what was known as seaming twine. The bombardment officer, Schiller by name, was ordered by Buttlar to climb out of the forward car to the covered catwalk, carrying a sailor's jackknife. Then, while the helmsman zigzagged *LZ.6* back and forth, Schiller took a general aim and hacked at the twine that held the bombs.

At this point we encounter two different stories. The British version stated that *Empress* became the target of a heavy salvo of bombs, whereas Buttlar said he had time to drop only one, and then a six-inch shell, fired by the cruiser *Undaunted* badly damaged his Zeppelin. He also claimed that the crew of the *Empress* fired rifles and machine guns, and later pointed out a number of rifle-caliber bullet holes in his gas cells.

Surprised to find other, and more formidable, vessels in the area, Buttlar wisely took *LZ.6* up into a cloud layer and moved about for another bomb attack. By that time he had fully identified off to the west two British cruisers and eight torpedo-boat destroyers that were steaming at high speed to join the impending action. From a height of about 2000 feet Schiller hacked at the twine again and the second bomb fell, missing a seaplane tender by only twenty yards. The British flotilla replied with shrapnel shells, and the smoke from the bursts swept through the catwalks and gondola of *LZ.6*, making the crew members hack and cough with the acrid effect.

Buttlar took her up to 3600 feet, and once in a cloud he steered south and darted from one patch of cloud to another. During this time he noted that the original straggler was still attempting to keep pace with the other vessels. He nosed down once more, and this time Schiller dropped the third 100-pounder about twenty yards ahead of the seaplane tender's bow. The British jack-tars could be seen popping at the dirigible with infantry rifles. The Zeppelin crew thought this an amusing gesture.

The German commander brought his airship down once more, determined to keep contact with the enemy. The cloud layer had thickened and the airship seemed heavy. It dropped unusually fast, and before measures could be taken they were down to 400 feet, directly over one of the seaplane carriers. Leaving Schiller to take the helm, Buttlar manned a machine gun while his chief engineer manned another. They sprayed the deck of the ship below, enjoying the sight of British sailors scattering for shelter. It was fun, but risky as the British cruisers opened fire with their heavy weapons.

"Take her aloft!" Buttlar yelled.

"I would, sir," the helmsman cried, "but there's something wrong. She won't respond."

Buttlar considered the previous shrapnel fire, and ordered a rigger to make an immediate inspection of all gas cells. After several anxious minutes, during which Buttlar took over the control car and tried to get back into the cloud cover, the rigger returned to report that all seemed well. All the ballonets were apparently filled, and there were no visible leaks or shrapnel damage.

Nevertheless, the dirigible continued to lose height, and the crew was ordered to release considerable water ballast. Buttlar then decided to attempt to work his way into Jade Bay where he might drop an extensive report, complete with detailed sketches, on the deck of the *Seydlitz*. His intentions were sound, but *LZ.6* kept losing height and although the engineer next made a complete inspection of the ship he could find nothing wrong.

The situation worsened even more, and as they came in sight of Jade Bay, Buttlar had to order a gravity tank containing six hundred pounds of fuel, dropped overboard. It almost fell on the Jade Harbor patrol lightship. Buttlar then had enough buoyancy to move up to *Seydlitz* and successfully drop a waterproof message wallet on the battle cruiser's quarterdeck, giving full details of the British Navy concentration off Helgoland.

Having carried out that duty, Buttlar next tried to steer for Nordholz, but only made that field after tossing off everything detachable. When they had landed, and a closer inspection had been made of the ballonets, the chief rigger discovered over six hundred tiny holes that had been made in the gasbags—by British Navy riflemen!

We now pick up the British seaplanes that had been launched from the seaplane tenders. Only seven of the nine planes could get off the water and take to the air. They sped off southward for Cuxhaven, while the surface ships had to stand by to await results. They first noticed a great increase in wireless traffic over the enemy's wavebands. Then a Zeppelin came over and tried to bomb one of the tenders, but was apparently driven off by antiaircraft fire from all the ships. They also reported that a German seaplane had flown over, dropped some bombs, but hit nothing but the waters of Helgoland Bight.

With all this as the background, it is only fair to report that the British raid was not a spectacular success; in fact the attacks on the Zeppelin sheds were a complete failure since none of the R.N.A.S. pilots could find them and there was very heavy antiaircraft fire to contend with. However, seaplane Number 136 had a profitable morning. It was piloted by Flight Commander C. F. Kilner with Lieutenant Erskine Childers as its observer. Kilner flew over the Schillig Roads and spotted a complete display of naval might—seven battleships, three battle cruisers, three light cruisers, ten destroyers, and four auxiliary vessels. He also reported a heavy concentration of shipping in the southern waters of the Weser, and a force of destroyers east of Wangeroog. The immediate effect of this particular flight was the frantic shifting of a large part of the German Fleet from Cuxhaven farther up the Kiel Canal, well out of range of the R.N.A.S.

(By coincidence, Erskine Childers had been an enthusiastic yachtsman and writer before the war, and his famous novel *The Riddle of the Sands*, published in 1903, had predicted German war preparations in these very waters. Later on he was awarded the Distinguished Service Cross. After his demobilization at war's end, Childers returned to Ireland where he had worked for Irish Home Rule before the war. He was soon elected to Dail Eireann as a deputy for Wicklow, and from this point on his life turned into a political tragedy. He opposed the Anglo-Irish Treaty of 1922 and supported De Valera in the Dail and joined the

Republicans when they took up arms. He was captured in Wicklow on November 10, 1922 and tried by a military court-martial on the technical charge of having possession of an automatic pistol without proper authority. He was found guilty of treason and executed by an Irish Free State firing squad on November 24, 1922.)

In the meantime the British surface ships were steaming back and forth over the launching area, awaiting the return of their aircraft. The first three came into sight about 10:00 A.M., or about three hours after they had taken off. They seemed to be in good condition and had no trouble making safe landings near their mother ships. Then it was noted that they were being closely followed by several enemy seaplanes out of Helgoland, and while the British seaplanes were attempting to taxi up to their derricks to be taken aboard, a new bombing attack began. A second Zeppelin (*LZ.5*, commanded by Hirsch) was seen hovering above, but her movements were so ineffectual they took little notice of her, and eventually the Zeppelin and enemy seaplanes moved off.

The British Navy men began searching for the remaining four seaplanes, and moved in closer to the Frisian Islands hoping to pick them up, but when it was apparent that the missing aircraft had by now run out of fuel, they decided to wait no longer and turned around for the return journey. However, a British submarine, *E.11*, that had been part of the heavier flotilla, remained off Norderney Gat to watch and wait. By good fortune she rescued three of the missing crews while German seaplanes tried in vain to bomb the undersea boat. A fourth pilot had force-landed with engine failure near a Dutch trawler and was interned in Holland for a short time, but managed to get to a Rotterdam dockside where he signed on as a seaman aboard a vessel heading for England, and in that manner returned to his homeland, ready and willing to fly again.

The attempted Cuxhaven raid was not garlanded with high success, but it made a deep impression on German airship policy as it was obvious to leaders like Strasser and

Eckener that unless England was soon bombed, the R.N.A.S. would eventually destroy every airship in its hangar before they could set out for London. In fact, there were some German military officials who were positive the Zeppelins would never be able to make effective attacks on England. But taunted by the raid on Christmas Day, Strasser and Eckener brushed aside all caution and put in motion a formal request to the Kaiser, asking him to withdraw his decision not to bomb London.

IV

THE DEFENSE OF LONDON

No matter what the orthodox military mind in Germany thought of Zeppelins, or their contribution to the Fatherland's determination to destroy England, the British had no intention of writing off the dirigible, or ignoring its potential. In early September 1914 Winston Churchill drew up the policy that was to guide the Admiralty in its task of defending the country from this aerial threat. This memorandum that was penned before the first bomb had fallen on British soil, represents the Churchill mind at its best, and indicates that the First Sea Lord had a remarkable anticipation of the problem.

He wrote: "There can be no question of defending London by artillery against aerial attack. It is quite impossible to cover so vast an area; and if London, why not every other city? Defence against aircraft by guns is limited absolutely to points of military value. The Admiralty and War Office, with the group of public buildings in the neighborhood, and the Houses of Parliament, constitute a military area, and are sufficiently guarded by the three guns mounted. The effect of these guns will be to compel the airship either to expose itself to dangerous fire or fly so high that accurate bomb-dropping would be impossible. Searchlights should, however, be provided without delay.

But, after all, the great defence against aerial menace is to attack the enemy's aircraft as near as possible to their point of departure.

The principle is as follows:

(A) A strong overseas force of aeroplanes to deny the French and Belgian coasts to the enemy's aircraft, and to attack all Zeppelin and air bases or temporary air bases which it may be sought to establish and which are in reach.

(B) In constant telegraphic and telephonic communication with the overseas aeroplane squadrons, we must maintain an intercepting force of aeroplanes and airships at some convenient point within range of a line drawn from Dover to London, and local defence flights at Eastchurch and Calshot.

(C) A squadron of aeroplanes will be established at Hendon also, in close telephonic communication with other stations, for the purpose of attacking enemy aircraft which may attempt to molest London. Landing grounds must be prepared in all the parks; railings must be removed and the area marked out by a large white circle by day and a good system of lighting by night. It is indispensable that airmen of the Hendon flight should be able to fly by night, and their machines must be fitted with the necessary lights and instruments."

Churchill also emphasized that all available guns be mounted at all key military and naval areas. He stated that London and other vital cities were to initiate blackout precautions. The public was to be warned and clearly advised of these precautions and instructed in means of taking shelter while enemy raids were being made. This matter of shelter was outlined further by the Commissioner of Police who took pains to warn the populace of the danger from falling fragments of shells when guns were firing at hostile aircraft. At this time, interestingly enough, no system of public air-raid warnings was being considered.

In December 1914 the *London Gazette* announced the appointment to the Royal Flying Corps of Captain Hugh C. T. Dowding of the Royal Artillery, who had been confirmed as a flying officer on conclusion of his pilot's course, and was seconded to the R.F.C. Twenty-five years later "Stuffy" Dowding became the Commander-in-Chief of Fighter Command during the Battle of Britain.

In the early plans the responsibility of London was in the hands of the Royal Naval Air Service, but the Royal Flying Corps had also taken a number of defensive measures, and the few aircraft they still had in England were made available in case of enemy raids. In fact, as early as October 1914 the Commanding Officer of Number 1 Squadron at Brooklands had received complete instructions from the Military Wing. In part they gave some details of the principle on which R.F.C. fields and equipment were prepared for their contribution to the defense of London:

Hounslow: Two B.E.'s with grapnels or bomb-boxes—at any rate one fitted with grapnels—will be available at Hounslow. (Grapnels are metal hooks that were to be lowered on steel cables and drawn through the covering of attacking dirigibles.) The B.E.'s will be sent to you shortly. Also, Captain Burdett will be posted to you. With these aircraft you will send eight men and one NCO, and they will be accommodated under the arrangements already made at Hounslow. *Joyce Green:* Two Henri Farman biplanes will be sent here. They will remain overnight and return to Brooklands if weather is suitable. Two good mechanics should go as passengers and should take with them rifles, grenades, flaring bullets for Martini carbines and a few hand-grenades with rope tails. The two officers and two mechanics will sleep at Joyce Green at night. A supply of flares is being arranged for by the War Office, fourteen for Joyce Green and fourteen for Hounslow. All machines will be in charge of a Flight Commander or an Acting Flight Commander, who should make arrangements for these two planes, and a light tender (motor van) should be put at his disposal.

Early in January 1915 the Chief of the German Naval Staff was given authority to bomb England, but again the Kaiser, perhaps with the Hague Convention in mind, and also because of his blood relationship with the British Royal family, stipulated that the raids be restricted to military targets and that London was not to be bombed.

The first raid by Zeppelins in which bombs were dropped on British soil occurred on the night of January 19-20, 1915, when two airships bombed Sheringham, Snettisham, King's Lynn, and Yarmouth. Four people were killed and sixteen injured, and during the next six months only six small raids were recorded. These did little damage. Then in the summer of that year three raids were made on London, and considerable damage was inflicted.

Through these wearying months it was realized that none of the air defenses was effective; in fact, from the point of view of the defense squadrons they were tragic. In seventy-nine sorties flown by defending fighters, eight aircraft crashed on landing in the dark, three pilots were killed in these crashes, and no Zeppelins were sighted.

These failures were soon obvious. Before the war only a few flights had been made by moonlight from the airfields of that day. Primitive flares made of waste, gasoline, and oil were laid out to indicate the landing path and the direction of the wind—nothing more. Generally speaking, these prewar flights were simply experimental, and made under ideal conditions by pilots who were skilled airmen of that period. No radio communication was available, and once aloft, the airmen were completely out of touch with the ground. Their aircraft were not too stable and likely to spin if the pilot gave too much attention to searching for his landing strip. Instrument, or blind-flying was several years away.

The artillery weapons were no more successful, and it was soon seen that the attacking Zeppelins must first be found by an "electric beam" (searchlight) before they could be fired at. Officials responsible for the antiaircraft guns explained: "When a beam has found a dirigible, that beam must continue to hold to it as it passes over London, or hand it over to another beam. The range of an electric light is considerably less than the range of a gun and may be sharply affected by atmospheric conditions. Then the gunner must know the range within very narrow limits of accuracy, for the range will change as the dirigible moves. There is also difficulty with aiming because sights are based upon range tables calculated for ground targets, and therefore they are inaccurate when the weapon is elevated to fire into the air."

The artillery defense had been placed in the capable hands of Sir Percy M. Scott, a Royal Navy officer and ballistics expert. He had invented several important devices that improved the accuracy of naval gunnery, and had served with distinction in the Boer War, the Boxer Rebellion, and had retired an admiral in 1913. He was brought back to take charge of the London defenses, a task that was almost beyond him as the most suitable weapon was a 13-pounder, a mobile gun that appeared to be as near what was required, as anything then coming out of Woolwich Arsenal.

Another point of interest, one with a pulp-writer's touch, lies in the fact that the British were laboring under a belief that the main gas cells of a dirigible were surrounded by an envelope that was filled with an inert gas, so that any bullets that penetrated would simply mix the inert gas with the hydrogen, and no blast would result. The Germans had caused this misconception to be carefully spread where it would be picked up by Allied agents.

To overcome this imaginary defense measure, British pilots were provided with light bombs and incendiary darts that it was believed would explode inside the main gas cells. All well and good, but the employment of these weapons severely limited the tactics of the aeroplane pilots who were expected to gain a position *above* the Zeppelins to make an attack. This was not only difficult to carry out, but because of the configuration of the standard biplane, the airship was, to a great extent, obscured from the pilot's view.

Eventually, the story of inert gas in the envelope was discounted, but for months it hampered the efforts of all British pilots, making their task almost impossible.

In early 1915 British production of aircraft was increasing in momentum, and many of the old country-fair machines that had been built solely for exhibition and city-to-city races were gradually weeded out. Designers were incorporating the ideas and suggestions of the active-service pilots into their new productions, and it was obvious that the true military aeroplane was well into its gestation period. Many of these machines were experimental, but they incorporated sound ideas and first-class workmanship. The armament men were planning the application of fixed and flexible machine guns. Controls were being simplified, and landing gear greatly improved. Looking back and thumbing through the old manuals of that day, one will see that the designers of the aircraft were far ahead of the armament staff, and setting a stiff pace for the engine manufacturers. In other words, the machines themselves were available, but the power plants were not efficient enough for general war purposes, and the gunnery could not keep pace with the progress of air-frame design.

In May 1915 the British War Office issued new instructions to all stations manned by the Royal Flying Corps, setting out the details of the aircraft and the armament that were to be kept in readiness against raiding Zeppelins. By now the R.F.C. had stations at South Farnborough, Brooklands, Hounslow, Joyce Green, Dover, and Shoreham. One machine was to be maintained constantly at "alert" at all fields, and the squadron commanders were advised that the aircraft most suitable for this purpose was the new Martinsyde Scout. This was a smart-looking biplane that at first was powered with an 80-horsepower Gnome rotary engine. It became an immediate success and was ordered in large quantities. It played an important role in the war all through 1915, or until the German Albatros and Halberstadt scouts proved to be somewhat faster. The Martinsyde was then improved with a Beardmore 120-horsepower, and later with a 160-horsepower Beardmore engine.

The armament for the available machines was listed as follows:

  6 Carcass bombs
 12 Hale Naval grenades
150 Incendiary darts
  5 Powder bombs
(Carcass bombs were simple iron cases filled with a suitable explosive. They were a variant of the old mortar bombs. Hale grenades were serrated-case grenades fixed to the end of a steel rod that was pushed down the bore of a rifle and fired with a special cartridge containing forty-three strands of cordite. Powder bombs were also a form of the incendiary bomb.)

Another Goldbergian bomb, described by Sir John Slessor in his memorable book *The Central Blue*, was a small oblong affair filled with gasoline and fitted with a secondary tube that carried an electrical detonator or igniter device. These bombs were to be released through a tube in the floor of the cockpit, and when the device exploded, a tangle of large fishhooks sprayed out of the top. According to their inventor, these hooks would grab the Zeppelin's envelope and the burning gasoline would complete the job. Slessor states no airships were burned, but several haystacks were destroyed.

It is interesting to note that up to this time it was not considered necessary to equip any of the anti-Zeppelin machines with rifles or machine guns.

Three Zeppelins took part in the historic attack of January 19, 1915. *LZ.3* was commanded by Kapitänleutnant Hans Fritz, *LZ.4* by Kapitänleutnant Magnus von Platen-Hallermund, and *LZ.6* by Kapitänleutnant Von Buttlar. The first two dirigibles had been docked at the Fuhlsbüttel sheds, but *LZ.6* had been berthed in the revolving hangar at Nordholz. These dirigibles were capable of remaining in the air for thirty hours. They had a gas capacity of 950,000 cubic feet, a ceiling of 9000 feet, and a speed of forty-five miles an hour, which shows how Eckener and Strasser had boosted Zeppelin capability during the previous six months.

Halfway across the North Sea, Von Buttlar's *LZ.6* had serious engine trouble and had to limp back home, but *LZ.3* and *LZ.4* made the Happisburg (pronounced "Hazeboro") light and continued on to Norfolk where they encountered snow squalls and poor visibility. Both airships cruised about seeking clear skies and a military target. They were first spotted from the ground by a young man in Ingham, Norfolk, who later reported that they looked like "two bright stars moving along some thirty yards apart." What he had seen were the navigation lights as the airships approached the British coast. At this point the two ships separated, and at 8:50 Lieutenant Fritz, who had managed to get up to 5000 feet, eventually found the town of Yarmouth. He dropped six 110-pound explosive bombs and seven incendiaries. One fell on a recreation ground, the second struck a flower garden, sending up a column of flame. No matter what Fritz aimed at he seemed to have bad luck, striking something unimportant.

On the other hand Lieutenant Hallermund took *LZ.4* toward the mouth of the Humber, but after crossing the coastline, he assumed he was over Grimsby whereas he had actually steered for Bacton in Norfolk. In his report he stated that he had been fired upon from the ground, so he dropped two incendiaries which only bewildered him with their glare. He turned and completely missed Cromer, and dropped two bombs on the little village of Sheringham. For the remainder of the night the skipper of *LZ.4* floundered about, completely lost, dropping the odd incendiary or high-explosive bomb whenever he believed he was over some important city. After venting his wrath on the village of Snettisham, Hallermund, still believing he was being fired on from the ground, dumped all his bombs indiscriminately, killing a woman and a little boy. On the way home he radioed that he had successfully bombed fortified places between the Tyne and the Humber. Both *LZ.3* and *LZ.4* managed to get back to Fuhlsbüttel although both dirigibles were coated with a thick veneer of ice.

The next morning the German newspapers reported full details of the raid, creating the wildest enthusiasm throughout the country.

But what did the people of Norfolk think of all this excitement? Was there panic? Were grim threats screamed? Nothing of the sort. Once the dead were decently removed, and the injured taken to hospitals, everyone went to bed as usual. The next morning people gathered in small groups, usually in front of some village church and compared experiences.

"All I can say is, it was the biggest sausage I ever saw in my life."

"It's too bad we didn't have some of them searchlights. We could have seen it all lovely, then."

"I'll swear the thing was flying sideways."

"Just like a church steeple that has been blown over and is floating away."

"I don't think it was a Zeppelin at all. I think it was just a big biplane."

But, as usually happened, a welter of spy stories followed, and any German pork butcher within fifty miles was an enemy agent who had used some mysterious signals to draw the Zeppelins to their target. There was the yarn about a car with a bright light attached to its roof; any windmill that turned erratically; and the mysterious lights flashing from church steeples, but there was no panic or frantic seeking of revenge.

World reaction to this first deliberate raid on undefended cities was most marked in the United States. The *New York Herald,* a very responsible newspaper, remarked in an editorial: "Is this the madness of despair or just plain everyday madness that has prompted the Germans to select for attack peaceful and undefended resorts on the English east coast? What can Germany hope to gain by these wanton attacks on undefended places and this slaughter of the innocents? Certainly not the good opinion of the people of neutral nations."

In contrast the Milwaukee *Free Press* ran glaring headlines proclaiming in high glee:

ZEPPELINS BOMBARD SANDRINGHAM
AS KING GEORGE AND THE QUEEN FLEE
Panic Grips Capital as Foe
Steers Course for London

This was concocted from the fact that the King and Queen had actually left Sandringham some days before to return to their London residence. The threatened Zeppelin raids had nothing to do with the move.

Across the North Sea the Berlin newspapers insisted that the attacks were made on "some fortified places," and several of them proclaimed (perhaps through the pen of Dr. Eckener): "German genius which has at last ended the legend of England's invulnerable insularity; no longer is she protected by the sea." The Zeppelins, it was predicted, would continue their attacks over England, "dropping death everywhere." The *Cologne Gazette* boasted, "We shall not allow these wonderful weapons, which German intelligence has invented, to grow rusty."

The crews of both airships were decorated with the Iron Cross on their return to Fuhlsbüttel, but they had little time in which to flaunt their decorations as both airships were wrecked in a storm over Denmark on February 17, 1915.

On February 26, *LZ.8*, commanded by Kapitänleutnant Helmut Beelitz, left her shed at Düsseldorf and headed for England, but strong headwinds forced her to land at an Army encampment field in occupied Belgium. On March 4 Beelitz tried again, but was trapped by a North Sea gale and blown out of control over Nieuport, and his brand-new Zeppelin was shot down by Belgian gunners.

At this point a touch of interservice rivalry cropped up. Feeling ignored, and jealous of Strasser's close association with the Kaiser's naval advisers, the head of the Army Air-ship Service planned a major raid or two on his own. He first had Hauptmann Ernest A. Lehmann, one of Count Zeppelin's early pupils, fly an Army Zeppelin, known as *Sachsen*, (actually *L.12*) from its new shed at Maubege on the Sambre River near the Belgian border to make a raid on the British East Coast.

On this sortie, made on March 17, 1915, Captain Leh-mann employed a new idea in dirigible reconnaissance, in which a Cologne machinist, a Herr Hagen, had conceived a method of lowering an observation car on a steel cable from the control gondola of the airship, by which means the Zeppelin could stay unobserved in a cloud bank. The observation car with an observer aboard was lowered to where a very complete reconnaissance could be made of the countryside or target area. Lehmann had had the Cologne machinist build an experimental model in which a butter tub, fitted with a stabilizing fin, was lowered by a hand winch on six hundred feet of cable. As a matter of record Lehmann himself gamely tried out the device and was satis-fied that the idea had great merit.

Aboard *Sachsen*, however, the device had been improved. The winch was powered, and its drum carried 2700 feet of steel cable through which an insulated telephone wire was entwined, so the observer below the clouds could report directly to the control car above.

On his trip to England Captain Lehmann ran into thick fog, but he cruised off the East Coast until nightfall. Shortly before midnight he crossed the coastline, but the fog was even worse there, so he ascended to 6000 feet. Still he could not find a break in the murk, so he continued to cruise about hoping to the find the River Thames, but had no luck.

Turning back for Calais, he found that at 3600 feet above the Channel the fog had dispersed, and he had a splendid view of Calais Harbor. He then decided to try out his observation car, and had the engines throttled back. An Army Staff officer, Oberleutnant Max von Gemmingen, a nephew of Count Zeppelin, volunteered to get aboard and try out the device. He was lowered for a distance of about half a mile, and then while suspended at 2600 feet over Calais, Von Gemmingen, unseen by the French people below, although they could hear the Zeppelin's engines ticking over, gave orders for steering over the enemy targets and the dropping of bombs. The effect was terrifying. The antiaircraft crews could hear the *Sachsen,* but could not see her, and had nothing at which to fire; what shells were expended were fired blindly with no effect.

After that fantastic trip, Von Gemmingen was awarded the Iron Cross, Second Class, for his daring, and it must be admitted this middle-aged gentleman more than earned it. He was not provided with a parachute, and no one knew exactly how reliable that reel of cable was.

There is a popular story, possibly of doubtful origin, that Commander Strasser once decided to try out the dangling observation-car idea, and had a duplicate apparatus installed in the bomb compartment of a new airship. He then went aloft to test it. The airship circled the field several times, and then rose to 3000 feet. Strasser's trial was watched by every airship commander and crew member on the field, each one probably wondering if he would be next for this chilling experiment.

All went well at first. Strasser climbed aboard the streamlined tub, and those below noted that the little car seemed to be greatly influenced by the slipstream of the dirigible. The car swung and spun, and then it was seen that the stabilizing fin had fouled the cable and for a minute Strasser seemed to be hanging almost upside down. Then the cable tangled as it was played out of the hand winch and great loops of it curled away from the observation car, but Strasser hung on grimly while everyone expected to see him tossed out and sent tumbling to the ground.

Finally, the stabilizer fin disentangled, the loose loops straightened out and the car dropped like a stone. Why the cable did not break under the strain and shock was a mystery, but it held securely, and the Naval Airship Service commander waved cheerfully, assuring everyone he was safe. Ignoring his frightening experience, Strasser was convinced the idea had real merit, and he ordered every Zeppelin to be equipped with a winch and an observation car.

As the weather moderated with the coming of spring, and encouraged by the delivery of *LZ.9* that replaced the *LZ.8*, Strasser put Kapitänleutnant Heinrich Mathy in charge, and ordered another attack on Britain. This raid, staged over the Tynside area on April 14, was only half-heartedly carried out; bomb damage was slight, and only one woman and a small child were injured. Some reports state the woman and child were killed.

The following night, April 15, three Zeppelins were sent out to East Coast targets. Strasser went along aboard *LZ.7* —actually in command of Oberleutnant Werner Peterson— to observe how his airships behaved under wartime conditions. *LZ.6* was commanded by Von Buttlar, and *LZ.5* by Kapitänleutnant Alois Böcker.

Again, the Zeppelin commanders reported stiff opposition, with searchlights pointing them out for British guns. All of them claimed to have suffered several hits, although again there were no searchlights available. Only three pom-pom shells were fired, all of which failed to burst in the air, and only exploded when they returned and hit the ground. A battalion of Sussex Cyclists fired a few token shots with their Lee Enfield rifles, but that was all. *LZ.5* dropped its bombs on built-up areas along the Humber River and returned with a few rifle-bullet holes in her gas cells.

Through that spring, British intelligence agents were checking on all new airship sheds being built in occupied Belgium, and marked places such as Gontrode, Evere, and Berchem-Sainte-Agathe for their attention.

At this point a British air hero steps into the scene. A quiet, shy man with clear eyes and a modest smile that hid an iron will and the heart of a lion, Lanoe George Hawker possessed an affectionate nature, and on the ground was more than generous with his friendship.

Born in December 1890, Hawker was somewhat older than the average R.F.C. playboy type. He began his teenage education at the Royal Naval College, but later transferred to the Royal Military Academy. He secured a commission in the Royal Engineers and was one of the first small group of officers selected for flight training. He was an adept pupil, and on March 4, 1913, was awarded Aero Certificate Number 453, after making his graduation flight on a Deperdussin monoplane.

When the war broke out, Hawker, by then a member of Number 6 Squadron, R.F.C., flew an R.E.5 across the Channel, and arrived in the war zone in time to see the fall of Antwerp.

He was one of the men selected to give some attention to the new Zeppelin sheds that were mushrooming all over Belgium, and on April 18, 1915, flying a B.E.2c biplane, he headed for the airship sheds at Gontrode. In a primitive rack he carried three melinite bombs that were nothing more than French .75 artillery shells fitted with guide vanes and a very temperamental nose cap; and a haversack of hand grenades.

As he arrived over his target he was greeted by a storm of ground fire, but he bored in, and then noticed a kite balloon that had been sent up for the purpose of signaling the approach of attacking aircraft. Hawker decided to tackle the balloon first, and flew over it while the observer shot at him with a Parabellum machine gun. The first two melinite bombs missed their target by the proverbial mile, so he went in much lower and tossed over half a dozen hand grenades, but with no better luck. He was still being harassed by the gunner in the balloon basket, so he dropped two more hand grenades on the big bag. They detonated where they would do the most good, and the *Drachen* exploded and started to flutter toward the ground. Hawker then circled, and using the smoke and debris of the balloon as a shield, made a run on the Zeppelin hangar. He scored a direct hit with his last melinite bomb and a new dirigible shed went up in flames.

The mission required about three hours, and on his return to his field at Abeele, Hawker counted almost forty bullet holes in the B.E. He was awarded the Distinguished Service Order for his one-man effort. Shortly after, Gontrode was abandoned as a Zeppelin base and redesigned as a Gotha field. Months later Hawker was honored with the Victoria Cross for his continued attacks and successful fights against the enemy, but his luck ran out on November 23, 1916, when he was shot down and killed in a memorable duel with the German ace, Baron Manfred von Richthofen.

The Germans persisted in their efforts to bomb Britain out of the war. There had been a time when the Naval Airship Service had decided that the most effective way to use dirigibles against London would be to organize fleets of twenty Zeppelins and have them concentrate over the target. It was calculated that under these conditions twenty Zeppelins, carrying three hundred incendiary bombs apiece could start at least a thousand fires, a situation that would completely thwart the London Fire Brigades. Recalling the attacks by Hitler's bombs twenty-five years later, this seems a fair estimate of the possibilities. Strasser and Eckener expected to lose at least one third of their airship fleet on every such raid, and were quite prepared to accept such losses, but they could have hardly taken into account the effect of such losses on all Zeppelin crews. As matters turned out, when airship losses reached 25 per cent, the raids on London were called off.

The new Zeppelin sheds erected in Belgium made it possible for the short-range Army airships to make hit-and-run raids against the Estuary sector of the Thames. In the early morning hours of May 10, 1915, *L.38*, commanded by Hauptmann Erich Linnarz, made an attack on Southend, but a salvo of unexpected gunfire forced him to take cover beyond Canvey Island. Although Linnarz was lionized and given the hero treatment in Berlin, he was something of a posturing martinet; if a story that has been told, retold, and revised time and time again, is to be believed. According to the version that seems to stand up to the various time brackets, he was so enraged by this hostile reception, that after he ordered his helmsman to take L.38 to a higher level, he took an engraved calling card from his wallet, and scrawled on it:

> You English! We have come, and
> we will come again soon, to
> kill or cure! Linnarz.

Some accounts have it that the card was simply signed, *"German,"* not *"Linnarz."*

This message that had been placed in a weighted streamer was found later on the sands near Canvey Island.

On his second raid over the Thames Estuary, Linnarz again casually floated about at 2000 feet where he was intercepted by Flight Sub-Lieutenant R. H. Mulock, who was piloting a Gnome-powered Avro, modified as a single-seater. Mulock thought he had a chance of a lifetime as he had been searching for raiding Zeppelins for weeks, and this was the first one to come within range of his guns. He opened fire with a Lewis, mounted on a metal peg, but after a short burst the weapon jammed, and before he could clear the stoppage, the dirigible had dumped a lot of ballast and climbed to a safer level. There was nothing for him to do but return to his base at the Westgate Air Station.

Linnarz did not know it at the time, but with that challenge of his on May 10, he had sealed the doom of another airship, L.37, the first dirigible to be shot down by a British airman.

On that same night in which Mulock attempted to fire on Linnarz's dirigible, another R.N.A.S. pilot was aloft. He was Squadron Commander Spenser Grey who was flying a Nieuport-11, a single-seater scout powered with a Le Rhone engine, when he encountered L.39, commanded by a Hauptmann Masium. Scrambling for height and position, Grey managed to get within a hundred feet of the belly of the dirigible and opened fire with a Lewis gun that was mounted on a bracket on his upper wing. At the same time, Flight Commander S. Bigsworth, who was aboard an Avro-504, also spotted L.39, and zipped along the top of its framework, dropping four 20-pound Hale bombs.

Amazingly, neither the Lewis gun ammunition nor the Hale bombs appeared to bother the airship, and eventually German antiaircraft gunners at Ostend drove off Grey and Bigsworth, and Hauptmann Masium managed to get his airship into some morning mist and head for Ghent. L.39 was somewhat damaged, but made her base with no further incident.

This annoying failure discouraged British airmen and caused considerable criticism, comment, and discussion. If a Zeppelin, filled with hydrogen, could not be brought down by bombs and machine-gun fire, what would put an end to the airship menace? One R.N.A.S. searchlight crew did, finally, catch a Zeppelin in the beam of its light, the first time an enemy aircraft had been illuminated over British soil, and so thankful were the authorities for this small favor, a special silver badge was devised and each member of the searchlight crew formally presented with one.

Surprisingly enough, the first British airman to down a Zeppelin is seldom mentioned in general histories of this all-important segment of military aviation. Even today, if you ask any elderly Englishman the name of the airman who brought down the first Zeppelin, he will with no hesitation of any sort reply, "Oh, that was that chap Leefe Robinson. He brought it down one night, and it fell all ablaze at Cuffley. Got the V.C. for it, he did. We'll never forget that night."

How easily they forgot a young Royal Naval Air Service pilot, Reggie Warneford, who on June 7, 1915, destroyed the Army dirigible L.37 over Ghent, whereas Leefe Robinson's victory was not scored until September 3, 1916. But Warneford made his "kill" over Belgium, and Leefe Robinson's was staged high above the outskirts of London where millions looked up and beheld the first of a series of defeats that eventually drove the military dirigible out of the skies. It is perhaps natural that all Britain should easily recall the finish of *SL.11*, and completely forget the destruction of *L.37*, but the oversight should be rectified.

Reginald Alexander John Warneford was a gay composite of the British Empire of those days. His parents were jovial Yorkshire folk who had shuttled about the world on engineering missions, and young Warneford, born in India, was schooled at the English College in Simla, but later went to England where he attended the Stratford-on-Avon Grammar School. The family next moved to Canada, and Reggie who had developed a mechanical skill, particularly with engines, joined the Merchant Marine and was serving with the India Steam Navigation Company when World War I broke out. He resigned immediately and made his way to England where he joined the 2nd Battalion of the much-publicized Sportsman's Regiment, an infantry unit consisting chiefly of well-known sporting and athletic figures.

There was considerable prestige in this regiment, but in England, as in several countries, it was found that most headlined athletes were psychologically attuned for sport only, not for war. Fearing the conflict would end before the athletes could be whipped into combat condition, Warneford applied for a transfer to the Royal Naval Air Service. Whether he was an ideal candidate has been widely discussed. His best friends have generally agreed that Reggie was too cocksure, inclined to be boastful, and frankly, no great shakes as a pilot. His first commanding officer, a Commander Groves, soon decided that this lad would break his neck long before he got into action. However, one or two intuitive instructors managed to curb his impetuosity, and by the time he had advanced to the Central Flying School at Upavon he had proved to be a daring young airman.

By May 1915 Warneford had won his R.N.A.S. wings and was shipped to Number 2 Naval Squadron, then located at Eastchurch (Thames Estuary). There his superior officers decided that he would be much better off where there would be some action to absorb his animal activity. He was sent across the Channel to Number 1 Naval Squadron, then under the command of Wing Commander Arthur Longmore who became an Air Chief Marshal in World War II. At Dunkirk Reggie continued his wild ways, resisting all discipline, and becoming the squadron nuisance. Longmore soon decided to turn him loose and let the Huns discipline him.

On his first flight out of Dunkirk he was given an ancient Voisin biplane, and an observer who, if he still lives, must remember that hair-raising experience. Shortly after taking off Warneford spotted a German observation plane circling over Zeebrugge. He went into immediate pursuit and ordered the observer to use the light machine gun with which he had been provided. They followed the enemy aircraft all the way back to its field, but by that time the British gun jammed, and ignoring the flight controls, Warneford tried to get into his observer's cockpit to remedy the stoppage. The antics of the plane under such conditions can be imagined, and it is related that Warneford had to help his observer climb down out of the plane when they returned to Dunkirk.

Wing Commander Longmore then provided Warneford with a Morane Parasol, a high-wing monoplane, originally designed as a two-seater, but which, in a few instances, had been modified as a single-seater and flown as a fighter-scout. Young Reggie was sent off in one of these machines to do his worst, and from all accounts, rolled up a remarkable record, chasing enemy planes, bombing gun emplacements, and attacking troop movements. So wild were these forays, Warneford soon wore out his mount, and Commander Longmore had to find another. In this it can be seen that Warneford was forming a service pattern that was to be followed by Captain Albert Ball and Lieutenant Frank Luke, a young Arizonian.

It was a month previously that Linnarz had hurled his childish challenge. The calling card became a taunt to the

R.N.A.S., and they were determined to take up the gaunt-let. Spenser Grey who had been aloft the night Linnarz had suffered his big scare, was given a special flight that was to be stationed at Furnes, just across the French-Belgian border. This was done to disperse the squadron equipment, now that Dunkirk had become such an obvious target. Grey's flight included Warneford, Lieutenant J. P. Wilson, and Flight Sub-Lieutenant J. S. Mills.

On the afternoon of June 6 Wilson and his flight were ordered to report to Dunkirk where Spenser Grey was hold-ing a conference. Hauptmann Linnarz's calling card was still on display, and Grey began with: "The Hun who dropped this might have played merry hell over England a few weeks ago. Mulock did his best, but Linnarz returned to his shed at Evere. We've got to do something about it."

"How do we know he's located at Evere?" Wilson in-quired.

"We have an Intelligence Division to learn such things."

Wilson started to get to his feet. "One good attack might be enough," he muttered.

"That's what Mulock said when he had to break off. Just blast them out of their bloody sheds."

Warneford confided to Wilson, "I've never been off the ground at night."

"Amazing! I thought you'd done everything with an aeroplane. Well, there's no time like the present."

At 12:20 A.M. of June 7 Wing Commander Longmore was warned by the Admiralty that three Zeppelins that had been over Britain were on their way back. Here was a chance of a lifetime.

Wilson's flight was warned and a broad plan, previously agreed on, was put into action. Warneford and another Sub-Lieutenant, Rose, were sent off in single-seater Mo-ranes. Wilson and Mills took big bomb-carrying Henri Far-mans to attack the Zeppelin sheds at Evere, near Brussels.

Warneford, who had never been off the ground at night, was flagged off first about 1:00 A.M. The Morane flew beau-tifully and Reggie was at 2000 feet before he realized what he had volunteered for. He stared wide-eyed all around and tried to find his small grouping of instruments. A length of scarlet worsted that was knotted to a center-section strut flicked insistently, and he knew from this primitive instrument that he was in a dangerous side-slip. Then, gradually, as his eyes grew accustomed to the yellow-gray nothingness beyond his Triplex windscreen, he could read all his instruments. Already he was at 3000 feet!

Rose was not so lucky. He became lost in the low mist, the light on the instrument panel went out, and he had to make a forced landing in an open field near Cassel where he turned over but was not seriously hurt.

Warneford searched for the rest of the group from Dunkirk, but no other aircraft appeared to be in the sky. He listened to the even *chug-chug-chug* of his rotary engine and felt his face being wasp-stung by condensation drips coming off the center section. He was fascinated by the poisonous-looking blue-yellow flame of his exhaust, a feature he had not seen before. He checked with his compass, made sure he was on the proper bearing, and began another search.

Content, if somewhat bored with the comparative inaction, Warneford kept a close watch, hoping to find two more sets of exhaust flame that would guide him to where Wilson and Mills were heading for their rendezvous. He wondered what an airship shed looked like from the air at night. Then, he suddenly saw a strange glow a few miles to the north. He squinted, and looked again. Although he was attracted by another blue-yellow exhaust he wondered what Wilson and Mills were doing up there near Ostend . . . and whatever was that long black mass floating above them?

Wilson and Mills had made immediate contact after taking off, and after clearing the low fog around Furnes, had headed for Brussels nearly seventy-five miles away. The skies were clear in that direction, and Wilson decided to fly straight for Evere which lay on the north side of the old Flemish city. Both Henri Farman pilots found their target with no difficulty. Wilson was soon caught in the blazing bar of a searchlight and some antiaircraft fire, but he used a flashlight to give the impression he was a friendly airman coming in for a landing. Uncertain what to do, the Germans did nothing, and Wilson made a clean run-in, released his rack of 20-pound bombs, making a beautiful pathfinder job for Mills who followed Wilson in. Between them they torched a great shed and an almost new dirigible, one marked L.38—the same airship flown by Hauptmann Linnarz on his raid on Britain. L.38 was an Army Airship Service dirigible, not to be confused with LZ.38 that appeared later on the Eastern Front, and after a forced landing at Seemuppen, Courland, on December 29, 1916, had to be dismantled and written off the books.

On this eventful night L.37, commanded by an Oberleutnant Von der Haegen, had been sent on a routine patrol with L.38 and L.39. L.38 returned early because of engine trouble, only to be burned in her shed by the R.N.A.S. airmen the next morning. There was nothing particularly important or offensive about L.37's mission. It had been arranged mainly to give a number of airship designers, specialists, and technicians from the Zeppelin factory some firsthand knowledge of the various problems experienced by the crews on active service.

L.37 was 521 feet long, and her eighteen main gas ballonets carried 953,000 cubic feet of hydrogen. She was powered by four 210-horsepower Maybach engines, and manned by a select crew of twenty-eight skilled airshipmen. For defense, her designers had provided four machine-gun posts that were built into the outboard engine gondolas. These positions gave good visibility, a fairly wide arc of fire, and efficient defense along both sides of the airship, but there was no gun position anywhere along the upper side of the dirigible.

After flying north for a few minutes, Warneford stared in amazement as he realized he had encountered a Zeppelin, but it seemed half a mile long. He had to twist his head from side to side to take in the leviathan proportions. Several glistening cars hung from its underside, and the gleam of the fantail exhausts indicated that the rubberized covering was daubed a yellow ocher. Warneford wondered what kept anything as large as that in the air.

But this was no time for cogitation. The Zeppelin's machine guns suddenly opened up and slugs clattered through the frail wing of Morane Parasol Number 3253. Somewhat puzzled, Reggie wisely heeled over and cleared out of range. It should be explained that this model of the Morane Parasol carried no machine gun of any kind. Many accounts of Warneford's exploit indicate that he may have had a Hotchkiss gun mounted on a convenient peg. Others state that with his own hands he had bolted a Vickers gun behind the propeller, and fixed a metal collar around the bases of the propeller blades, as had French ace Roland Garros some weeks before. Thus he was provided with a fixed, front-firing gun. This is most unlikely, for in his official report, to be added to this chapter, Warneford makes no mention of firing a machine gun of any kind. There is also some question whether the aircraft-type of Vickers was available by early June 1915.

The fog was clearing and the Ostend-Bruges Canal was sharply defined below, and with that position clear in his mind Warneford decided that the dirigible was heading for Ghent, but suddenly the big snub-nosed airship shifted course and came straight for him. Two more streams of tracer-flecked machine-gun fire were threatening. Two more bursts came from the forward gondolas and converged only a few yards from the Parasol. The R.N.A.S. pilot gave the Le Rhone all she could gulp, and tried to climb, but the crisscrossing tracers penciled in a definite warning, so Reggie had to peel off and dive.

As he studied the situation he may have turned to a light Belgian carbine, carried in a leather boot beside his wicker seat. He may have steered the Morane back into a position below and behind the mighty elevator and rudder framework. He may have gripped the control stick between his knees and triggered a few .303 shells at the massive target. He may have, but this is strictly conjecture. Many historians have provided Warneford with a machine gun and/or a carbine, but there is no definite proof he was so equipped. We do know he had six 20-pound bombs in a simple rack that could be released one by one by a toggle and wire device.

Warneford stalked *L.37* for several minutes, but whenever he came within range or view the German gunners sprayed the sky with long bursts of Parabellum fire, and he was driven off time after time.

L.37 began to rise fast, for Von der Haegen had apparently dumped some water ballast over Assebrouck, leaving Warneford still scrambling to get above his present 7000 feet. Von der Haegen then increased his speed and nosed around for Ghent. Although he knew he was outclassed, Reggie refused to give up the chase, and he settled down, determined to keep the dirigible in view, and hope to gain some much-needed altitude.

Von der Haegen was obviously racing for safety, and while he maintained his height, Warneford was helpless, but the German airship commander realized this was no ordinary patrol and he fretted about his passengers, the technicians, when he should have concentrated on maintaining a safe tactical procedure.

At 2:25 A.M. the Morane pilot, still stalking and trying to get above the Zeppelin, was cheered to see the big airship nose down and apparently head for a break in the 7000-foot cloud layer that spread toward Ghent. By now Reggie had browbeaten his Morane up to a position where he could use his 20-pound incendiary bombs. In a few minutes *L.37* was actually below him and for the first time he saw that its upper cover was painted what seemed to be a dark green, and he was thankful no gun turrets were showing along this upper panel.

Again, he was astonished by the size of this monster as he moved in for an attack glide. She was so big he felt he would have no trouble in making a landing on her topside.

Below, Ghent lay a dull smudge, and when the gnatlike Morane nosed down for that 500-foot-long upper panel he must have felt slight and puny against the aerial leviathan.

He set a straight course along the top of the airship and began pulling the bomb toggle.

"*One . . . two . . . three!*" he counted and felt the Morane jerk with the release of each bomb. He fully expected the Zeppelin to explode immediately, but nothing happened!

"*Four . . . five . . .*" he continued to count, and then a blinding explosion ripped through the upper cover, baring the blackened tracery of the framework.

Whongff!

Spellbound, Reggie continued his run-in until the little Morane was swept up on a savage belch of flame and concussion. She whipped over with a violence that would have hurled Warneford out of his cockpit had it not been for his safety belt. He gasped in astonishment, rammed the stick forward and tried to force the aeroplane into a dive. Chunks of burning framework hurtled by as he floundered out of that aerial convulsion and streaked down through a curling pall of choking smoke. Over the next few minutes he was absorbed in skimming clear of the debris, getting back on an even keel, and frantically adjusting his air and gas mixture to dampen out a series of warning pops from the Le Rhone engine.

A few minutes afterward the doomed airship fell on the Convent of St. Elizabeth in the Mont-Saint-Armand suburb of Ghent. One man on the ground was killed and several badly burned, but the helmsman of the Zeppelin had a miraculous escape. According to some eyewitnesses he jumped clear of the tumbling wreckage at about two hundred feet, landed on a roof of the convent, crashed on through as though it had been made of matchwood, and landed in an unoccupied bed, suffering only minor injuries. He was the only man aboard the ill-fated airship to survive. Again we encounter several versions of the helmsman's escape, but the most persistent, and more likely, is that he stayed with the gondola that carried him safely through the roof of the convent and deposited him somewhat dazed on a lower floor. However, survive he did, and is said later to have opened a beer hall where for years he related his adventure and confirmed Warneford's official account.

But what about the young British pilot who was now tossed across the flame- and smoke-streaked sky with a recalcitrant engine? He gingerly tested his plane controls and gradually brought the Morane back on an even keel. He fully expected his monoplane wing to part company from the fuselage, so violent had been the concussion. Then, when the Le Rhone began to behave and respond, she snorted her wrath and quit cold. Warneford watched the gleaming wooden prop wigwag to a halt and he had to ram his nose down to prevent a stall.

He did not have to look about, he *knew* he was at least thirty-five miles inside the German lines. There wasn't an earthly chance of stretching a glide, and it was obvious that the best he could hope for was a safe landing, and a long spell in a German prison camp.

Despite the darkness, the unfamiliar topography, and the lack of any ground lighting, Reggie landed his beat-up Morane safely in an open field—a turfed stretch shielded along one side by a long strip of woods. There was an old farmhouse nearby, but no one emerged to question his arrival, and no German troops appeared to take him prisoner. His initial impulse was to destroy the Morane, but he first tried to find out what had caused the Le Rhone to stop.

What now occurred may be a legend, but it was often told in those days. Warneford was a better than average mechanic and certainly knew the rotary engine, and it took him but a short time to discover that a length of fuel line running from the tank to the fuel pump had broken. There was still enough fuel to get him back across the line, either to Dunkirk or Furnes. A quick search through his pockets produced a cigarette holder. The wide outer end was perfect for making a temporary repair, and the two ends were bound secure with strips of his handkerchief.

In his official report, hurriedly scribbled after his arrival back at Furnes, there is no mention of this, just "I was forced to land and repair my pump." Obviously, there was more to it than that for it must have taken some substitution and improvisation. In fact, Reggie spent about twenty minutes remedying the break and starting the engine again. An experimental tug on the prop assured him that fuel was being drawn from the tank to the carburetor device used on rotary engines. Fortunately, the engine was still warm, and after running through the starting sequence twice to draw vapor into the cylinders, Reggie cut in the switch and snapped her over. The Le Rhone caught immediately, and he had to scramble to duck under the wing and climb into the cockpit, but all went well. He taxied around for a good take-off and in minutes was roaring away.

As he approached the coast again he flew into more fog, so he cruised up and down until he found a hole and glided through. He had little idea where he was, and on landing was told he was at Cape Gris-Nez, ten miles below Calais. He was welcomed warmly, given more gasoline and permitted to call his squadron headquarters at Dunkirk. He told his story briefly, and was advised to sit out the bad weather and return when it had cleared.

His official report is as follows:

Wing Commander Longmore.

Sir,

I have the honour to report as follows: I left Furnes at 1:00 A.M. on June the 7th on Morane No. 3253 under orders to proceed to look for Zeppelins and attack the Berchem Ste. Agathe Airship Shed with six 20-lb. bombs.

On arriving at Dixmude at 1:05 A.M. I observed a Zeppelin apparently over Ostend and proceeded in chase of the same. I arrived at close quarters a few miles past Bruges at 1:50 A.M. and the Airship opened heavy maxim fire, so I retreated to gain height and the Airship turned and followed me.

At 2:15 he seemed to stop firing and at 2:25 A.M. I came behind, but well above the Zeppelin; height then 11,000 feet, and switched off my engine to descend on top of him. When close above him, at 7000 feet I dropped my bombs, and, whilst releasing the last, there was an explosion which lifted my machine and turned it over. The aeroplane was out of control for a short period, but went into a nose dive, and the control was gained.

I then saw that the Zeppelin was on the ground in flames and also that there were pieces of something burning in the air all the way down.

The joint on my petrol pipe and pump from the back tank was broken, and at about 2:40 A.M. I was forced to land and repair my pump.

I landed at the back of a forest close to a farmhouse; the district is unknown on account of the fog and the continuous changing of course.

I made preparations to set the machine on fire but apparently was not observed, so was enabled to effect a repair, and continued at 3:15 A.M. in a south-westerly direction after considerable difficulty in starting my engine single-handed.

I tried several times to find my whereabouts by descending through the clouds, but was unable to do so. So eventually I landed and found out that it was at Cape Gris-Nez, and took in some petrol. When the weather cleared I was able to proceed and arrived at the aerodrome about 10:30 A.M. As far as could be seen the colour of the airship was green on top and yellow below and there was no machine or gun platform on top.

> I have the honour to be,
> Sir,
> Your obedient servant,
> (signed) R. A. J. Warneford,
> Flt. Sub-Lieutenant.

By the time Warneford returned to his squadron the news that a German Zeppelin had been sent down in flames had seeped out of Ghent, and within hours his name was ringing from one end of the Empire to the other. His photograph was flashed on hundreds of theatre screens to the delight of cheering audiences, but that afternoon, in keeping with the traditions of the Silent Service, Commander Spenser Grey of Number 1 Naval Squadron posted a notice that read:

> *Though weather has been extremely*
> *unsettled, our pilots have been*
> *active and busy.*

Within thirty-six hours King George V awarded the Victoria Cross to Warneford, and the French government added their Cross of the Legion of Honor, but Flight Sub-Lieutenant Warneford lived only ten more days to enjoy the laurels of victory. He was sent to Paris on June 17 to be decorated, and after the ceremony was ordered to Buc to pick up a new Farman biplane. The machine had been assembled hurriedly, and most of its standard equipment had not been fitted.

An American newspaperman, named Henry Needham, had asked to go along to Furnes where he planned to write a special story about Warneford and his Zeppelin victory. Reggie cheerfully agreed, and they climbed into the biplane and took off. Almost immediately, the Farman started to pitch and behave strangely, finally rolling over completely out of control. When it was on its back Warneford and Needham were thrown out and killed. Some reports have it that Reggie had made a wild take-off that had been too much for the Farman; the tail was wrenched off and the rest of the machine fluttered over on its back. It was also said that neither man had bothered to fasten his safety belt.

Following Warneford's victory, the war news and rumors were well garnished with reports of other Zeppelin conquests. One of the most fantastic, that persisted for weeks, was that of a Frenchman who had tried to down a dirigible over Paris by using a machine gun. When that method of attack failed, he boldly rammed the raider in midair by flying his Morane Bullet straight through the aluminum framework, crashing out the other side. After that, so the story went, the Zeppelin folded in the middle and dropped in a French cornfield. There was no truth in the report, but faked photographs of this astounding adventure were on sale for weeks throughout France.

V

ZEPPELINS IN NAVAL WARFARE

Determined to prove the worth of his dirigibles, and perhaps to retain the hold he had on the more ebullient correspondents of the Berlin press, Strasser made the most of every opportunity to put his Zeppelins into the air.

Less than a week after the first raid on Britain, the first big naval action was fought, the Battle of the Dogger Bank —second in importance only to the Battle of Jutland. In this historic engagement an airship played a small part, and it must be admitted provided some information for the German surface fleet.

On January 23, 1915, Admiral Franz von Hipper set sail from the Schillig Roads with four battle cruisers, four light cruisers, and nineteen destroyers with orders to reconnoiter the Dogger Bank, a noted shoal in the North Sea. He could not know that the Royal Navy's wireless intelligence had decoded messages passing back and forth from Wilhelmshaven to the German High Seas fleet, and not only knew that Von Hipper was sailing, but exactly where he was heading.

Alerted by this information, the Admiralty on the morning of January 24 sent Admiral David Beatty with five battle cruisers to the area where Admiral von Hipper was to arrive at 8:15 A.M. It is not clear how the German admiral was advised, but realizing he was expected, he decided to run for home, arguing in his own mind that conditions were not favorable. His sudden about-face left the *Blücher,* his weakest vessel at the rear of his line.

Making the most of this opportunity, the faster British ships steamed within range and quickly crippled the *Blücher,* but, in compensation German shellfire disabled Admiral Beatty's flagship HMS *Lion.* Then there ensued a period of mild confusion when British communications broke down, and the German squadron was able to make its run back to Wilhelmshaven, leaving *Blücher* to her fate. She was sunk and provided one of the most spectacular pictures of naval warfare to come out of the campaign.

Kapitänleutnant Hirsch was carrying out a routine patrol in *LZ.5,* and was advised of the action when he picked up a message from Admiral Hipper shortly after 10:00 A.M. Steering for a point 145 miles northwest of Helgoland, Hirsch came upon a panorama of naval action. He saw the fleeing German warships belching their smoke cover, and a number of British destroyers attempting to break through with torpedoes. While pondering on what action to take, Hirsch came under fire from several British light cruisers that were trying to move in from the north side of the concentration. With that, *LZ.5* climbed into the clouds, and there lost track of the important developments. Hirsch completely missed the situation as it effected *Lion,* and thus did not advise Hipper that the British flagship had been disabled. He did, however, see *Blücher* go down inside a circle of British destroyers. Some time later the British claimed that *LZ.5* had dropped a number of bombs close to the destroyers that were rescuing German survivors, but the Kaiser's government attempted, later, to prove that these bombs had been dropped by "an interloping seaplane out of Borkum."

On his way out of the battle Hipper had asked Hirsch how many British battle cruisers were still in action and the Zeppelin commander replied, "Four enemy battle cruisers still in action," and with that Hipper sent in an advance claim that he had sunk HMS *Tiger*.

It should be stated that all the blame was not Hirsch's. He must have lost track of *Lion*, or did not realize she was in difficulty. Also, up to that time there were no definite rules, or naval doctrine to be employed by airship captains during fleet actions. Second-guessing would have it that *LZ.5* should have attempted to stay over or near the British ships and carefully observe their movements, rather than trying to act as a rearguard for Hipper's force.

On the night of February 16, Strasser was advised that there were British naval patrols steaming off the Norwegian coast, and he took a wild chance on making an attack on any British shipping or men-of-war that might be encountered. Earlier, during the autumn of 1914 *LZ.3* and *LZ.4* had flown to within sight of the Norwegian coast on several occasions, but such flights could be hazardous in winter. Strasser felt the flight was worthwhile, however, and he sent out *LZ.4*, under Kapitänleutnant von Platen-Hallermund, and *LZ.3*, commanded by Kapitänleutnant Fritz in threatening weather with orders to search for enemy ships as far north as the Skagerrak. Within a few hours both airships were in serious trouble without ever seeing any enemy surface craft.

LZ.3 was the first to report that she was in dire straits, and asked for aid from German destroyers. Engine after engine failed and Hallermund was forced to beach her on the Danish island of Fanö. The dirigible buckled in the middle, but her crew of sixteen managed to get to the ground and then set fire to the airship, before they were interned.

LZ.4 was no more fortunate. The weather caused her engines to fail one by one, and she was driven toward Blaavands Huk on the Danish coast. A sudden down draft slammed the nose of the airship into the heavy surf, ripping away two gondolas, and eleven members of the crew had to leap overboard and thrash their way ashore through the freezing sea. There was no time or opportunity for landing procedure, and when these men had left the airship, the lightened craft whirled away and disappeared in the darkness. Four machinists, still in the aft gondola, were carried off with the hulk, and it was presumed they went down with *LZ.4* somewhere in the North Sea. Hallermund and the other survivors, one man with a broken leg, surrendered to the Danish police.

This double loss staggered Strasser, as he was said to be especially gifted in predicting weather, but this southerly gale had completely eluded him. He also came to appreciate that in cold weather the airships and their crews suffered severely in the thin air of high altitudes. There were times when the liquid in the magnetic compasses, which was said to be 44 per cent alcohol, first turned a thick, muddy brown, and then froze at temperatures of zero to six degrees below zero. On one occasion aboard *LZ.44* the fluid in the air thermometers separated, the gas thermometers did not function at all, and the rudder cables went slack and jumped off their sheaves in the cold of high altitude. While making their first raid, the crew of *LZ.46* had trouble with the compressed oxygen (it had been contaminated with glycerin) and the men preferred to work without it. As a result, the helmsman collapsed several times, the machinists were incapacitated, and the warrant quartermaster apathetic toward his duties. In contrast, the men who had taken a great deal of oxygen to stay alert, became violently ill from the effects of the glycerin.

Appreciating that the Germans must eventually use their airships for more important work than purely tactical reconnaissance above the High Seas Fleet, the British Harwich Force attempted several new strikes against the dirigibles. They now had a Sopwith seaplane, one based on the type developed for the early Schneider Cup races, which they hoped to put up to destroy the gasbags. This aircraft, powered with a 100-horsepower rotary engine, could reach a speed of 87 miles per hour, and was armed with a single Lewis gun mounted on the upper wing to fire almost directly upward. Though these Sopwiths required thirty-five minutes to reach 10,000 feet, there were a few factors in their favor, particularly in the summer months when the ceiling of the Zeppelins was somewhat lower.

As mentioned before, the Harwich Force was augmented by *Engadine*, *Riviera*, and the newly converted *Ben-my-Chree*, and were to deliver the aircraft as close to the scene of attack as possible.

On May 3 the British attempted to attack a German naval wireless station at Norddeich, not far from Hage, but general conditions prevented water take-offs. The surface ships saw no Zeppelins either, although *LZ.9*, commanded by Kapitänleutnant Heinrich Mathy, experienced a thrilling encounter with a British submarine. He had missed the surface vessels, but shortly after noon he was flying at 900 feet about twenty miles northwest of Terschelling Island when he spotted four submarines cruising on the surface, obviously steering for stations in Helgoland Bight. Submarine *E.5* was the only vessel that carried a deck gun, but her crew put up such a display, Mathy thought all four subs had opened up. He took *LZ.9* up to 3300 feet, and three of the submarines dived, probably figuring out the Zepp commander's game. The fourth stayed on the surface and watched as Mathy took a position directly overhead, but once bombs were spotted, *E.5* started to dive. Four 110-pound bombs, fitted with delayed-action detonators burst close to the diving sub, and Mathy reported seeing air bubbles and an oil slick. He honestly believed he had destroyed the British boat, but she was not damaged in any manner. By the same token, the young commander of *E.5* believed he had hit the Zeppelin and so reported.

Mathy headed toward the southwest, merely as a ruse, and returned at 1:15 P.M. Still flying at 3300 feet he came upon another submarine and moved in to attack from astern. *E.4*, a second sub, had surfaced about half a mile away, so Mathy dropped five bombs fitted with immediate-impact fuses, and believed he had scored a direct hit. Again, he was overconfident, but *E.4* did receive a severe shaking that loosened many rivets in the conning tower structure. The commander of *E.4* reported later that he had spotted *LZ.9* through the canted prism of his periscope, and was actually well below sixty feet when the bombs exploded.

Later in the afternoon Mathy spotted another British submarine that turned boldly toward his airship and used its deck gun until the dirigible was almost overhead. Then it dived before Mathy could get into position to deliver bombs.

On May 11 an interesting experience was logged by the Harwich Force in another vain attempt to bomb Norddeich. While steaming through the western portion of the North Sea Commodore Reginald Tyrwhitt's lookouts spotted a Zeppelin about seventy miles away and rather low on the eastern horizon. They attempted to launch a Sopwith seaplane off *Ben-my-Chree,* but the improvised launching platform collapsed when the plane's engine was started, and *LZ.9,* the Zeppelin seen on the horizon, was undisturbed and went on to bomb four British submarines fifteen miles west-northwest of Texel. This encounter was reminiscent of the one on May 3; no subs were damaged, and the airship received no hits.

Early in June the Zeppelins began to take their Navy work seriously, making several protective flights over the minesweepers, and on one occasion *LZ.5* warned that three light cruisers were proceeding southeast, so the minesweepers and their protective destroyers sped away and evaded the British warships. Böcker who was in command of *LZ.5* on this flight received something of a fright when he first came upon these cruisers at low altitude and low visibility; the Britishers put several explosive shells very close, and *LZ.5* had to climb quickly to 4000 feet and dart into cloud cover. The light cruiser *Arethusa* quickly swung her Sopwith seaplane overboard and the pilot got her beautifully off the water, climbed away, and gained fast on *LZ.5.* As the pilot looked back toward his ship from about 1800 feet he saw smoke being discharged by some destroyers which he mistook for a recall signal, and returned to his ship, thereby possibly sparing Böcker's Zeppelin.

In the early evening of July 3, Tyrwhitt's force suddenly appeared in the German Bight with the intention of launching fighter seaplanes to intercept Zeppelins, and as an alternate assignment to make reconnaissance flights over the Ems River and Borkum. A German submarine reported three light cruisers and sixteen destroyers supporting *Engadine* and *Riviera*.

Admiral Hugo von Pohl, who had been given command of the German Naval Staff, took no action, beyond ordering an extensive air reconnaissance, and the next morning six airships took off with orders to seek and destroy the British seaplane carriers. By early dawn the British force stood off the Dutch island of Ameland where the Short seaplanes were put over to make the sixty-mile flight to the Ems and Borkum. One launched off *Engadine* split her propeller against a roller and had to be hoisted aboard. Four actually got away, but two returned in a short while with engine trouble.

The Zeppelins ran into difficult weather for high-altitude flight, and had to keep well clear of the British ships, so their reconnaissance was not too accurate. Kapitänleutnant Odo Loewe reported only a light cruiser, twelve destroyers, and two seaplane carriers. He could not tell whether the seaplanes had been launched, and it was not until 6:51 A.M. that he reported seeing a single seaplane land alongside one of the carriers, and be taken aboard.

This was the only Short to reach Borkum, and return. The crew could only report that they had seen no transports gathering there. The other seaplane, after flying over Juist and Borkum, entered a cloud layer and apparently became lost. It failed to return to the British squadron, and had to land near a Dutch trawler that took the pilot and observer into Holland for internment.

Kapitänleutnant Joachim Breithaupt in *LZ.6* was following Loewe when he spotted a number of British destroyers, a cruiser, and the two seaplane carriers. He had to drop considerable ballast, including two tanks of fuel and a large bomb, in order to rise to 5200 feet before he dared to move in to attack, but even at that altitude he came under heavy antiaircraft fire, so he kept clear of the opposition. Below, the intruders turned and steamed toward the west, so Breithaupt decided to follow, but on spotting a Norwegian steamer he went down again to make a close examination of her house and national flag. While cruising at 150 feet he suddenly found himself under heavy shellfire; two destroyers he had decided were German, were British, but, fortunately, he was able to turn away fast and slip into cloud cover.

Three other Zeppelins that had been alerted by Loewe's first message proceeded west together, and at 7:20 A.M., *LZ.10* spotted five destroyers and a cruiser that immediately took up the chase and drove her eastward. *SL.3* (a Schütte-Lanz type) identified one seaplane carrier, a light cruiser, and twelve destroyers. *LZ.11* also found the squadron lurking off Ameland, and Von Buttlar who had proceeded deep into the west, later claimed to have come upon a covering force that included a battle cruiser of the *Indomitable* class. He completed this fable by reporting that the battle cruiser had fired a volley of twelve-inch shells that had driven him back east. Actually, no British capital ships were anywhere near the Harwich Force.

The four Zeppelins had unwittingly flown into a trap, but the trigger failed to snap. As they approached, *Engadine* tried to launch three Sop seaplanes, but the rip-tide sea was too rough, and the plywood floats broke up before the aircraft could clamber into the air. Two of them went to the bottom, but the pilots were rescued. The third Sop pilot was able to wallow back to the derrick and snatch at the launching tackle.

It can be seen from all this that neither dirigibles nor heavier-than-air craft had yet proved their worth in actual military operations. The Zeppelins were handled too cautiously, or were not properly fitted into the tactical picture.

9. Kapitanleutnant Heinrich Mathy, Germany's greatest Zeppelin commander who was killed when his *LZ.31* was shot down over Potter's Bar, Middlesex, by Captain W. J. Tempest.—IMPERIAL WAR MUSEUM PHOTO.

10. Invalided out of the Army after being wounded at Ypres, the then Second Lieutenant W. J. Tempest, found his glory in the RFC, and flying an old B. E. 2c by downing Mathy, Germany's Zeppelin hero.—IMPERIAL WAR MUSEUM PHOTO.

11. The notorious B.E. 2c biplane, affectionately known as The Quirk, probably one of the worst aircraft to see service in World War I, and yet with all her faults she was to bring the Victoria Cross to three pilots who were assigned to fly her.—WHITEHOUSE PHOTO.

12. Three Zeppelin killers. Left to right, William Leefe Robinson, W. J. Tempest, and Lieutenant Fred Sowrey who destroyed *LZ.32* which fell near Billericay.—WHITEHOUSE PHOTO.

13. The wreck of *LZ.12* at Ostend, after being forced down in the Channel as the result of British gunfire over Dover. The damaged airship was towed into Ostend on the morning of August 10, 1915, but she exploded and burned while the crane attempted to lift the hulk out of the water, shortly after this photograph was taken.—FRIEDRICH MOCH PHOTO.

14. Heavier armament, the 20-mm. Becker air-cannon which was mounted on Peter Strasser's ill-fated *LZ.70*. This one was mounted in the port window of the control car. Another was set up in the starboard window.—FRIEDRICH MOCH PHOTO.

15. A typical scene in a Zeppelin shed. Here is *LZ.52* in her Wittmund-haven hangar. The airship in the background is possibly the *LZ.49*. —FRIEDERICH MOCH PHOTO.

16. The wreckage of *LZ.33* shot down by Lieutenant A. de B. Brandon. The Zepp crew destroyed their airship and tried to reach the British coast, but were all captured by a British country policeman riding a bicycle.—IMPERIAL WAR MUSEUM PHOTO.

Their crews returned jubilant, not realizing how close they had come to disaster, and Breithaupt of *LZ.6* bragged that the airship force had beaten back a large-scale air attack planned for the German Frisian coast. "Not one enemy aviator reached a German target," he wrote in his autobiography.

There was little, or no, glory for the German High Seas Fleet, for it had made no move to go out and engage the Harwich Force, and as a result Strasser's airships garnered all the headlines. While their reconnaissance reports were either sketchy or inaccurate, they had provided some tactical advantage, which Admiral von Pohl failed to utilize. It is true that by orders from the Kaiser he had to withhold from combat all battleships and cruisers that might have been sent out to destroy the light British force, but under these ideal circumstances, a reasonable risk should have been assumed.

On the other side of the coin, the British were sadly disappointed with the showing of their seaplanes, for it was realized that a heaven-sent opportunity had been lost. Considerable money and time had been squandered to provide mother ships and naval escort, but the improvised aircraft had failed miserably, and back in London there was much discussion concerning the actual worth of such aircraft, and it was not until January 1916 that any further seaplane-carrier operations were attempted against the enemy.

At Wilhelmshaven, Admiral von Pohl, still haunted by the possible loss of any major surface ships, soon placed responsibilities on the Airship Service that were beyond their capability. For instance, on August 6 when the auxiliary cruiser *Meteor* was ordered out to spread a minefield outside the British Grand Fleet base at Cromarty (Outer Hebrides), he would not risk any major naval vessels to escort her out of the German Bight, but placed her safety in the hands of the commanders of the airships, destroyers, and submarines. This was to result in another naval tragedy.

Under this plan *SL.3* went off to act as a scout ahead of the minelayer, but a predicted storm caused officials to re-

call the Schütte-Lanz airship, and, in fact, on the way back
SL.3 had to fly through a heavy rainstorm, and absorbed
so much water practically all ballast had to be jettisoned
to keep her in the air. As a consequence, on landing at Nordholz in a thunder squall she was almost unmanageable, and
hit so hard she was out of service for three weeks.

The skipper of *Meteor* bravely laid his mines, attacked
and sank a British armed boarding steamer, and then
headed back for Wilhelmshaven. By the morning of August
9 he was steaming through the outer edge of the German
Bight. All would have gone well, but Commodore Tyrwhitt
had gathered together five light cruisers of the Harwich
Force and two light cruisers from the Grand Fleet, and being advised of the movements of *Meteor* had moved at high
speed from the south and west to cut the auxiliary cruiser
from the sanctuary of Jade Bay.

Again, Admiral von Pohl did not seize a golden oppor-
tunity. He must have known that the British would attempt
to cut off the minelayer, but instead of sending the High
Seas Fleet to sea, he simply gave orders for the Airship
Service to carry out a strong air reconnaissance. In response,
LZ.7 took off from Tondern, followed by *PL.25* (a Parse-
val-Lanz type) to look for *Meteor* off Horn's Reef. About
9:00 A.M. a German seaplane reported Tyrwhitt's force off
Terschelling, which needled Von Pohl to order the High
Seas Fleet to "heightened preparedness," while Strasser
and the Leader of Submarines were ordered to send out all
available units.

This tragedy of errors was highlighted by an incident experienced by Kapitänleutnant Max Dietrich who commanded *LZ.7*. About 10:00 A.M. Dietrich spotted what he
reported to be a "black-painted merchant ship" that carried
no distinguishing marks, and would not answer recognition signals. This was the ill-fated *Meteor,* but Dietrich
failed to identify her, so he turned south and left her to her
fate. He did, however, receive the seaplane's warning, and
by 11:00 A.M. had found Tyrwhitt's force about seventy-
five miles northwest of Helgoland and reported that it was

made up of four armored cruisers and one destroyer. He did his best at this point and radioed the position, speed, and course of the British vessels; he even tried to lure them into following and attacking him, but Tyrwhitt had other ideas.

Aboard *PL.25*, commanded by an Army officer, Hauptmann Kuno Manger, Dietrich's message was finally decoded, and Manger steered for the reported position, and by 1:00 P.M. *LZ.7* and *PL.25* were moving along parallel courses and saw the British force maneuver into a line abreast formation as they steamed for the coast of Jutland. They were now putting on twenty-nine knots, and *PL.25* was soon left far behind, and a short time later *LZ.7* had to give up the chase, for the Zeppelin was boring into a twenty-two-miles-per-hour head wind, and there was nothing Dietrich could do but sit above and watch the British trap close in on *Meteor*.

At 2:00 P.M. the skipper of the minelayer saw the British cruisers coming up from the south and west, and he had no choice but to set explosives, open the sea cocks and take to the boats. The Royal Navy had scored another victory, right under the nose of Admiral von Pohl, without firing a shot. The incident, small as it was, must have had a telling effect on the responsible officers of the High Seas Fleet command. In this instance the airships had contributed nothing more than a radioed warning that prompted the skipper of *Meteor* to spare Tyrwhitt the unpleasant duty of sinking a helpless enemy vessel.

In the ignominy of the tragic situation, Admiral von Pohl, who still was hampered by the pusillanimity of his Emperor, reacted psychologically and immediately exaggerated the importance of the dirigibles and their significance in naval warfare. He elevated the Naval Airship Division to a permanent arm of the Fleet. He was not so sure about future co-operation between airships and submarines, but he considered it to be urgently necessary to give priority to the erection of more airship sheds by every possible means. Up to this time airships were being built at a good rate by the Zeppelin and Schütte-Lanz firms, and the Navy program had reached eighteen airships, and by June of 1915 there were that many sheds built or under construction, and it had become necessary to have two or more sheds available to accommodate airships that could not land at their home bases. On June 17, it was decided to erect six double hangars, all of the same dimensions—790 feet long, 197 feet wide, and 110 feet high. For this project Dr. Eckener and a number of Admiralty officials spent more than a week studying sites in the vicinity of Bremen, and finally settled on an open area near the village of Ahlhorn, about sixty miles from the sea. Here four sheds were completed by September 11, 1916. The reason for their giant size was that plans were under way for the construction of new and greatly enlarged dirigibles; in fact as early as April 3, 1915, the first million-cubic-foot Zeppelin was nearly ready for military operations, and the Admiralty had ordered the airship firms to produce designs for even larger ships. The Zeppelin Company eventually developed a two-million-cubic-foot monster that was powered with six engines.

Why this devotion to, and belief in, the dirigible? In mid-1915 the aeroplane was still considered a frail novelty, not to be taken seriously by professional military men. With its great success as a commercial project prior to the outbreak of the war, the Zeppelin had impressed the military and civilian mind alike. There was a great demand for military airships along the Eastern Front, in Poland, and even from the Imperial Headquarters in France, so the airship companies were encouraged to erect new and larger factories everywhere. Exaggerated estimates of the damage inflicted in the early raids on Britain caused German authorities to believe that it was only a matter of time and equipment until they could plan the complete destruction of London.

On June 15, 1915, the French Air Force staged an aeroplane raid on Karlsruhe and Baden, and this impudence so shocked Admiral Bachmann, Chief of Naval Staff, he sought a conference with the Kaiser, hoping to win permission to engage in unrestricted air warfare on London, the heart of the Allied coalition. General Erich von Falkenhayn, Chief of the General Staff, was somewhat in accord, but suggested that they wait until the Navy and Army Airship services could be increased to a large squadron apiece, and accompanied by fighter and bomber planes. Von Falkenhayn also recommended that these forces be placed under Army control.

This needled the Navy officials who by now had four airships of the new *LZ.10* class, and felt that they were ready to begin a complete raiding program against London. Bachmann approached Chancellor Theobald von Bethmann-Hollweg and gained his support, but with the stipulation that the London financial district be attacked only on weekends, and that all historical buildings be spared. Owing to weather problems it was obviously impossible to restrict raids to any particular day of the week, and because of the distribution of London's historic architecture there could not be such bombing accuracy. All this Bachmann later put to the Kaiser, and with that the Emperor gave his permission for unrestricted air warfare, although he hoped that St. Paul's Cathedral and the Tower of London could be spared.

After the *Meteor* incident, Strasser ordered a five-airship sortie to assemble about ten miles north of Borkum, and by 2:50 P.M. on August 10, 1915, the five Zeppelins were on a westward course, led by Strasser aboard *LZ.10*. At 3:50 *LZ.9*, under Loewe, cut away from the formation and headed for the mouth of the Humber, and as it turned out, Loewe was the only skipper to get anywhere near his objective. He arrived over Goole, but believing he was approaching Hull, dropped most of his bombs, killing sixteen people and destroying some dwellings and warehouses. He turned in a typical report of daring heavy gunfire and causing serious damage to the Hull docks.

The rest of the formation, heading south, ran into bad weather that was mixed with thunder squalls, making the airships heavy, and they had to drop much of their ballast.

The weight situation became so serious, all code and signal books were lead-weighted and dropped into the sea. However, Strasser still hoped to attack London, and by signal light ordered all airships to remain together until 9:45 when they were to bomb the London docks and the City area independently.

Their determination was admirable, but not one of the Zeppelins even saw London that night. Mathy in *LZ.13* had to turn back with engine trouble, and while limping home had to jettison 120 incendiary bombs to lighten his ship. *LZ.10*, crawling about through stacks of heavy rain clouds, spotted an area of the Thames, and her skipper Oberleutnant Friedrich Wenke decided he was well over eastern London. He released all his bombs and thought he saw "several burst among shipping."

What really happened was that twelve of his projectiles dropped on the airfield of the Eastchurch Naval Air Station on the island of Sheppey at the mouth of the river. Von Buttlar in *LZ.11* concluded he was over Harwich on the Essex coast and hurriedly dropped his bombs when guns, mounted at Lowestoft more than forty miles from Harwich, opened up. Most of these bombs fell into the sea where British coast-watchers reported them as water flares.

LZ.12, commanded by Oberleutnant Werner Peterson, crossed the British coast at Westgate, south of the Thames, but her commander thought he was well to the north over the Norfolk coast, and reported he had passed Yarmouth, Lowestoft, and the Ordfordness Lighthouse. After cruising about he finally decided that Dover was Harwich, and that there was little chance of reaching London, so decided to make his attack there. He off-loaded all his bombs which included two 220-pound and twenty 110-pound explosive and seventy incendiary bombs, but only three of them, all incendiaries, fell inland where they injured three men, but did little property damage.

One of the Dover guns, a three-incher, managed to fire ten shells, and one apparently hit *LZ.12* aft. Peterson dumped all his water ballast and bolted for home. Cells 3 and 4 had been cleanly hit and both lost their gas before patch repairs could be made, and the airship began to sink rapidly. Around 2:40 A.M. all available spares, machine guns, rations, etc., were jettisoned but even with these measures it was apparent that Peterson would not regain his North Sea base at Hage. He decided to try for occupied Belgium, but even this was beyond range, for LZ.12 was sinking fast. Then all wireless equipment was tossed out, but by 3:40 A.M. the ship settled stern first on the foggy Channel. They tried to cut away the aft gondola that was under water, but leaking hydrogen and oil fumes knocked out the mechanics assigned to the task, so Peterson decided to await rescue by surface craft, and planned to set fire to the hulk as soon as his crew could be taken off.

A German torpedo boat crept out of the fog and its commander explained to Peterson that he was only a short distance from Zeebrugge. Peterson asked for a line, and a hawser was fixed to a mooring point under the bow, and over the next eight hours LZ.12 was towed to the docks at Ostend, where Peterson planned to have the airship immediately dismantled and shipped back to her factory.

Once the news had spread that a German Zeppelin was down at sea, three British R.N.A.S. pilots took off from Dunkirk to finish her, but their attempt went for nought. Their bombs failed to damage further LZ.12, and one of the airmen was shot down and killed. Later, six planes tried to set her afire as she lay at Ostend, but no hits were scored.

Meanwhile, the dismantling work proceeded. Two of the gondolas were detached and hauled ashore, but when the forward section of the hull frame was being swung over a pier, it exploded and burned. The after section, however, was salvaged.

VI

MATHY, THE ZEPPELIN HERO

Despite this unsuccessful venture, Strasser was undaunted and on the afternoon of August 12, he sent off four more airships on a raid over England but only two of them reached their objective. Wenke, again commanding *LZ.10*, headed for Harwich, this time clearly identifying Woodbridge, Ipswich, and was able to pick out Harwich. He continued on and released his load, later claiming to have damaged seriously the electric power plant and the railroad station of the well-known naval base, but the British reports stated that only two houses were destroyed.

Von Buttlar, commanding *LZ.11*, first appeared over North Foreland but found no target worthy of his attention, so decided to return to his base and save his explosives for future operations. On reaching a point some forty miles west of Den Helder on the Dutch coast, he had to change course to avoid several thunderstorms, one over Rotterdam, another over Amsterdam, and a third over the Texel and Terschelling islands. Uncertain which course to take because of the severe lightning, Buttlar finally determined the storms were heading out to sea, so he tried to run around them, taking a northerly route. By the time he reached the Dogger Bank it was clear that he was in serious trouble. Around 2:00 A.M. *LZ.11* was caught in a violent updraft, and then as suddenly dashed toward the sea. Heavy rains lashed the hull envelope, bolts of lightning flashed in all directions, and every metal object aboard the airship glowed with bluish St. Elmo's fire.

(St. Elmo, an Italian corruption of St. Erasmus, is the patron saint of all Mediterranean sailors who regard St. Elmo's fire as a visible sign of his guardianship.)

By great good fortune, Buttlar managed to keep his ship below "pressure height," the altitude at which diminishing atmospheric pressure would allow the gas to expand to the point where it would completely fill the cells. Had this occurred, hydrogen, passing through the pressure valves, would have been ignited by the electrical discharges, and LZ.11 would have exploded and burned in the air.

Through good airmanship—and his share of luck—Von Buttlar brought his ship safely home.

On August 17 four more Zeppelins were sent out with definite orders to bomb the City of London. Two of these ships had serious mechanical trouble and had to turn back before they reached England. Von Buttlar in LZ.11 produced another dramatic, but totally fictitious, account of how he bombed London, but he was never at any time within forty miles of the British capital. Twenty-one of his bombs were scattered about Ashford in Kent, from where he turned north for Faversham and an Admiralty gunpowder factory located there. Facing no ground opposition of any kind, he dropped forty-one bombs in nearby fields.

Wenke, aboard LZ.10 was more successful as far as navigation was concerned, for he actually did reach London, the first Naval Airship commander to do so. Wenke had steered a true course for the Orfordness light, and from there used a number of small villages that still displayed lights, and by 10:35 P.M. he picked up the nimbus of London looming like an aurora on the southwest horizon. One hour later he set the stage for his attack on the city. He thought he bombed the metropolis between Blackfriars and

London bridges and reported that great buildings collapsed and big fires were observed, but he had hit the Leyton railroad station, damaged a tramcar roundhouse, and destroyed a number of small houses. Ten people were killed and forty-eight wounded. Why he thought he was over the center of London is a mystery, but this type of wishful thinking seemed to be an inborn characteristic of German airmen in both World Wars.

On September 3 Strasser sent out four more Zeppelins, one of which was *LZ.10*, now commanded by Kapitänleutnant Klaus Hirsch, but shortly after taking off, this commander reported that he was returning and planned to land at Nordholz at 3:30 P.M. A ground crew was ordered to stand by, but *LZ.10* never appeared. (Strasser later made a service report in which he stated that Hirsch apparently had encountered "a circumscribed local thunder storm" somewhere off Cuxhaven.) About 3:20 P.M. personnel at the Nordholz base spotted what appeared to be an airship, and then saw a large flash of flame and heard an explosion. In a few minutes a report by telephone stated that a Zeppelin had fallen in flames near Neuwerk Island. Coastal batteries near Cuxhaven had a clear view of the disaster, and a sentry who had watched *LZ.10* struggling shoreward with the upper portion of her hull shrouded by clouds, said he had seen a flash of lightning and with that a jagged flame that burst from the hull. Others saw the fire spread until the nose of the airship tilted down and she began to dive at about 80 degrees, and eventually piled up on the tidal flats, and burned in great clouds of smoke.

It was thought that in the vortex of the storm *LZ.10* went over pressure height and the cells must have been valving gas at the time of the lightning flash. Hirsch and his crew of nineteen perished; only eleven bodies were recovered.

Taunted by the example of this German Navy effort, the Army Airship Service decided to contribute to the planned destruction of London, and on the night of September 7

military airships *L.74,* and a Schütte-Lanz, listed as *SL.2,*
set off to bomb Britain's capital. The Schütte-Lanz that had
been rebuilt following a damaging forced landing in a training flight, put on a spectacular show, striking at Millwall,
Deptford, Greenwich, and the Woolwich docks. But on her
return, engine after engine failed until only one was turning
a propeller. Creeping on at a much-reduced speed, *SL.2*
made an attempt to land at the Berchem-Sainte-Agathe
base, but fell, instead, on a small house which penetrated
inside the rigid hull. A kitchen fire was burning in a small
grate, but by miraculous luck the chimney was forced up
between two gas cells, and a vent shaft carried away the
heat and any sparks from the hearth below.

L.74 dumped most of her 4400-pound bomb load on a
set of greenhouses at Cheshunt, an urban district of Hert-
fordshire, thirty-five miles north of London, and as a result
when her skipper Hauptmann George did come upon London, he had only one incendiary bomb left which was deposited on a shop in Fenchurch Street with no spectacular
results.

Strasser was inflamed with the Army's comparative success and immediately ordered another four-airship attack.
LZ.9, commanded by Loewe, was assigned to a benzol plant
at Skinningrove on the north Yorkshire coast. (Benzol is a
grade of crude benzene.) As usual, the Zeppelin commander floundered about trying to identify the towns and
districts below. Utterly bewildered with what he swore were
"false streets laid out and lit up like the real thing," he
dropped explosives where he thought the benzol plant was.
In this instance Loewe abounded in luck, for one incendiary
actually hit the benzol house, but failed to pierce the con-
crete cover. A high-explosive bomb that fell within ten feet,
broke a water main and cut electric light cables, but did no
damage to the storage shed. There were 45,000 gallons of
fuel on hand at the time, and had they been ignited the
whole complex would have gone up in flames. Another bomb
from *LZ.9* landed on the roof of a TNT store—but failed to

explode. There was considerable noise, much excitement, but no casualties.

The airships assigned to the southern sector of the raid, *LZ.11* and *LZ.14* were handicapped by engine trouble, and only Kapitänleutnant Heinrich Mathy's *LZ.13* actually reached London.

This raid which was carried out over September 8–9 was to make Mathy the newest wartime idol in Germany. He made his landfall at Wells-on-Sea on the Norfolk coast by 8:35 P.M., but wisely stood offshore for an hour awaiting the cover of darkness. At 9:45 he cruised over King's Lynn and from there followed the Ouse River, picked up the Bedford Canal, and used the small villages that were lit up as gay as any peacetime evening, so that by the time he was north of Cambridge all he had to do was to head for the glow of London that arched up from the southern horizon.

At 11:40 Mathy dropped five bombs as he approached from the northwest, chiefly to check his bombsight. He was able to identify Regent's Park and saw many good targets spread out before him. He had visited London in 1909 and knew what he was looking for.

He dropped two incendiaries in Upper Bedford Place, but there was little damage. He sent down a high-explosive which shattered much glass in Queen's Square. A heavy bomb hit Theobald's Road and wrecked a small bank. Another landed on the steps of Lamb's Conduit Passage, and fragments of shell casing killed a man standing outside a pub. A bomb that struck an apartment farther along killed four children.

Mathy had one 660-pounder in his rack, the largest bomb to be hauled to Britain, and shortly after midnight he dropped it in the center of Bartholomew Close. The blast, concussion, stone fragments, and flying glass caused considerable damage, but it was the textile warehouses and the crooked lanes north of St. Paul's that had the worst damage. Wood Street, Silver Street, Addle Street, and Aldermanbury were soon ablaze. Their soft goods warehouses were badly damaged and required the services of twenty-two fire engines to quell the conflagration.

Throughout all this tumult and carnage, the London gunners tried manfully to put up some defense, but most of their guns were outranged. Mathy, making his run out, was much impressed, however, and soon took *LZ.13* up from 8500 feet to 11,000 feet, and sought cover behind a light layer of cloud. Twenty searchlights snapped back and forth like blades of giant broadswords as Mathy tried to put his last four bombs on the Liverpool Street Station. One of these tore up a section of track, two missed the station, but hit two motor omnibuses that brought the death toll for this particular raid to twenty-two. This was the greatest damage, £530,787 worth, inflicted by any Zeppelin or aeroplane raid during the whole of World War I.

Kapitänleutnant Mathy was wildly acclaimed for this success, and Karl von Weigand of the New York *World,* who interviewed him in Berlin, wrote such a laudatory article that for weeks Mathy was said to have been as popular with Americans of German-descent as he was in his native land.

Heinrich Mathy, born in Mannheim, was thirty-two, tall and slim, a severe Naval officer who always wore his cap dead center. He entered the German Navy in 1900 and put in much service aboard destroyers. In 1913 he transferred to the Naval Airship Service and quickly became a very reliable skipper, flying *L.1* and *L.2* in prewar days and contributing much to the infant science.

With the declaration of war, the invasion of Belgium, and the prospects of naval action with the High Seas Fleet, Mathy transferred back to the surface fleet and skippered a destroyer. But with the German Navy obviously bottled up, he heeded Strasser's call, and returned to Zeppelins in January 1915. He first commanded *LZ.9* and then took over *LZ.13*, and by the time he made his historic raid on London he had logged more than one hundred dirigible flights. He was an especial favorite of Count Zeppelin, and after the raid on September 8–9 was hero-worshiped by every member of his crew and the German public.

Believing they had the secret of bringing Britain to her knees, Strasser and other officials of the Naval Airship Service decided to raid London again on September 13 when three Zeppelins were sent off, but only Mathy in *LZ.13* managed to evade a bad thunderstorm and reach the English coast. Shortly after midnight he found himself over Orfordness where he was soon picked out by searchlights mounted at Harwich, and British guns opened up with shrapnel and incendiary shells. One came up vertically, pierced the gangway, tore through Cells 11 and 12, and took out a fuel line and a wireless power cable.

Seeing he was unwanted, Mathy turned back to sea to dump his bombs to lighten his ship. The port engine had a broken wrist pin and had to be switched off. The mechanics tried to patch the punctured cells, but they had emptied quickly, leaving *LZ.13* in a dangerous condition. Mathy took a course for the nearest friendly shore, risking a flight over Holland, to save his ship and his crew. He dumped 1750 pounds of valuable fuel, and managed to reach his berth at Hage by 5:20 A.M. He could have waited for sunrise to warm and expand his remaining gas, but more thunderstorms had been predicted, and he decided to risk an immediate landing. He jettisoned more oil, water, and spare parts in the Ems River, but despite these precautions *LZ.13* dropped hard and damaged several important girders, gondola struts, and propeller shafts. However, all this was remedied within four days. It was then discovered that Mathy's airship had been hit by a six-pound shell fired from a gun set up at Felixstowe, across the harbor from Harwich.

It is interesting to note from official records that these raids on Britain, announced joyously by the Naval Airship Service, did not completely impress Staff officers of the German Army. General von Falkenhayn pointed out on September 12 that the Army Zeppelins had been limited to bombing London's docks and harbor works, and their captains had been ordered to avoid damaging any part of the City of London. Actually, Von Falkenhayn feared the British would retaliate in some spectacular manner, but Admiral Franz von Holtzendorff who had succeeded Admiral Bachmann as Chief of Naval Staff, was anxious to press the advantage the Naval Airship Service had attained. On September 14 he issued a directive which stated that "in the future the air raids should be restricted *once more*, as far as possible, to those parts of London on the banks of the Thames, as to which no restrictions had been made by the German authorities, and that the northern quarter of the city inhabited chiefly by the poorer classes should as far as possible be avoided."

With this stricture the Commander-in-Chief of the German High Seas Fleet decided to call off the gunnery raids until the next period of the new moon, and employ the dirigibles in assisting the minesweepers in clearing the German Bight.

October brought an assurance of darker nights, and Admiral von Pohl ordered Strasser to raid Liverpool's docks, pointing out that supplies being purchased in the United States were beginning to pour through this West Coast port. Inclement weather kept the airships in their sheds until October 13 when it was considered that conditions were reasonable enough to risk another venture against London.

Airships *LZ.11, LZ.13, LZ.14, LZ.15,* and *LZ.16* were assigned to this mission, three from Nordholz and two from Hage. They assembled in the afternoon and were soon above a solid overcast at 2600 feet. From Ameland they headed for the coast of Norfolk with the intention of flying from Haisbrough to Cambridge and attacking London from the north. Mathy, who was in command, spread his airships for safety and took the lead to London. Von Buttlar aboard *LZ.11* strayed somewhat and at 9:30 P.M. was over Bacton, Norfolk. Further inland *LZ.11* came under fire from a mobile machine-gun section, upon which her skipper jettisoned his bombs on several villages, and on his return to Nordholz reported that he had flown up the Thames and bombed West Ham and some docks at Woolwich.

Joachim Breithaupt in *LZ.15* was over Britain for the first time, and he boldly set course for London and by 9:10 the glow of the city directed him straight to his target. A mobile 13-pounder at Broxbourne attempted to put up a barrage, but Breithaupt replied with three explosive bombs, one of which knocked down some gunners with its concussion.

The German commander thought that this gun was set up at Tottenham on the northern fringe of London, so he steered west to pick up a tail wind, jettisoned two tanks of fuel and rid himself of most of his water ballast, enabling him to rise to 8500 feet. He then ordered top speed and headed for the city. A wartime panorama of unusual detail was thus outlined for the people of London.

The airship was clearly seen crossing the Thames as she was picked up almost immediately by two searchlights. The big guns added to the Wagnerian scene as the silver dirigible nosed its way from over New Palace Yard to Green Park. Breithaupt and his crew had a different view. Although he later said it was indescribably beautiful, it must have been fantastic and disconcerting as shrapnel burst all around, pasting sequins against the velvet sky. Then, from the gondolas they could see their bombs bursting in the streets while British guns snapped slim tongues of flame. When they raised their eyes from below and looked around they saw balanced on searchlight beams the other airships of the formation, "all clearly recognizable against the starlit sky."

Breithaupt headed straight for the heart of London. He made Charing Cross his first impact point, and headed for the Bank of England with intent to plaster Fleet Street and Ludgate Hill. His first bombs struck the theatre district north of the Strand. The historic Lyceum Theatre, where Henry Irving and Ellen Terry had acted, was hit. A bomb dropped in Wellington Street, fractured a gas main and set fire to the escaping gas. Seventeen people were killed in that blast. York Street was also hit, as was the front of the Waldorf Hotel. One bomb fell in the Kingsway, a few hit the Inns of Court, and one incendiary torched the robing room at Gray's Inn.

It was at this point that Commander W. Rawlinson's 75-millimeter antiaircraft gun, previously mentioned, went into action from the Honourable Artillery Company's grounds in Finsbury. One shell that exploded at a level of 7200 feet startled Breithaupt, but luck was with him as the gun could not be elevated above 83 degrees and LZ.15 was able to fly through the "dead circle" of the weapon. As Breithaupt headed eastward Rawlinson's gunners got off a second round that burst uncomfortably close to his airship.

Now let us change cockpits to see what the defense was doing during this particular raid, and for this we shall turn to Sir John Slessor's book *The Central Blue*. At the time Slessor, who later became Marshal of the Royal Air Force and Chief of Air Staff, was a none-too-experienced second lieutenant in the Royal Flying Corps who had been assigned to an airstrip laid out at Sutton's Farm, some sixteen miles from London; actually in Essex. This primitive aerodrome became the famous Hornchurch base from where many R.A.F. pilots took off to fight the Battle of Britain a quarter of a century later.

Lieutenant Slessor had ferried a B.E.2c from the Daimler factory in Coventry with orders to join Second Lieutenant R. Yates, a member of Number 23 Squadron and a Lieutenant Jenkins of Number 14 Squadron who were sitting things out at this bosky dell. Since he was on hand, and had brought a new aircraft, Slessor was told to stay on and send Jenkins back to his unit where he would be available for any posting out to France.

Earlier on this day, October 13, Slessor had tossed a coin with Yates to see which one of them should have the honor of taking off should a Zeppelin appear over Britain. Slessor "won" and Yates hied himself back to the nearby pub where the commissioned officers were billeted. Four of the Zeppelins had crossed the British coastline near Bacton in Norfolk, sometime between 6:15 and 6:40 P.M.—according to coastwatchers. Buttlar dropped his high explosive in some fields outside Norwich and returned to his base, claiming to have flattened West Ham, and Woolwich Arsenal.

Led by *LZ.15*, the four dirigibles did finally reach London. Breithaupt, in addition to this honor, also may claim to have commanded the first airship to be fired on by a gun that hurled a shell fused to explode at a predetermined height. A product of French artillery, this weapon had only a few days before been mounted in Paris. It was borrowed, hauled across the Channel and established with the new Mobile Anti-Aircraft Squadron, commanded by Colonel Sir Alfred Rawlinson. The gun was set up near Hampstead.

Back at Sutton's Farm Lieutenant Slessor was talking with the tenant farmer, Tom Crawford, admiring the agricultural machinery, and giving a few minutes to the gunners who were wiping the grease off a brand-new 13-pounder. By 9:00 P.M. he returned to the hangar where a folding cot had been set up, slipped off his field boots and curled up with a blanket.

The time brackets in all these various reports are most confusing. Slessor states in his book that it was nine o'clock when he turned in, whereas in another book, *Raiders Approach!* by Squadron Leader H. T. Sutton—no relation to the owner of the farm—it is claimed that Slessor was warned of the enemy raid by 7:30 P.M., but the visibility was not too good and ground mist or fog was moving in from the river and as Slessor had been off the ground at night but once previously, he was advised to wait to see if conditions improved. In this version the young lieutenant then took to his cot.

Meanwhile, in London proper, Colonel Rawlinson, anxious to try out the weapon he had borrowed from the French, found himself sitting around, unable to make a move as his gun teams and drivers had been dismissed to their billets and were not expected to report for their night watch until 9:00 P.M. Somewhere amid all this the British radio watch had picked up a signal from *LZ.15* that was intended for *LZ.10*, and from this they predicted that some of the raiders were south of Harlow in Essex. Fortunately,

LZ.15 made a cautious, wide sweep, skirting the north of
London, a move that gave Rawlinson a ghost of a chance
to get his weapon into action. When his gunners finally
turned up, London was treated to a violent spectacle of a
high-speed (fifty-seven miles per hour) motor lorry bearing a bristling gun and a crew of wild-eyed artillerymen
racing through Finchley Road and Oxford Street as though
the devil possessed them.

By now *LZ.15* was somewhere over Edgeware and had
turned to make her raid on the most vulnerable city in the
world. At Sutton's Farm Slessor had received a telephone
call from the War Office ordering him to get into the air
and see what he could do about this swarm of Zeppelins
that was converging on London. The voice on the other
end was that of Lieutenant Colonel W. W. Warner, a family
friend who less than six months before had been instru-
mental in getting Slessor his R.F.C. commission and flight
training.

"Four or five Zeppelins have crossed the coast, and were
last spotted in the vicinity of Thetford. We believe they
are making for Thetford," Warner explained.

"Yes, sir. Immediately, sir."

"How is the weather there?"

"Well . . ."

"It doesn't look good here at Whitehall, and if it is at
all risky you are not to take off. I'll leave it to you," the
lieutenant colonel explained. "However . . ."

Warner issued some general orders to the effect that if
Slessor did get off safely he was to patrol at about 10,000
feet for as long as his fuel would allow.

Getting off was comparatively simple as a flare path was
quickly laid down, but like young Warneford, Slessor was
somewhat blind at first and flew only by instinct. Then,
gradually some degree of night sight enabled him to pick
out the subdued glow of the big city, for a total blackout
was unthinkable in those days.

Colonel Rawlinson, still leading his convoy, screeched
into Holborn where they were held up by a road that was

under repair; a tangle complete with barriers, piles of materials, discarded tools, and a watchman's shed. The first car threw one barrier in all directions, and then a London bobby, about to arrest the lot, suddenly realized that this could be something connected with the Defense of London program, so he quickly tore down a second barrier, and the artillery convoy lurched through.

By now *LZ.15* was almost directly overhead and Rawlinson's crew pulled up, set up their gun with commendable skill and smartness and actually fired two rounds at the raider before it roared off in another direction. As mentioned, this particular weapon could not be elevated beyond 83 degrees, which left a wide dead-zone circle above, in which any target was safe. On reaching Hyde Park and identifying his position by the gleam of the Thames River, Breithaupt began releasing his bombs.

Lieutenant Slessor, who had started to climb from the field at Sutton's Farm, soon spotted what looked to him like the hull of a transatlantic liner sitting stationary above the glow of the city. He was the only pilot sent aloft that night who spotted a dirigible, but he never had a chance to try out the comical fishhook bombs.

As he climbed, urging the best from the 90-horsepower R.A.F. engine, he next found himself caught in the beam of a London searchlight just when he was about 1000 feet below *LZ.15*, and Slessor saw sparks and gouts of flame flash from the airship's engines. He realized he had been spotted, and that the airship commander had decided to head for home.

The airship did, in fact, suddenly nose up, and at what seemed an alarming speed, swung away and then climbed for more altitude. Breithaupt had dropped every pound of his ballast in his effort to keep clear of the British plane below.

Years later Slessor and Breithaupt met at the R.A.F. Club in London where they talked about their wartime experiences. The German airship commander admitted that he had been sitting up there quietly listening for the beat of aeroplane engines when he first spotted Slessor's plane. In fact, in his first report he stated that while he had been trapped in the beams of "a large number of searchlights" four aeroplanes had threatened as dozens of AA guns had surrounded him with bursting shrapnel. The aeroplanes, according to Breithaupt, all endeavored to reach the airship and shoot her down with incendiary ammunition. (There was no such bullet in those days.)

As stated above, Slessor was the only British pilot to spot LZ.15 and even he had never been anywhere near a position from which he could attack the Zeppelin. All he could do was sit there and watch the massive form roar away and disappear into the darkness that made a bowl over the low gleam of the British metropolis. Slessor did his best to follow, but soon lost the dirigible in the clouds, and then to his disgust was lost himself. Below, he next identified the area of his old school Haileybury, and from there, after frantically fluttering back and forth in the sable night, finally picked up the Thames and followed it westward until 10,000 feet below he finally spotted the faint welcome of a flare path. All would have gone well, except for the concern of one of the searchlight men who with good intentions decided to add his light beam to the landing strip just as Slessor was making his final glide in. The Zepp-chaser was partly blinded and wound up in a turnip patch, wrenching his undercarriage, splintering a wingtip and ripping out an aileron.

This was Slessor's first operational sortie, making him the first British pilot to intercept an enemy aircraft *over Great Britain*. To him, it was an amateurish effort, but it was an important beginning to what was to evolve into the air defense organization that broke the heart of the Luftwaffe twenty-five years later. Slessor never flew another Defense-of-London patrol in what the British know as the Kaiser's War. A short time later he was rushed out to Mudros Harbor on Lemnos Island, the base of the Gallipoli campaign. After ten days in that theatre of operation, he embarked for Egypt with Number 14 Squadron to take up the defense of the Suez Canal.

This is how it was in the Great War.

Heinrich Mathy in *LZ.13* had hoped to drop a few bombs on the waterworks at Hampton, and after the release of that load he knew he could gain enough height to risk an attack on London proper. But visibility and slack navigation kept him from the Cambridge area until 8:30 P.M. While over Hatfield northwest of London he was harried by an anti-aircraft gun, so he dropped four 110-pound bombs in retaliation. He did not reach the Thames at Staines until about 10:30, and from there set out for Hampton.

He missed the bend of the river and instead flew along the Wey River and at 11:30 was over the village of Shalford. He released four parachute flares, but only one opened to furnish illumination, and with that he decided that Shalford *was* Hampton. He crossed the village three times, dropping explosive bombs, believing he was pounding pump houses and power stations, but actually inflicting only minor damage to a few private homes.

Satisfied with that effort, Mathy turned northeast for London, and over Bromley on the southeastern edge of the city almost collided with *LZ.14* that was commanded by Alois Böcker. He then headed for what he thought were the Victoria Docks, and his bombardier pulled the plug, releasing the rest of their load, including a 660-pounder. These fell on Woolwich Arsenal, but, fortunately for the British, comparatively little damage was done.

Böcker in *LZ.14* crossed the coast between Norwich and Thetford where he was fired on, so he steered for Woolwich via Chelmsford, but in the excitement, and in trying to avoid other airships, he somehow steered southeast, crossed the lower Thames at the Isle of Sheppey, continued on until 10:15 when he reached the sea near Hythe in Kent. Here began another epic of bewilderment. Mistaking the English Channel for the mouth of the Thames, he bombed what he thought to be Woolwich and the dock facilities in that area.

Instead, his nine explosive bombs dropped on an Army camp that overlooked the Channel. Fifteen soldiers were killed and eleven wounded. How Böcker found his way back to London is a mystery, but he did, and still insisted he had bombed Woolwich. At 12:20 A.M. he floundered about over Croydon where he dropped the rest of his bombs, damaging a number of private houses.

Werner Peterson, commanding *LZ.16*, began his program of trouble shortly after they were crossing the North Sea. He had pulled a toggle to release a forward water-ballast breech in order to bring the airship to an even keel, but most of the 220 pounds of water had poured out on the control-car roof. Several gallons had sloshed down the ventilator set up over the wireless transmitter, and the operators spent the night dismantling, drying, and assembling the set. As was to be expected, a number of short circuits were experienced while important messages were being transmitted. In fact, the set was not fully operational until early the next morning.

Nevertheless, Peterson continued on, passed over Norwich and Cambridge and reached London in time to spot *LZ.15* brightly illuminated in the searchlights over the city. Making the most of the attention being paid Breithaupt, Peterson took the bold course and started dropping bombs, "hitting some factories and railroad yards in Stratford, East Ham and West Ham," or so he thought. Actually, *LZ.16* was over the town of Hertford, some twenty miles north of London, where nine people were killed and fifteen injured. This was the toll of his eighteen explosive, and thirty incendiary bombs that were scattered across the town and out through the countryside.

Fog came up and hampered the journey. *LZ.13* (Mathy) found herself over the island of Vlieland where she was fired on by Dutch guns, but she evaded the cannonade and reached her base during the early morning of October 14. *LZ.11* and *LZ.16* also returned safely, but *LZ.14* was kept aloft for nearly five hours waiting for the fog to break and permit her to get in at Nordholz. *LZ.15* with Breithaupt never did get back to her base. Although the craft had reached Nordholz by 10:00 A.M. she had fuel for only two hours flight. At 11:40 the ground staff sent up a captive kite balloon to mark the position of the airship base, and Breithaupt forced his airship down time after time. Although he reached the 300-foot level, he could see no trace of the ground. Two of his engines had failed, and the other two were giving trouble because of water in the gasoline. By noontime Breithaupt knew he must land somehow, and he forced her down to 250 feet but still could not find the ground, and had no idea where the sheds or gas tanks were in relation to the kite balloon. He lowered landing ropes, hoping someone would spot them, but they brought no response. He now had no choice but to valve gas and hope for the best.

LZ.15 wallowed through the murk and finally smacked down hard on the moorland near a railroad track. Most of the gondola struts were fractured, a main ring and some longitudinal girders were broken and there were only thirty-six gallons of fuel in the tanks. A ground staff walked the airship three miles, and sheltered her at Nordholz. A week later repairs had been made so she could fly back to her own shed at Hage.

This raid on October 13 was one of the deadliest of the war. Seventy-one people were killed, and 128 injured. But ensuing winter weather drastically reduced Zeppelin air activity, and this first full-squadron raid on London was the last for almost a year.

Winter made its demands on the flight schedule, and eased Britain's problems. There were southeast gales, thick weather, and meteorological conditions that contributed to the questions of condensation. Mathy also reported to his superiors that the British blackout was becoming more complete, and their gunnery defense was improving.

But we must forgive some of their failures, particularly in navigation and identification of particular areas. Aerial navigation was not much more than surface-nautical navigation applied to flying. There was little reliable radio co-operation or accurate triangulation. Airships were being hurriedly built, crews quickly trained, and, most important, the Maybach company was hastily turning out engines, most of which proved to be complete duds. By late 1916, more than two years after the start of the war, the company still had not worked out all the bugs in their 240-horsepower HSLu engine that had been designed to replace the 210-horsepower C-X, produced early in 1914.

The HSLu was lighter, more powerful, and believed to be more efficient, but for months the airship mechanics had to bear with fractured crankshafts, broken connecting rods, faulty crank bearings, wrist pins that overheated, melted and "froze," and these failures were only slightly allayed by fitting air scoops to carry air from the slipstream into the crankcase.

Some flights were attempted during the bad weather, possibly as training for the new crews. During the latter part of November the airships were sent out to cover the mine-sweepers in the western sector of the German Bight. On one of these forays Peterson in *LZ.16* had an engine breakdown. The mechanics dismantled the Maybach, removed a frozen wrist pin, and they carried on. By noon fog enveloped them, and Peterson had to turn back, flying at 130 feet above the sea. A propeller bracket broke while he was trying to land at Hage, and another engine failed when the spark plugs oiled up. But this young skipper managed to set his airship down safely near the village of Hilgenriedersiel, three miles from the base at Hage. A ground force walked it back to the shed, and another hair-raising experience was logged.

A new airship, *LZ.18*, was delivered to Max Dietrich who attempted to fly her from Löwenthal to the North Sea. Bad weather inland forced him to seek shelter at an Army field at Hanover where he stayed for thirteen days awaiting a clearance, and then managed to get to Tondern. He berthed *LZ.18* in one of the new double sheds there, and the next morning when a ground crew was topping off a gas cell, an explosion occurred, setting the new Zeppelin afire. Before the war ended five other airships burned in this same double hangar.

All through December and early January the schedule was blanked by foul weather. Even scouting or training flights were few and far between, and while the airships stood in their unheated sheds they became beaded with moisture, and condensation lowered the value of the fuel, high humidity drew much of the lift from the hydrogen, and the gas cells had to be refilled time and time again.

But all this delay, idle time, and frustration gave the Naval Airship Service authorities hours to plan new bombing forays on the British Isles.

In order to appreciate much of the action that takes place aboard a military dirigible, the reader should clearly visualize the positions of various members of the crew, their duties, and their general range of action. In the early types, such as *LZ.3*, a crew of sixteen was carried. Six, including the captain and his executive officer, were accommodated in the forward, or control gondola, seven were in the hull cabin amidships, and three, chiefly machinists, were carried in the aft gondola. Personnel in these power cars spent much time there, but occasionally it was necessary for them to make inspections or use the galley or lavatory conveniences in the main hull. To get there they had to climb up a metal ladder connecting the gondola with the main catwalk above, a move that necessitated their clambering up or down in the open space while the airship was proceeding at high speed.

In the later models, such as the *LZ.13*, sixteen crewmen were carried, but nine worked in the aft gondola under exactly the same conditions while the remaining seven carried out their duties in the forward, or control cabin. Aboard airships of the "Thirties" class, from *LZ.31* on, the crew was composed of twenty men, of whom ten worked in the forward control car, three in the amidships engine gondola, and seven in the larger power gondola aft.

For all dirigibles there was in addition a ground staff of twenty-four skilled hands.

A Zeppelin crew usually included the commander, the observation officer, two helmsmen, two radio operators, a sailmaker, and possibly a dozen machinists or mechanics who serviced the engines, maintained the ballast tanks, and watched the gasoline systems. The observation officer directed the airship's maneuvering before and after landing, as the commander was fully occupied in the control gondola. In flight the observation officer was in charge of communications, the radio sets, and took the responsibility of coding or decoding messages. During an attack he assumed the post of executive officer, or second-in command, just as he would have done had he been aboard a surface warship.

Navigation was the duty of the officer steersman, under the commander's authority. He kept the course, registered the speed, and checked their positions on the chart. During landing proceedings the steersman used the telegraph system to communicate orders to each engine gondola. The chief engineer was responsible for the testing of engines, and fuel consumption, and his post usually was in the rearmost engine gondola. The men in charge of the elevators also directed the use of the ballast, and when action permitted they might man searchlights or machine guns. Under normal flight conditions they would take turns acting as lookouts.

With the development of the "height climbers" which were received early in 1917, the crewmen encountered all the discomforts of thin air and sub-zero temperatures, and it was found that their physiques were not always equal to the task. Climbing the ladders from the gondolas to the interior catwalk was most exhausting, and many of the men had to take to their hammocks after a very ordinary move from one portion of the airship to another. Anywhere above 13,000 feet the men suffered marked acceleration of respiration and cardiac activity. Pulse rates of 120–150 a minute were not uncommon. Dizziness was generally apparent, and practically all suffered painful headaches. Men who had to haul 66-pound drums of gasoline either to the main tanks or to retrim the ship; or walk up and down the twenty-degree gangway on their duties became so weary they had to pull themselves along by available handholds. Some of these uphill climbs measured 295 feet, and the job of pumping fuel from tank to tank by hand often put experienced men in their hammocks for the rest of the trip.

One can then perhaps imagine the drama, the terror and physical exhaustion the men of the Zeppelin service experienced every time they went on a raid. If their ship came under attack, all these horrors were multiplied. They had to carry out their duties in that mad cavern, illuminated by vague or blinding lights. They staggered along narrow catwalks, clinging to handrails that were grease-swabbed, zero-cold, or not where they were supposed to be. Enemy attack provided new and frightening sounds, failure of engines, or communications, and that ever-present dread of hydrogen fire. Enemy attack might take the form of flame-spiked hornets, snapping from girder to girder, or it could be the impact of heavy shells tearing out important segments of the framework. Every raid created a new dread. Every new sound produced an added terror. Every new pattern of light brought a reminder of a cigar-shaped projectile, garlanded in flame, plunging toward some peaceful spread of English countryside.

Yet brave men willingly volunteered for this insane duty, for duty is what they owed to an Emperor and their Fatherland. Back home their children marched back and forth to school singing a tuneful ditty that ran:

> *Zeppelin, flieg,*
> *Hilf uns im Krieg,*
> *Fliege nach England,*
> *England wird abgebrannt.*
> *Zeppelin, flieg!*

A literal translation goes:

> *Fly, Zeppelin,*
> *Help us in the war,*
> *Fly to England,*
> *England shall be destroyed by fire.*
> *Fly, Zeppelin!*
>
> DR. ADOLF SAAGER.

VII

THE DEFENSE BUILDS UP

By late 1915 Warneford's heroism was forgotten, and the newspapers were inundated with letters from their readers demanding to know when the raids, considered a "gross impertinence," were going to be stopped. The public concern was reflected in political debates that, at best, enlivened the House of Commons, but all Arthur Balfour, then First Lord of the Admiralty, could promise was that no matter how many times the Zeppelins raided London, they would never shake the nerve of the British people — a memorable compliment to all Londoners, but these fine words did nothing toward halting the continued threat of high-explosive bombs and incendiaries.

Lord Horatio H. Kitchener, Secretary of State for War, was more of a realist and certainly far from supine. He was made of more practical sinew. He did not believe that only the poverty-stricken populace and the immigrant aliens scurried down the Underground railway warrens when the Zepps came over. He fully appreciated the psychological effect on the general public, and knew what the lowering of morale could do to the munitions-production program.

Early that summer Lord Kitchener sent for Sir David Henderson, Director General of Military Aeronautics, and in his articulated-eyebrow manner demanded to know what was being done about the Zeppelin raids.

"Home defense in this field rests with the Royal Naval Air Service," Henderson explained.

"What is the Royal Flying Corps doing?"

"Their chief job is in France, but we are gradually setting up fields, communications, and modifying aircraft that will allow the R.F.C. to take over some of the burden."

"I hold you responsible, Henderson," Kitchener growled.

Sir David then explained that in this emergency all trained R.F.C. pilots who were awaiting overseas assignments were to be retained in England, and as many as possible posted to the defense of London. It was presumed from all previous experiences that the next Zeppelin raids would be carried out during the second week in October, and that the raiders would avoid the defenses around the Thames Estuary, and approach the city from the northeast, and on this premise suitable dispositions had been made of searchlights, guns, and aircraft.

A corps of coastal observers was organized, among whom were a number of blind men who had volunteered, and were selected because it was thought they had developed a keen sense of hearing; in many cases this proved to be true. New telephone and telegraph communications linked these outposts with the War Office, and an additional line of 13-pounders with their own searchlight system was drawn about the northeastern suburbs of London.

The aerodromes at Joyce Green and Northolt, previously mentioned, were complete and properly manned by late 1915. Another was set up at Hainault Farm, four miles north of Romford, and another farm, farther south at Hornchurch, was requisitioned. This was then known as Sutton's Farm.

The aircraft were mainly B.E.2c biplanes, modified as single-seater, night-attack ships. This meant that the front seat usually occupied by an observer was covered over temporarily with fabric and an extra fuel tank was fitted in this passenger space. Power was supplied by a 90-horse-power Royal Aircraft Factory (RAF) engine that gave a reported top speed of 93 miles per hour, and a service ceiling of 11,000 feet. It was as good a machine as could be provided at the time, although latter-day historians are prone to place it in the "crate" category, ignoring the fact that in 1915 there were few, if any, other aircraft with a superior performance in night operations. It was sound structurally, easy to fly, and, coincidently, three of the Victoria Crosses awarded to British airmen in World War I were won while they were flying in B.E.2c's.

The Defense of London planes were fitted with two bomb racks, one under each wing, that accommodated eight 20-pounders. There is no evidence that any were equipped with a machine gun, although the original model—the two-seater—was fitted by now with a Lewis gun mounted at one of two positions. (1) It could be mounted near the forward-seated observer (if one was carried) who had to fire outside the arc of the propeller, or through the tangle of struts and flying wires. (2) It could be mounted, in the case of a single-seater arrangement, on a peg near the pilot who, at best, could fire it only forward through a very limited arc drawn between the tips of the propeller and the inner set of interplane struts. By late 1915 there still was no interrupter gear available for B.E.2c aircraft. They were being reserved for the new Sopwith 1½-Strutter, the first British two-seater to be equipped with a front-firing, interrupter-gear gun.

By early October 1915, then, the Defense of London system had four R.F.C. fields with sheds, landing tees, machines, and pilots. In fact, at Joyce Green they had one S.E.4a, a single-seater designed by H. P. Folland, who was to have a hand in the development of many British fighters over the ensuing years. This machine was a sleek biplane with I-type interplane struts, and racing wings equipped with full length ailerons that could be used as landing flaps. In the first version Folland provided a molded celluloid cockpit canopy, but none of the R.F.C. pilots of the day would risk flying beneath it, so it had to be discarded.

Power was furnished by a 14-cylinder, 160-horsepower

Gnome engine that gave the machine a top speed of 135 miles per hour, making it the world's fastest aircraft at that time. The Gnome engine, however, proved to be unsuited for military work and had to be replaced with a 100-horse-power Monosoupape Gnome that cut the speed to 92 miles per hour. It was one of these modified models that was sent to Joyce Green, but how it fared has not been recorded. We do know that a landing accident brought about the discarding of the type, and Folland apparently set to work to produce what was to become the famous S.E.5.

We have, therefore, a military situation in which a 70-miles per-hour Zeppelin with a ceiling of 12,000 feet was to be intercepted and destroyed by an aircraft, the B.E.2c, said to be capable of 93 miles per hour, which would seem to give the pilot a reasonable chance to chase and over-take the dirigible, but it took almost an hour for him to reach 12,000 feet, even if this were possible when the plane was being flown as a single-seater. And, as has been noted, to attack with bombs or incendiary darts, the airplane would have to attain a position *above* the dirigible. Only in cases of advance warnings, given in plenty of time, was there any hope of putting an aeroplane high in the sky in time to intercept the oncoming raider and destroy it.

The program of the air defense of London was made very clear to all concerned. A chain of observers was deployed across the northeast sector of London, and if any of these men observed a dirigible in the sky, they were to fire rockets of a certain color that would indicate in which direction the raider was advancing. Once any of the observers had reported an airship approaching London, the Home Defense Headquarters was to inform all defense fields, and one aircraft was to be sent up on a specific order. It was presumed that the warning would come soon enough for the pilot to reach an altitude of 8000 feet. At this level he was to patrol over his own field until he spotted a hostile airship, upon which he was to take offensive action. If no airship appeared within ninety minutes, he was to return to his field, fire a green signal light to indicate his approach, await a like signal response that the landing area was clear, upon which the ground crew would ignite a number of flares to outline about three hundred feet of runway. The actual field was about five hundred yards square.

The flares were simply five-gallon gasoline cans with the tops cut away, and were filled with a mixture of kerosene, gasoline, and machinists' waste and lit with ordinary pocket matches. Once the aircraft had landed, the cans were turned over on their open ends, and in that manner quickly doused.

The defense of Britain built up slowly. True, considerable constructive thought had been given to the situation before 1914, but nothing practical could be developed until enemy aircraft appeared overhead to attack the spread of undefended cities. Until October 1915 when Strasser's dirigible commanders were enjoying the first fruits of their planning, Britain's air defense was still in the hands of the Admiralty and the War Office, a situation that provided little in the way of practical co-operation, since it is well nigh impossible to get a military and a naval man to see matters from the same viewpoint.

The first break came in March 1916 when the defenses were assigned solely to the Royal Flying Corps. It was also decided that more searchlights would be needed to illuminate the big dirigibles for the night fighters. It had been shown that one searchlight could not hold a 70-miles-per-hour airship very long, as the raider would soon fly out of the range of the beam. Two concentric circles of searchlights were established around London to overcome this, and nine electric tramcars were fitted with searchlights to be moved from point to point.

Royal Flying Corps pilots, assigned to this defense, told Sir David Henderson they believed that in the event of a six-Zeppelin attack on London, they could down at least three of them—if the observers and searchlight crews played their part. Although he was a cautious man, he wished to believe this and showed his faith in these young men by forming what was to be known as the 18th Wing, R.F.C., that included all air defenses of London under Colonel F. V. Holt.

Sutton's Farm was established on a permanent basis as one of the ring of airfields around London. Others included Hounslow, Wimbledon Common, Croydon, Farningham, Chingford, Hendon, Northolt, and Hainault Farm. Each field was provided with two B.E.2c's, and two night-flying pilots. Some twenty aircraft and their pilots had been taken from several training squadrons, but all had retained their squadron identity, a situation that could not guarantee any workable cohesion. It soon was evident that the planes and pilots should be established under a single command. By February 1916 the Defense-of-London pilots, planes, and searchlights were placed under the control of Major T. C. Higgins who was commanding Number 19 Reserve Squadron at Hounslow. One month later ten Home Defense squadrons were authorized and the aircraft at Sutton's Farm, together with the other detached squadrons around London, became part of what was to be Number 39 Home Defense Squadron, and Major Higgins set up necessary headquarters at Hounslow.

But again, such a scattering of force was unmanageable so Major Higgins reduced the perimeter of fields from seventy-six miles to fifteen by concentrating all aircraft at Hainault Farm and Sutton's Farm. This was accomplished by establishing two flights of six aircraft each and accommodating them at the two fields. At the same time plans were made to form a third flight at Woodford, Essex, and at long last a compact organization was available.

But with all this planning and training for the inevitable, the Zeppelins enjoyed another halcyon year through 1916. The newer, larger, faster airships, carrying more gas cells were reported to be able to reach 21,000 feet (somewhat of an exaggeration), and that the crews were being provided with an oxygen-supply system that would help them to endure such thin-air altitudes. It will be seen in later pages that much of this was enemy propaganda, but the performance of the dirigible was being improved, month by month.

The British antiaircraft guns had no such range and through the first six months of 1916 forty-six Zeppelins crossed the British coastline between Yorkshire and Kent. London was attacked twice during this period, and although the R.F.C. put up commendable numbers of aircraft, only one Zeppelin fell before a British airman's guns, but this memorable victory was the turning point in the grim struggle to counter the enemy's air offensive.

With the approach of 1916 the German General Staff and the Chief of the Naval Staff concentrated on new and broader plans for bombing England. All raids were to be made by as many airships as possible, and even Army Zeppelins were to participate whenever feasible. To facilitate the planning, Great Britain was to be divided into three operational areas. *England North* meant Edinburgh and the Tynside area. *England Middle* referred to Liverpool and the valley of the Humber. *England South* took in London, and secondarily the Yarmouth sector. Strasser admitted that an attack on Bristol was almost out of the question and Southampton could be reached only by airships leaving from bases in occupied Belgium.

On the afternoon of January 31, 1916, nine Zeppelins took off for England, and on this occasion, Strasser elected to lead the pack. He was aboard *LZ.11*, and the object was to attack England, Middle or South, and if at all possible, seek out Liverpool.

They ran into deep fog over the North Sea, and as they approached the English coast this changed to rain clouds and some snow that iced up the outer covers. Star fixes were impossible and they had to make the most of radio bearings to determine their positions. Most of the airships finally reached the coastline well to the south, and none of them actually reached the west coast. Ground mist and low fog over England further hampered navigation, and as a result two commanders claimed to have bombed Liverpool. Others reported that they had hit Sheffield, Nottingham, Goole, Yarmouth, and Immingham. No bombs actually fell in any of these places, though defense throughout the Midlands was virtually nonexistent. People were killed, some property damage was incurred, but no target of military importance was found.

Max Dietrich, Heinrich Mathy, Alois Böcker, and Werner Peterson, as well as Peter Strasser, took part in this raid, and all of them turned in highly questionable reports of their adventure, and not until British newspapers published details of the attack, did any of them know where they had been.

Kapitänleutnant Herbert Ehrlich aboard *LZ.17* provided a typical report of this raid, but it must be admitted he was plagued with bad luck. Early that afternoon *LZ.17* broke a piston ring that "froze" to the cylinder wall, and the frosty-fingered mechanics spent hours dismantling the engine to clear the obstruction. Then, by 6:00 P.M. a wrist pin melted and the starboard engine refused to put out required power for any reasonable periods, but Ehrlich bravely set course for the Humber. He believed he had crossed the coast at about 8:00 P.M. for a searchlight had bored through the overcast, making him think he was over an industrial area. Other glows below were thought to be blast furnaces, so he made two runs over these targets, claiming to have silenced a battery and to have bombed the town of Immingham in Lincolnshire.

What really happened was that *LZ.17* drifted in over Sheringham, Norfolk, at 7:40 P.M., and was picked up by a naval searchlight mounted at Holt. Ehrlich actually dropped his bombs in nearby fields.

A tragic conclusion to this raid was suffered by Odo Loewe, commanding *LZ.19* who had remained over England for nearly nine hours. Being in charge of a brand new Zeppelin, Loewe probably felt he would be expected to make a special attempt. He, too, was plagued with HSLu engine trouble but managed to cross the coastline at Sheringham at 7:20 P.M., and then headed for Burton-on-Trent.

Next, he went for the suburbs of Birmingham, but his bombs fell on an unimportant area. From this point on engine trouble increased and apparently he wandered about over the Midlands, and did not cross the British coastline until 6:30 A.M. In the meantime he had pleaded with Nordholz and Bruges to give him bearings, and at one time he was located between King's Lynn and Norwich. In his attack report, radioed about 5:30 A.M., Loewe stated that at midnight he had been over the British west coast, but because of foul visibility had turned back and "over Sheffield dropped 3500 pounds of bombs."

By 6:41 A.M. *LZ.19* was plotted near the Haisbrough Lightship, and three flotillas of German destroyers were alerted to move out for search and rescue. Two hours later *LZ.19's* radio operator reported they were near Borkum Island with three engines out of order, but radio bearings indicated that *LZ.19* was farther west than that, or some twenty-two miles north of Ameland.

The hours passed, but nothing more was heard from Loewe. Searches of all kinds were sent out. There was no trace of the new Zeppelin. Other airships were ordered out to look for her, but fog and erratic winds kept them in their sheds.

On the morning of February 2 German destroyers picked up one of *LZ.19's* fuel tanks about twelve miles north of Borkum, and when it was examined it still contained ten gallons of gasoline. Then the Dutch authorities announced that an airship had appeared low over Ameland late in the afternoon of February 1, and their sentries and gunners had repeatedly fired on her, and she finally vanished in the mist. It was generally agreed later that this gunfire had further crippled Loewe's airship, and she was driven out to sea by a rising south wind.

Then ensued a drama, pathetic, poignant, and tragic. On February 3 a German Army wireless station located at Lille picked up a message that explained that a British trawler had sighted the wreck of a Zeppelin about 110 miles east of Flamborough Head, Yorkshire. German newspapers, published over the next few days, were outraged to learn that the British trawler captain, after moving in close enough to the floating hulk to speak to members of Loewe's crew, had then backed off and sailed away, leaving them to their fate. The trawler in question was the *King Stephen* whose skipper argued later that had he rescued the nineteen men of the German crew they could have overpowered his nine hands, and forced him to sail for some German port.

This was a point that came up time and time again during World War I, and again in World War II. Second-guessing would have it that the captain of the *King Stephen* might have rescued the airship crew and risked having to put them ashore in Germany, with the understanding that he, his crew, and their vessel would be released and escorted to where they could have returned home safely.

Nothing more was ever heard of Loewe or the *LZ.19.*

Although the Germans lost one airship on this raid, credit could not be claimed by the London defenses; it was the Dutch military which had poured concentrated rifle fire into the floundering Zepp. Strasser was determined to continue the attacks, but in the face of the failures of the HSLu engines he begged the German Naval Aviation Department to order modifications in these power plants, and by March 4, 1916, *LZ.15*, *LZ.16*, *LZ.17*, *LZ.20*, and *LZ.21* were taken out of service, and their engines removed for shipment back to the Maybach factory. The machinists' mates were also posted there for further training.

This left Strasser with only *LZ.11*, *LZ.13*, *LZ.14*, and a few earlier models powered with the 210-horsepower C-X engines with which to carry out his program, but he knew that by the end of March he would have the first of the 2,000,000-cubic-foot giants, the six-engined dirigibles that had been ordered from the Zeppelin Company the previous July. Not only that, he then suggested to Admiral Philip, Chief of German Naval Aviation, that he channel all but two of these super-Zeppelins, as British agents were to term them, into the Naval Airship Service. This left the Army with the earlier models which, in fact, were quite suitable for their short-range missions.

On the afternoon of March 31 Strasser sent seven Zeppelins to attack the main target in southern England—London. Two of them had to turn back off the Dutch islands, but Mathy in *LZ.13*, after studying the atmospheric conditions, decided to get rid of some bombs on an explosive depot at Stowmarket. He actually reached this area at 9:45 P.M., but on dropping a flare to find his target, he aroused an anti-aircraft battery that opened fire. Mathy replied with several bombs, but succeeded in breaking only a few windows. Turning away, he made a sweep to the west and then tried to find Stowmarket once more, but again the British gunners were alert and scored a telling hit. Cell Number 10 amidships was pierced and half its gas had escaped before the damage was found. A short time later Cell Number 16, well forward, was found to have been holed, so Mathy wisely turned for home, dropped the rest of his bombs near Lowestoft, and made it back safely to Hage by 3:30 A.M.

Breithaupt, aboard *LZ.15*, apparently returned to service; crossed the British coast at about 7200 feet and headed for London by way of Ipswich and Chelmsford. In order to reach a safer altitude he dropped all available ballast, but could not get much above 8000 feet. London was well blacked-out, but the gleam of the river was a tremendous help. As he crossed Dartford searchlights crisscrossed the sky and ground guns opened up. A shell from the first salvo scored a direct hit amidships and there were several moments of anxiety aboard *LZ.15*, but nothing serious transpired. Breithaupt swerved north and dumped fifteen large explosive bombs to lighten his load, all of them falling in open fields near Rainham.

The British defense was getting into gear. The redoubtable Mathy had already been driven off with severe damage, and now Breithaupt was hurrying away from the prime target with a great gash in his cover, and for the first time the commander of *LZ.15* sensed that a British aeroplane, or aeroplanes, were somewhere above him. In fact, a Second Lieutenant Ridley, flying out of Joyce Green, was the first to give chase, and was able to fire twenty rounds of regular ammunition before *LZ.15* disappeared in the dark. A few minutes later Breithaupt was again caught on a cone of searchlight gleam, and came under heavy antiaircraft fire from a gun set up at Purfleet, which eventually scored a hit that tore a great gash in the airship's main envelope.

Second Lieutenant Alfred de Bath Brandon who had taken off in a B.E.2c from Hainault Farm next spotted *LZ.15* as it was trying to evade the searchlights. He made three separate attacks with a box of explosive darts, incendiary bombs, and his machine gun. This combined attack apparently created much damage. In part of his eventual report (still in the Imperial War Museum file) Brandon stated:

I continued and circled in front of the Zeppelin, and turned round to get in its rear, and on going past, there was a tremendous amount of machine-gun fire going on. At this point I switched off my lights, and continued in my direction for two or three hundred yards, and then turned and got in line with the Zeppelin. I was then about 500 feet above it; I closed the throttle and volplanned toward the Zeppelin; the nose of my machine was pointed about quarter way from the rear. I then got an incendiary bomb, and in trying to get it into the tube I had to take my eyes off the Zeppelin, and on looking up again I was astonished to find that in a very few seconds I would have passed it, so I quickly placed the incendiary bomb in my lap, and let off No. 2 and No. 3 lots of darts. I did not hear any report from this. I concluded that the Zeppelin was, in reality, coming toward me, so I opened up the engine again and turned completely round, and followed a southerly course, continuing for some considerable time, as I thought the Zeppelin had got a good start. In the meantime I turned on my lights again and I was at 8,000 feet for some time and saw nothing, and then dropped to 6,000 feet and cruised around for considerable time without seeing any further sign of the Zeppelin.

Breithaupt was in dire straits. His *LZ.15* was damaged seriously; the amidships Cell 11 was empty, Cell 12 forward and Cell 9 aft were both leaking. Cell 16 in the bow was also empty which made the ship nose-heavy. Breithaupt realized that his only sanctuary was Belgium. He had jettisoned all of his bombs and all but four hours of fuel. Next, the heavy machine guns, engine covers, and spare parts went over, but despite these emergency efforts it was obvious that *LZ.15* was doomed to end in the sea. Breithaupt's secret documents were wired to the radio stool and dumped into the Thames, and finally after reporting, NEED IMMEDIATE ASSISTANCE BETWEEN RIVER THAMES AND OSTEND, the wireless instruments were tossed overboard.

At 12:15 A.M., wallowing along at 500 feet, *LZ.15*'s framework buckled in two at Rings 7 and 11 and the airship nosed into the sea about a mile from the Kentish Knock Lightship.

Six armed trawlers steamed up out of the night and another *King Stephen* was in the making as one trawler opened fire. But on the arrival of the British destroyer *Vulture* the gunnery was discontinued and Breithaupt and his crew taken off, not, however, until they had obeyed an order to strip off all their clothes, and embark not more than three men to each boat bringing them to the destroyer. *Vulture* tried to tow *LZ.15* ashore but the hull framework broke up and the wreckage sank off Westgate, Kent.

The prisoners were landed at Chatham where they were interrogated by a Major Trench of the Royal Marines, who at the time headed Admiral Sir Reginald Hall's Naval Intelligence Division. Trench had once been imprisoned in Germany for more than two years on a charge of espionage, and he had a full command of the German language, so, understandably, was able to reap some small reward in his interrogation of Breithaupt and his crew. Afterward the officers of *LZ.15* were sent to the famous Donnington Hall, a luxury lockup where British soldiers waited on and provided batman service for a special group of enemy officers. Donnington Hall was one of the features of British propaganda, and wads of illustrated material were dropped over the enemy lines by R.F.C. airmen with the intention of enticing German soldiers to desert and enjoy this form of aristocratic incarceration.

For the next five days Strasser sent out his Zeppelins daily to raid England, and one of the most "outrageous" exploits was the bombing by Böcker of the Leith works of Messrs. Innes and Grieve's whiskey warehouse where £44,000 worth of Hieland Nectar was destroyed. What was most distressing was that Böcker was really looking for the Forth Bridge or the Rosyth dockyard.

All this marked the high point in Strasser's planning. By April 6 a steady pattern of bad weather was experienced, and he took this opportunity to have all airships laid up for maintenance and engine overhaul. At the same time the Staff of the Naval Airship Service relaxed, and completely taken in by the repeated, exaggerated reports of the destruction wrought on Great Britain, sent a formal report to the Kaiser on April 11, 1916, which read in part as follows:

At Grimsby, in addition to the Post Office and several other houses, a battleship in the roadstead was heavily damaged by a bomb, and had to be beached. At Kensington an aeroplane hangar was wrecked, near Tower Bridge a transport ship was damaged, in Great Tower Street a factory was wrecked, and north of the Tower a bomb fell in George Street only 100 meters away from two anti-aircraft guns. It was reported that a big fire had broken out at West India Docks, and that at Tilbury Docks a munitions boat exploded (400 killed). Specially serious explosions occurred at the Surrey Commercial Docks and at a factory close to the lower road, at which shells were filled with explosives. A railroad train already loaded with these shells was stated to be completely wrecked.

Such statements presaged the beginning of the end. Not one word of the above was true, but the reports were willingly believed by the Supreme War Lord and the German public, so wishful thinking continued to determine national policy, or until the German Navy was forced to shake off its dream of using Zeppelins to blast or burn Great Britain into submission.

The destruction of *LZ.15* and the reports of Mathy having been driven off with ground gunfire damage, eased the dread of Zeppelins for a time and raised the morale of the 18th Wing, but with the advent of August when the raids began again in earnest, the general public demanded visual evidence that Zeppelins could be destroyed. There was a period when sound minds inquired, "Why can we not meet Zeppelins with Zeppelins?" Few thought aeroplanes were the answer for it had been painfully obvious over the past year or so that dirigible airships were not easy to deal with, and calling them "German sausages" in no way uncovered any vulnerability. Where British airships were to come from to send up against the Zeppelins was never clearly answered.

But the airmen of the 18th Wing refused to be daunted. For one thing they stuck to their night flying despite the fact that on one occasion in January 1916, of the fifteen machines that took off, eleven crashed and three pilots were killed. Four months later ten aircraft were sent up from the same aerodrome on night operations and all ten returned safely.

But a more important die was cast. The original 20-pound high-explosive and 16-pound incendiary bombs were dispensed with, and the explosive darts invented by a Commander Rankin of the Royal Navy were introduced. These were loaded into a metal box and could be discharged when the aeroplane was directly above a Zeppelin. But here, again, it will be seen that the scattering of such projectiles could be made only from above the dirigible, and, as yet, British aircraft could not always reach these commanding levels. So they turned back to the machine gun (Lewis), trusting that sprays of rifle-caliber bullets would so pepper the gas cells the Zeppelins would have to hurry home before all buoyancy was lost. They did not know, or refused to believe, that all Zeppelins carried sailmakers who had quick-sealing patches for repairing such leaks while in flight.

Eventually, some headway was made toward the production of a true incendiary bullet that could be fired from a machine gun. The path had been rugged and had led down many time-consuming detours.

There also was a time when British authorities were convinced that the Germans had eliminated the danger of hydrogen fire by producing a double-walled gas cell, a belief that caused the abandonment of the search for an incendiary bullet for a while. As early as August 1914 John Pomeroy had submitted details for an explosive bullet but the British War Office saw no necessity for such a round, and Mr. Pomeroy returned to his home in Australia. Fortunately, by December 1915 the Ministry of Munitions had decided that there might be some value in his invention.

About the same time other officials took a second glance at a phosphorous bullet devised by Mr. J. F. Buckingham of Coventry, England, and an explosive bullet invented by Squadron Commander F. A. Brock of the Royal Naval Air Service. Commander Brock was a member of a famous English family which for years had manufactured fireworks and pyrotechnics for public celebrations, and his explosive bullet was exactly what was required, as it blew fairly large holes in the outer covers and gas cells of the Zepps, and the following rounds of Pomeroy or Buckingham would ignite the escaping hydrogen.

By the spring of 1916 one million rounds of Brock, Pomeroy, and Buckingham ammunition were ordered for all .303-caliber machine guns, and these rounds were available to the Home Defense squadrons by the summer of 1916. A German airship commander said later, "This pattern of incendiary ammunition was an invention of the devil!"

Something was finally done about efficient cockpit lighting for the night-flying pilots. Not only were small electric lights run in, but all instruments were made luminous. On the airfields the rough-and-ready lighting system to set up a flare path was improved to some extent by the provision of what were called Money flares in which an asbestos wick set in a wire frame was saturated with paraffin (kerosene) oil, affording a standard and steady flame that could be lighted or doused quickly, and the pattern for setting them out was standardized throughout the command.

If only British aircraft designers could have provided high-speed, fast-climbing planes, the Zeppelin problem would have been solved within weeks. But across the North Sea German dirigible squadrons were receiving newer, bigger, and more efficient airships. In fact, these monsters, carrying 1,949,000 cubic feet of lifting gas, represented the greatest advance in airship construction made throughout the war. The first of this series, *LZ.30*, was 649 feet long, 78 feet in diameter and stood 90 feet, 10 inches above her gondola bumpers. She was powered by six Maybach HSLu engines, two of which were mounted in small gondolas set on either side of the hull amidships. She carried five tons of bombs and at one time had brackets for ten machine guns.

Number 39 Squadron, based at Sutton's Farm, had adopted every facility and weapon available, and on the night of September 2, 1916, one of her lieutenant pilots staged an epic patrol that was never matched until 1940 when British fighter pilots took off from Hornchurch in the memorable Battle of Britain.

Continuing his frantic attacks on England, Strasser sent out no less than twelve Zeppelins on the afternoon of September 2 to raid England-South with the idea of concentrating on London. In fact, he sent every available dirigible, except *LZ.31* and *SL.9*. In the pack were Army airships *L.90*, *L.97*, *L.98*, and a new *SL.11* which brought the total number to sixteen—so far the greatest raid of the war, and one which was to mark the turning point in the history of the Zeppelin as a major weapon.

The weather was hardly ideal; the wind was from the southwest, and on approaching the enemy coast the airships encountered rain and snow. Several reported icing conditions, and two raiders failed to reach England at all. The Army airship *L.98*, commanded by Ernst A. Lehmann, who became one of Dr. Eckener's co-workers in the postwar days, reached Gravesend on the Thames and came under heavy fire from guns at Tilbury and Dartford. Quite shaken, he dropped his bombs on what he believed to be some important London docks. On his turn around to fly home, his airship was spotted by Lieutenant William Leefe Robinson of Number 39 Squadron, but Lehmann darted into some clouds before Robinson could get within machine-gun range. Some 621 high-explosive bombs and 202 incendiaries were dropped by the Zeppelins before the night was over, but not one fell in the Metropolitan area of London.

Lieutenant William Leefe Robinson (sometimes written Leefe-Robinson), like Reggie Warneford, had been born in India of British parents, and when his family returned to Britain, he was enrolled at St. Bee's School in Cumberland, a small academy that was to produce three winners of the Victoria Cross. As a youth he had traveled extensively in France and Russia, but by August 1914 he had entered Sandhurst Military College. On graduating he was gazetted to the Worcester Regiment, but by March had become disenchanted with infantry training and transferred to the R.F.C. where he first served as an observer. On May 9 of that year while on a patrol over Lille, he suffered an arm wound, and on recovery was given pilot training at Farnborough, and gained his ticket the following September. After various postings he eventually joined Number 39 Squadron at Sutton's Farm.

A slim six-footer with a pleasant smile, curly hair, fair of complexion, Robinson was a mischievous devil in his free time. He appeared to some of his acquaintances to be shy and quiet-spoken, but he was a memorable practical joker, a fierce stunt merchant, and positively mad when turned loose with an automobile. In other words, Robinson was typical of the playboy pilots attracted to the Royal Flying Corps in those days.

Robinson had been sent aloft on the day in question

through a plan set up by GHQ Home Forces which had now taken over control of the Home Defence Wing. The squadron orders planned for each flight to send one aircraft out on patrol at two-hour intervals during a raid. The order was first issued at 11:00 P.M. and Lieutenant Robinson went off to patrol a line between Sutton's Farm and Joyce Green. Lieutenant Brandon took off from Hainault Farm to cover the area between his field and Sutton's Farm. Lieutenant C. S. Ross, out of North Weald, was responsible for the line North Weald-Hainault Farm. A second trio of patrols took over an area incorporating Sutton's Farm, Hainault Farm, Joyce Green, Farningham, and North Weald.

Robinson was to encounter Lehmann's *L.98* first when she was illuminated by searchlights and under fire in the vicinity of Finsbury Park and Wood Green. Lieutenant J. I. Mackay out of North Weald and Lieutenant B. H. Hunt of Hainault Farm also spotted Lehmann's airship, but she managed to escape, and become enveloped in cloud cover. The greater glory was to come to Robinson whose official report, scrawled at Sutton's Farm, gives some conception of this memorable encounter.

The report, still on view at the Imperial War Museum in London, reads as follows:

"I went up at 11:08 P.M. with instructions to patrol between Sutton's Farm and Joyce Green. I climbed to 10,000 feet in 53 minutes. I counted what I thought were sets of flares—there were a few clouds below me but on the whole it was a beautifully clear night.

"I saw nothing until about 1:10 A.M. when two searchlights picked out a Zeppelin about southwest of Woolwich. The clouds had collected in this quarter and the searchlights had some difficulty in keeping up with the aircraft. By this time I had managed to climb to 12,900 feet and I made in the direction of the Zeppelin which was being fired on by a few anti-aircraft guns, hoping to cut it off on its way eastwards. I very slowly gained on it for about ten minutes —I judged it to be about 200 feet below me and I sacrificed my speed in order to keep my height. It went behind some clouds, avoided the searchlights and I lost sight of it. After about fifteen minutes of fruitless search I returned to my patrol.

"I managed to pick up and distinguish my flares again. At about 1:50 A.M. I noticed a red glow in the northeast of London. Taking it to be an outbreak of fire I went in that direction. At about 2:05 A.M. a Zeppelin was picked up over N.N.E. London (as far as I could judge). Remembering my last failure, I sacrificed height (I was still at 12,100 feet) for speed and made nose-down for the Zeppelin. I saw shells bursting and night-tracer shells flying around it. When I drew closer I noticed that the anti-aircraft fire was too high or too low, also a good many rose 800 feet behind—a few tracers went right over. I could hear the bursts when about 3,000 feet from the Zeppelin.

"I flew to about 800 feet below it from bow to stern and distributed one drum along it (alternate new Brock and Pomeroy). It seemed to have no effect. I therefore moved to one side and gave it another drum along its side—without much apparent effect. I then got behind it (by this time I was very close—500 feet or less below—and concentrated one drum on one part underneath. I was then at a height of 11,500 feet when attacking the Zeppelin. I had hardly finished the drum when I saw the part fired at glow. In a few seconds the whole rear part was blazing. When the third drum was fired there were no searchlights on the Zeppelin and no A.A. was firing. I quickly got out of the way of the falling Zeppelin and, being very excited, fired off a few red Very lights and dropped a parachute flare.

"Having little oil or petrol left, I returned to Sutton's Farm, landing at 2:45 A.M. On landing I found that I had shot away my machine-gun wire guard, the rear part of the center section, and had pierced the main spar several times."

Thus had Lieutenant Robinson, Flight Commander of B Flight, Number 39 Squadron, R.F.C., given London the thrill she had long yearned for. Millions of anxious watchers saw *SL.11* fall slowly, spreading a brilliant glare over miles of British countryside while a number of German naval airships were still making their approach across Cambridgeshire, Norfolk, and Suffolk.

A tragic coincidence marked this victory. *SL.11* was commanded by Hauptmann Wilhelm Schramm, a German Army officer who, according to some records had been born in London, and had gone to his finish while attempting to bomb his birthplace. Schramm had come in over the Crouch River at about 10:40 P.M. from where he went into a diversionary sweep in order to approach London from the north. By 1:10 he was seen over St. Albans, and a few minutes later had dropped his first bombs on London Colney. Turning southward he then peppered the northern suburbs until he was picked up by searchlights at Finsbury Park. Although there were six pilots of Number 39 Squadron in the air at the time, Lieutenant Robinson was the first to get within firing range. The wreckage of *SL.11* fell in the village of Cuffley.

Though Number 39 Squadron had hung up its first night-flying victory, London and vicinity did not get off scot free. The bomb total was 38,979 pounds which included sixty incendiaries weighing 4559 pounds. Four civilians were killed and twelve injured, but the monetary damage was said to be well over £21,000.

L.90 which went in from south of the Naze, Essex, stopped her engines at 11:20 P.M., and lowered her observation car. The mechanism ran wild, the cable snapped, and the sub-cloud car with about 5000 feet of cable fell near Manningtree. The airship crew then dumped the winch which when found indicated that they had tried to jam the gears by ramming metal bars into the teeth. Years after the war a film company in Hollywood produced a motion picture based on Zeppelin operations in wartime and in one sequence showed a German Zeppelin commander ordering his crew to cut away a dangling observation car with its occupant when enemy gunfire indicated that a higher altitude would be expedient. Actually, no such cruel jettison task was ever carried out, and the British stated clearly that there was no observer in the car when it was found, and that it had undoubtedly fallen through some accident.

LZ.16, which had been in the van on the approach to London, was commanded by Kapitänleutnant Erich Sommerfeldt, and on the way in he had encountered considerable rain, so he dropped three explosive bombs on what appeared to be a locomotive. They fell near Kimberly Station on the Great Eastern Railway, ten miles southwest of Norwich. As he moved on toward London, Sommerfeldt counted more than forty searchlights fanning back and forth over the capital, and when he moved in for his attack he saw *SL.11* burst into flames.

LZ.16 was lucky to get away for she was spotted by another pilot of Number 39 Squadron, but her commander put on full speed and escaped to the northeast.

Peterson, aboard *LZ.32*, was over Tring, twenty miles to the northeast when Schramm's dirigible corkscrewed down. He had made his landfall at Cromer where his airship had iced up in the snow squalls, so he dropped eight 110-pound bombs, mainly to trim his ship. By midnight he had to drop a fuel tank when he believed he was over Newmarket. He prepared a fictitious report that he had attacked London somewhere near Kensington and started several fires. He did nothing of the kind. When he was near enough to appreciate the spread of searchlights and heavy gunfire, he turned east and dumped his bombs on Ware. He then steered northeast and crossed the coast near Lowestoft.

Oberleutnant Kurt Frankenberg, aboard *LZ.21* was over Hitchin when *SL.11* went down, and with her destruction, he decided he could not reach London "in the face of a freshening south wind," so he turned back to bomb Norwich. He reported later he could not find that city so dropped all his bombs on Sandringham where he might have damaged the Royal Family's Norfolk home, but his contribution fell in open fields. On the way home *LZ.21* lost an engine with a cracked cylinder. Two hours later the port engine also broke down with a defective magneto which in turn cut off all radio power, leaving Frankenberg in an unenviable position over the North Sea, but after several more mechanical problems, the early morning sunshine warmed his lifting gas and, cruising slowly at 10,700 feet, he eventually staggered to his home field.

And so it went. Zeppelins, creeping through rain, snow, and sleet, finally crossed the English coastline, but few were able to reach a worthwhile target. They became lost, and, as usual, their commanders decided they were miles from where they actually were. The defenses of London, both guns and searchlights, had been manfully strengthened, and the destruction of Schramm's *SL.11* took the boldness out of most of them. So ended the greatest bombing effort the German airship services were to make throughout the war. Thirty-two tons of bombs were carried, but only seventeen tons could be accounted for on British soil. A new airship and a trained crew of sixteen men had been lost, a setback which cost the German public about $970,000.

The next day, Sunday, September 3, all of London turned out to view the wreckage. The early morning newspapers said it had fallen at Cuffley, and every road, lane, and railroad leading into that rural hamlet was packed with the curious who arrived in carts, motorcars, on foot, and via bicycle. The grim, blackened framework lay across a beet field near the Plough Inn. The four Maybach engines were in different parts of the field, all more or less battered. The crankcase of one had apparently been hit by a shell fragment, for a shapeless hole had been plugged with a ball of machinist's cotton waste, proving that *SL.11* had been hit before Lieutenant Robinson sent her down. *SL.11*, a Schütte-Lanz airship, was built on a wooden framework, braced with steel wire, and much of the girder structure was burned or badly charred.

Typical of the British when individual exploits are concerned, the early morning newspapers which carried broad headlines on the destruction of *SL.11*, made no mention of the young man who had scored so dramatically. The news columns bore details of the ground defenses, the efficacy of the searchlights, and the fact that the casualties and damage had been disproportionate to the number of Zeppelins engaged in the raid. Lieutenant Robinson's name was not mentioned for many hours, but on September 5, three days after the epic event, it was announced that Lieutenant W. Leefe Robinson had been awarded the Victoria Cross, Great Britain's highest military honor.

Lieutenant Robinson soon became a popular public hero. His jaunty photograph appeared everywhere. Money rewards amounting to £3500 (about $17,000 in those days) had been contributed by British businessmen for the first airman to shoot down a Zeppelin over Britain.

Tradition in top London military circles has long held that no British officer should accept monetary rewards in such circumstances, and for a time there was a mild furor when Robinson was given his check. A War Office regulation was soon passed that put a stop to any such public acknowledgment. Romance also came Lieutenant Robinson's way. Within a short time he became engaged to pretty Joan Whipple, widow of a captain of a Devonshire Regiment who had been killed during the early days of the war.

As so often happens in wartime, Robinson did not long enjoy his many rewards. When the Zeppelin menace began to fade, he was promoted to a captaincy, and given a flight with Number 48 Squadron, R.F.C., which had just been formed to use the new Bristol Fighter, Britain's premier two-seater fighter. This new aircraft was so advanced in performance, armament, and all-around capability, R.F.C. authorities had no idea how to incorporate it into the offensive pattern. During the first few weeks when the Bristol Fighter appeared on the Front, it was employed inefficiently, and for a time some people thought the machine would never win a place for itself, particularly as a two-seater fighter.

On April 8, 1917, about seven months after being awarded the Victoria Cross, Robinson took his six-ship flight across the lines of the Western Front, and, according to popular fancy, immediately ran into—you know whom—

none other than Germany's ace flier, Baron von Richthofen, who was leading four other planes of his famous *Staffel*. In the ensuing melee, the Bristol Fighters attempted to maintain a tight formation, just as all British two-seater fighters had done over the previous months. They were cut to pieces, and four of the Bristols were shot down. Had they been flown as individual fighters to make the most of their speed and performance, the situation could have been reversed, but these are factors that can be learned only by experience. Captain W. Leefe Robinson was one of the pilots shot down and had to land in enemy territory, but a study of Von Richthofen's log fails to disclose that the Red Knight had anything to do with this particular fight. He did shoot down a Bristol Fighter on this particular day —two in fact—but neither belonged to Number 48 Squadron.

Nothing was heard of Captain Robinson until April 11 when it was reported that he had been killed, but he turned up later at a prisoner-of-war camp at Holzminden. At this infamous laager Robinson came under the jurisdiction of Hauptmann Karl Niemeyer, who, as part of his routine of torture, taunted him about his misfortune, and swore to make him suffer for having caused the death of Wilhelm Schramm, who had been a personal friend.

Captain William S. Stephenson, a twenty-one-plane ace of Number 73 Squadron, R.F.C., and a friend of the writer, tells of meeting Robinson at Holzminden in August 1918. Captain Stephenson had, himself, been shot down a few days previously. Although he had been wounded in a leg, Stephenson had no intention of being cooped up in a prison camp, and as he has since explained, he suggested to Robinson that he "accompany me to a more salubrious area." They made a break, and after several days of scurrying through the Black Forest—always with the idea that they might get back to "where we might find new mounts with which to take another pot at the devils"—they were captured. This was not the first time for Robinson and he was again tucked away in solitary, but Bill Stephenson tried once more, and this time, making the most of his previous experiences, managed to get back to his squadron, then located at Hénin-sur-Cojeul, southeast of Arras.

But luck was not with Robinson, and in the closing weeks of the war when Germany's fortune waned, he was transferred from camp to camp, each one more disciplined than the one before, and his health deteriorated until he was a pathetic invalid.

He was among some of the first prisoners-of-war to be returned to England after the Armistice, arriving there on December 31, 1918. He immediately contracted the dread influenza that had been sweeping across the British Isles earlier that year, and in his wretched physical condition could not withstand the ravages of the scourge. Captain Leefe Robinson died on January 17, 1919.

(Captain Stephenson has explained that there was a Hauptmann Niemeyer, the commandant of the reprisal prisoner-of-war camp at Holzminden, where past or prospective escapees were imprisoned. Niemeyer had lived in Milwaukee, Wisconsin, and had returned to Germany about 1912.

"I do not think he singled out Robinson, as far as I am aware," Stephenson writes. "But he was a sadist well selected for the job of multiplying any fancied wrong the British inflicted upon German prisoners of war. He was the first so-called human I ever saw who literally foamed at the mouth. Once, after discovery of a tunnel system under the very area on which we were standing, he screamed: 'Gentlemen, you think I know nothing, but I assure you I know damn all!' and then was obviously astonished to note that we were amused by this declaration.")

VIII

ZEPPELINS AT JUTLAND

At this point we must retrace our steps, for no history of the wartime Zeppelin would be complete without a fair appraisal of the dirigible and its contribution to Germany's naval operations that worked up to its peak during the Battle of Jutland. The spring of 1916 saw this contribution at its best, for it was during these months that the High Seas Fleet put on its most formidable effort. At this time, too, it will be recalled that German U-boats were attached to the Fleet because on March 6 the Kaiser had bowed to world opinion and had decided against the program of unrestricted warfare on merchant shipping.

Intelligence furnished by both the Zeppelins and the U-boat flotillas had warned Admiral Reinhard Scheer that it was quite possible the British were preparing an attack on the Tondern airship station. Then, co-operating with the Irish Rebellion of Easter Sunday, April 23, thousands of captured Russian rifles were shipped into Tralee Bay, southwest Ireland, by submarine. Sir Roger Casement, renegade British statesman who was involved in this venture was captured and eventually executed. But so important was this anti-British movement Admiral Scheer planned to bombard the town of Lowestoft in England to draw the attention of the Royal Navy from the activities across the Irish Sea.

Therefore, late in the morning of April 14, a bombardment force made up of a number of battle cruisers, sailed from Jade Bay and were followed by a number of dreadnoughts. Then *LZ.7* flew from Tondern to act as escort for the battle cruisers as they steamed out of the German Bight. On the way out the *Seydlitz,* flagship of the force, struck a mine, and for a time it was thought she had been torpedoed. But Kapitänleutnant Karl Hempel commanding *LZ.7* radioed that he had not seen a torpedo track, nor any trace of an enemy submarine. *Seydlitz* managed to stay afloat and *LZ.7* escorted her back to her mooring, and then went to her own dock at Hage. Lowestoft was eventually shelled by four battle cruisers for about six minutes, and then they turned their attention to Yarmouth where a few hit-and-run rounds were blasted off.

On the way back, this surface force was covered by *LZ.9* which was flying at only 2500 feet. There also were several B.E.2c biplanes out of Great Yarmouth in that area, and while their pilots pressed home their attacks with some vigor, their fire bombs all missed. Had they been provided with incendiary ammunition there might have been a different story.

From that time on Strasser pursued a continual program of raids, some fairly effective, some complete wastes of fuel and bombs, but no major strikes were registered. True, the weather was inclement, the British batteries and searchlights were being handled with greater skill and efficiency, and defense aircraft were becoming more tenacious, but it should have been obvious that the program was no longer worth the effort expended.

On May 2 Strasser sent eight of his airships to attack England-North, with particular attention to be paid to Rosyth, the Firth of Forth Bridge, and any concentration of vessels of the British Fleet. They left Tondern, Nordholz, and Hage and picked up a tail wind that enabled them to make fifty knots, but later as they climbed for a safe altitude, they encountered southern winds and were then warned of a low-pressure area forming over England. Because of this, six of the eight dirigibles went to alternate targets in the Midlands; only *LZ.14* and *LZ.20* attempted to carry out the original orders.

LZ.23, the first Zeppelin to cross the British coast, for some unexplained reason dropped an incendiary bomb on Danby High Moor that set fire to a wide patch of heather. Spotting what looked like a blazing target area, Peterson in *LZ.16* moved in and dumped most of his bomb cargo on the same spot. He then reported seeing the town of Stockton completely engulfed in flames. This came to the attention of another Zepp commander and he too made a run-in and bombed what he thought was a blazing city, while Peterson sat above and reported "well-placed hits on buildings and clearly recognizable railway embankments."

Heavy snow clouds moved in and many of the Zeppelins made the most of this heath fire and dumped everything they had into the glare. *LZ.17* apparently made a light attack on Skinningrove and then dropped the rest of her load on "a coastal city to the east," which may have been Saltburn.

Meanwhile *LZ.14* and *LZ.10* heading for Scotland had run into heavy weather of rain squalls mixed with snow that caused icing conditions and *LZ.14* was beaten down from 9000 to 6000 feet. Then for a time the weather cleared and Alois Böcker in *LZ.14* decided there were two enemy warships directly below, and dropped five large bombs, and reported that both vessels had gone to the bottom. A short time later, blanketed between snow clouds, he decided he was over Edinburgh, but oddly enough, did not drop any bombs, but headed for home. British authorities plotting the course of this Zeppelin reported that it had actually been over the Firth of Tay, not the Firth of Forth, and her bombs had dropped in an open field near Arbroath.

Franz Stabbert in command of *LZ.20* had planned to head for the Firth of Forth by way of Dundee, and appears to have dawdled about between 7:00 P.M. and 10:45 P.M. taking radio bearings and dropping water flares while hopefully seeking his target. By 11:20 he encountered icing conditions, and was forced to drop ballast and some fuel tanks as he groped blindly through dense fog. He tried to determine his position by radio but discovered that his iced-up antenna was so weakening his signals, none of his appeals reached Germany.

About 1:00 A.M. the sky cleared and Stabbert was shocked to find that a southeast wind had carried him as far as Loch Ness in the Scottish Highlands. There was nothing to do but turn for the east and hope he could cross the coast before first light. To justify his journey he dropped seventeen of his bombs on some lights that he took to be a mine complex; it actually was Craig Castle (Inverness) the roof of which was damaged and several windows blown in.

Staggering on, hoping to cross at the Firth of Forth, Stabbert was next plotted over Peterhead some one hundred miles to the north and by 6:00 A.M. he finally made radio contact with his field at Nordholz, and to his dismay realized he was dangerously close to the Orkney Islands. Making a further contact with the steamer *Holland*, he knew he could not possibly reach Germany with what fuel remained. Nordholz advised him to head for Denmark where they would try to provide aid by means of destroyers that might take the airship in tow. But the SSE wind increased to forty miles per hour, and knowing that Denmark was still ten hours away, he was then advised that they had only five hours of fuel in the tanks. And to add to their problems, the chief machinist reported that two of the engines threatened to stop at any minute.

Stabbert had no choice, and he set course for a point on the Norwegian coast south of Stavanger. His code books, documents, and other important papers were lead-loaded, and dropped into the sea. The radio console was tossed overboard, and finally, buffeted and tossed about by turbulence coming off the coastal mountains, *LZ.20* moved in slowly for a landing. With no ground crew to take her landing ropes, she was in dire peril. Attempting to get down on the beach was out of the question because of down drafts off the mountains, so Stabbert brought his ship in over a fjord. She landed hard, since she was more than two tons heavy, and the struts of the forward gondola were shattered, leaving the car dangling on a few wires.

A sea anchor was put over, but it failed to hold the dirigible into the wind and she started to drift toward a high cliff. With that, panic broke out, and eight men, including Stabbert and his executive officer, leaped overboard. This left the elevator man alone in the control car, and thus lightened the airship rose and drifted toward a spit of land. She scraped over the cliffs, tearing off the aft gondola, and Wilhelm Tinchon, the elevator man, and four other members of the crew were unceremoniously tossed out on Norwegian soil. With her back broken LZ.20 drifted away, a pathetic hulk with three men still at their posts in the gangway. These three slashed at the gas cells, and the complete wreck finally settled on the sea.

Meanwhile other airships of this raid were also floundering about in the hostile weather. They encountered thunderstorms, rain squalls, and hail which in turn decorated the ships with patterns of St. Elmo's fire. Ice, slithering from the upper covers, fell into whirling propellers and was batted back through the envelopes to slash the gas cells.

LZ.17 with a jammed radio antenna had long sparks of static electricity jetting at her gondolas and frame. With only two-thirds of her power available and burdened with a soaked envelope, LZ.23 started to nose down for the sea, but prompt action jettisoned water ballast, machine guns, ammunition, and fuel tanks and she just managed to climb back to safety. LZ.11 also lost a gas cell to flying ice and her crew had to trim the stern-heavy ship by shifting bombs and sending a number of men to the nose of the framework. LZ.14 and LZ.21 went through the same experience and were lucky to get back to their sheds. (To overcome this situation, heavy canvas ice shields were fitted later to the

outer covers above the propellers, but they were not completely satisfactory as they often were riddled by these
flying ice missiles.)

The Battle of Jutland, history's greatest naval engagement, was in the making. Each side had planned to trap
the other into a situation whereby they could fight it out in
an area and under conditions advantageous to itself. Both
adversaries sent out decoy or diversionary squadrons. Both
did what they could to scout out the general situation, but
fate was to play the most influential role.

On the morning of May 3 when Strasser's weary Zeppelins were struggling back to their bases, the British seaplane carriers *Engadine* and *Vindex,* escorted by a small
force of light cruisers and destroyers, set out to make the
long-expected attack on the airship sheds at Tondern. At
the same time it was hoped this minor thrust would entice
the German High Seas Fleet to steam out of Wilhelmshaven
and become trapped under the guns of the Grand Fleet.

The seaplane venture was a great disappointment. Eight
Sopwith "Baby" seaplanes failed to get airborne. One
smashed into the wireless antenna of a destroyer and
crashed. One that did get off had to turn back with engine
trouble. Another, succeeding in getting clear, flew to Tostlund, but failed to find Tondern because of the mist, and
dropped one bomb that unfortunately fell on Danish soil.
This R.N.A.S. pilot then returned to his mother ship.

The abortive raid aroused the German Fleet, however,
and by 8:50 A.M. on May 4 LZ.7 was sent out from Tondern
with orders to make a scouting foray toward Horns Reef.
LZ.9 also took off from Hage and her skipper Hauptmann
August Stelling cruised north from Terschelling toward
Horns Reef, but could not report anything of value. Kapitänleutnant Karl Hempel in *LZ.7* first reported when he
was sixteen miles off Sylt, and by 10.39, after taking a compass bearing, figured he was twenty miles SSW of Horns
Reef Lightship, but he made no further report and Strasser
thought he perhaps had radio failure, but when Hempel did

not return to Tondern by 2:00 P.M. he was reported as overdue.

A complete hunt, led by *LZ.14* that had been repaired after her recent experiences over Britain, was made and by 7:23 P.M. she reported no trace of *LZ.7*, and started home fifty minutes later. Within an hour *LZ.14* was in dire trouble herself and almost crashed into the sea when, after meeting a strong downdraft, her elevators jammed and her skipper had to jettison much water ballast forward and stop all engines to keep from nosing into the water. *LZ.14* did not get back to Tondern until 5:20 A.M. the next morning.

LZ.7, so it was learned a week later, was even more unfortunate. At 11:30 A.M. on the morning of May 4 Hempel had flown to within sight of two British light cruisers *Galatea* and *Phaeton* that were part of the force escorting the seaplane carriers. The British warships opened fire and put on flank speed to chase the dirigible for about half an hour. Hempel, surprisingly, spent most of his time drawing the British light cruisers in, but made no report of the contact or the position of the enemy ships. Believing they were wasting time, shot, and shell, the two light cruisers started to turn away, and at that moment saw the Zeppelin nose down and plunge in flames into the sea.

Neither *Galatea* nor *Phaeton* cared to risk going too close to the burning wreckage for fear of enemy submarines, but a British submarine *E.31* surfaced nearby and rescued seven survivors. It was then learned that one of the last shells fired had pierced a fuel tank and started a fire that had destroyed the big dirigible. Fate played her first trick when Hempel failed to make a contact report, and because of that the German High Seas Fleet did not sortie until late that evening, or long after the British flotilla had turned back for its base.

The weather continued to conspire against them and Strasser decided to keep all airships grounded and serviced for a surface-fleet operation against Sunderland. It was hoped this hit-and-run bombardment would draw small portions of the British Fleet into an area patrolled by a number of German U-boats, but again the weather refused to co-operate and the original scheme had to be abandoned.

Some historians have explained that the inability of the Naval Airship Division to cover the High Seas Fleet in the western part of the North Sea, may have determined in a negative way the place as well as the time of the Battle of Jutland, but how valid this belief may be is difficult to state. What we do know is that the British Admiralty knew something was under way, and before midnight of May 30, 1916, the British Grand Fleet and the Battle Cruiser Fleet were at their predetermined positions, whereas Admiral Scheer did not sail until the early morning of May 31.

Much has been written, pro and con, concerning the value of the German Naval Airship Service's contribution to the Battle of Jutland, but the fact remains that because of the weather the airship captains were unable to furnish rational reports, and their contrary messages set up considerable bewilderment. Many bold efforts were turned in but none of these provided Admiral Scheer with any information of tactical value. Several British historians have claimed that it was the scouting of the Zeppelins that saved the German High Seas Fleet from total destruction, but these claims have been discounted time and again.

The airships did not distinguish themselves. They saw nothing of the battle itself, and the good effort turned in by Korvettenkapitän Viktor Schütze, aboard *LZ.11*, was canceled out by the shocking errors of Kapitänleutnant Robert Koch in *LZ.24*. The British, too, were deprived of any valuable aerial reconnaissance since their *Campania*, mounting a flying deck for launching two-seater seaplanes, aircraft-carrier style, using a wheeled trolley under the floats, was by an amazing quirk of fate not advised when the British Fleet sailed from Scapa Flow. Thus, the one vessel capable of launching a two-seater with a pilot and a trained wireless observer, was denied her role in the historic action. What important part she might have played has long been a topic of conversation when Naval intelligence men meet in their wardrooms.

Thus, the Battle of Jutland was fought in the old-fashioned manner of the days before directional wireless or radar.

Five Zeppelins were detailed to take off during the early morning hours of May 31 to carry out a strategic reconnaissance in advance of Scheer's fleet which was steaming up the Jutland coast. The airships were to swing out in an irregular semicircle from the southern tip of Norway to a point halfway between the West Frisian island of Texel, and Cromer on the Norfolk coast. As if in opposition to Strasser's plans, the weather turned unpredictable, holding the dirigibles in their hangars until early afternoon, and keeping them from their scouting sectors at a time when they might have contributed much to Admiral Scheer's intelligence. It was 3:30 P.M. when the German battle cruisers first made contact with the British off the Danish coast. All through that afternoon both sides pounded each other. *Indefatigable* and *Queen Mary* went down, and there was a short period when the battle fleets of both sides exchanged rounds during the oncoming dusk, a time when Scheer might have been cut off from his base and forced into a vital action by the next morning. But the British were fighting blind, and the German Admiral forced his way through the British destroyer flotillas and found himself with a clear course back to Wilhelmshaven.

The airships sent out to act as scouts saw nothing of this action. *LZ.14* and *LZ.23* which presumably were somewhere in the area ran into poor visibility. Kapitänleutnant Otto von Schubert commanding *LZ.23* did receive radio reports of the action somewhere around 5:00 P.M., but he was unable to find any evidence of the battle. *LZ.14* was also nearby, and these two remained over the Dogger Bank hoping to make contact with *LZ.9*. It was learned later that *LZ.9* had turned back about 4:30 when her starboard propeller had sheared off. *LZ.16* had remained practically stationary off the Dutch coast.

As the evening progressed, and Admiral Scheer realized the seriousness of his position, he sent a message to Strasser asking for an early reconnaissance off Horns Reef. The radio appeal was never received in Germany, but was intercepted by British Naval Intelligence, which, amazingly, did nothing about it. After all, this was a very dangerous message to send, and had it been carefully analyzed, Admirals Beatty or Jellicoe would have known Admiral Scheer's intentions, and might have taken immediate action in that area. This was another example of how important matters can go wrong at critical periods during a vital engagement.

During the night of May 31–June 1 the first quintet of Zeppelins returned to their sheds and five more were standing by with orders to proceed to the same stations and continue the reconnaissance patrols. The weather improved somewhat and visibility was considerably better, and two of the airships heading out on the northward sector actually saw some of the confused fighting taking place below. At 1:06 A.M., Koch aboard *LZ.24*, noted some gunfire while flying just under the overcast in the Horns Reef Lightship area, but when he steered in that direction the gun flashes died away.

Kapitänleutnant Martin Dietrich in *LZ.22* also saw some of this action as he was in the vicinity at 3:10 A.M. when the battleship *Pommern* was hit by a British torpedo and went down, following a tremendous explosion. Koch in *LZ.24* continued north and made a number of contacts with the enemy some fifty miles west of Bovbjerg, but his reports were so hurried, unclear, and at times garbled that Admiral Scheer finally came to the conclusion that Admiral Jellicoe had divided the British battle fleet, and that one half had been seen by Koch in Jammer Bay, when in fact there was no such situation. In later weeks it was concluded that Koch had spotted a convoy of merchant ships. By good fortune Scheer put more reliance on reports from Korvettenkapitän Viktor Schütze aboard *LZ.11*. This Zepp commander had made contact with the British Grand Fleet shortly before dawn and it was he who carried out the only reliable reconnaissance during the battle. He accurately identified various vessels and gamely kept in touch during the development of the final situation.

At the same time, the appearance of *LZ.11*, for she was clearly seen, caused some consternation in the Grand Fleet. Beatty, with six battle cruisers, had hoped to find Scheer by dawn, not knowing that the German admiral had already escaped into the swept channel at Horns Reef. Thus, when *LZ.11* appeared in the sky HMS *Indomitable* made every effort to blast her out of action, by firing 12-inch armor-piercing shells. This was taken up by the British 3rd Light Cruiser Squadron, all trying to down this snooping dirigible. The gunfire, heard well to the east by the battle fleet, aroused some hope that Beatty finally had caught the enemy, and as a result they, too, turned in that direction. Schütze, of course, had no idea how well he was doing, but his reports must have enabled Scheer to continue on with some sense of security until he was clear of all Royal Navy opposition.

Still uncertain of the fleet supposed to be in Jammer Bay, Scheer presumed that the warships being reported by Schütze might possibly be reinforcements from the English Channel, for the commander of *LZ.11* had reported no signs of battle damage on any, and declared that they seemed to be maneuvering at high speed, which indicated that they had taken no part in the previous day's engagement. Then by 5:07 A.M., convinced that all was well, Scheer signaled all of his ships to "run in by squadrons," having decided not to bring to action the British forces reported by Schütze, "since an action in the present circumstances and with insufficient air reconnaissance promised no success." By 7:30 A.M. he had radioed Strasser: "Airship reconnaissance no longer necessary."

Another plan to use Zeppelins in a master design to trap the British Fleet into a U-boat ambush was put into play in the middle of August. Scheer planned a bombardment of Sunderland on the English coast which it was hoped would draw the Grand Fleet within torpedo range of nine U-boats spread in two lines off Northumberland and Yorkshire. Again, as in the Jutland planning, a number of Zeppelins were first to search for the British fleet and furnish airship reconnaissance.

The initial part of the plan was put into action on August 18 when Zeppelins were sent out on weather-reporting missions, and as a result of these forays the High Seas Fleet put to sea at 9:00 P.M. that evening. Early the next morning, no less than eight airships took off, led by LZ.32 with Strasser aboard. These aircraft were carefully assigned to special segments of the North Sea, some to watch the Firth of Forth, some to keep an eye on Scapa Flow, some to cover the Tyne and Humber, and one or two to warn of any British naval forces that might come up from the English Channel.

There was nothing much to report from the Scapa Flow area or from the northern area of the Scottish coast. The British had guessed from monitoring German Navy radio signals that the High Seas Fleet was preparing to sail by August 18, and with that Jellicoe had moved out of Scapa Flow with the Grand Fleet during the afternoon of the 18th, and in doing so had passed the northern patrol boundary long before the Zeppelins were in their assigned positions. Then at 9:30 in the evening of August 18, Beatty with his battle cruisers had moved out of Rosyth to rendezvous with Jellicoe, and by 11:30 that night the Harwich Force of light cruisers and destroyers also sailed to take up its post.

By daybreak of August 19 Jellicoe and Beatty met some one hundred miles ENE of the Firth of Forth, and together moved south. The Harwich Force coming up from the south was finally spotted by Kapitänleutnant Eduard Prölss aboard LZ.13. Although hampered by heavy cloud conditions, he eventually picked up the Tyrwhitt squadron while flying at 1000 feet. Heavy antiaircraft fire forced him into the clouds but he did warn Scheer that two enemy destroyer flotillas with a cruiser squadron following, was about seventy miles off Lowestoft. At the time Tyrwhitt was temporarily steering southwest, and with Prölss' information Scheer decided that they were in no way related to the Grand Fleet; that they were heading for the Channel, and that so far the British had no idea what was going on. Later Prölss spotted the Harwich Force on an ESE course and assumed they were simply on patrol along the Belgian and Dutch coasts, and Scheer agreed.

In the meantime four airships on the northern segment were still proceeding toward their patrol line, and Admiral Hipper, in *Moltke*, at 9:00 A.M. ordered *LZ.11* to cover ahead of the Number 2 Scouting Group. This revealed that visibility was worsening off the English coast, and the clouds were down to 650 feet. *LZ.31* reported several thunderstorms, but *LZ.21*, well to the south, found good visibility through scattered clouds.

Admiral Scheer enjoyed his first break when submarine *U-52* torpedoed *Nottingham*, a light cruiser of the battle screen. Then at 8:00 A.M. Jellicoe, wary of this submarine menace, reversed his course and turned north, and thirty minutes later the British battle cruisers turned to join him. This move was spotted and reported by another submarine, *U-53*, when she was able to report in some detail the strength of the force now eighty miles east of Farne Island. This report, decoded by 10:40 A.M., was the first Scheer knew of the disposition of the British Fleet.

Now the Zeppelins moved into the picture again. Mathy, commanding *LZ.31*, was moving toward *U-53*'s position, and despite the low-cloud ceiling and rain squalls, he risked being spotted and shot down before his lookouts could even find the surface vessels. In fact, he came upon the light cruiser screen of the battle cruiser fleet where antiaircraft fire forced him into the clouds. Dropping down again he found two light cruisers and two destroyers, but these were soon lost in the rain. Farther to the north he encountered what he took to be the main body of the British Fleet, but he was deceived by Beatty's temporary change of course, and could not believe that it was actually still inside the airship patrol line. Scheer, too, decided that this was an isolated group, and ideal proof that the British did not suspect they were at sea.

Mathy put on a good show, but by noon he became involved with a fleet of fishing smacks and decided that the British warships had again turned south, which they had. During all this Admirals Jellicoe and Beatty sensed they were being shadowed and watched, as well they might, which may account for the fact that they continued to steam north for a period of two hours, and then turned south again. Had Jellicoe kept to his northerly course he would have intercepted the German Fleet by 1:00 P.M. Again, a mischievous fate had played a trick on the British naval commanders.

But Scheer was also moving blindly, for in spite of the spread of airships he had no idea he had missed a major engagement with the Grand Fleet, so he decided to continue his plan for the shelling of Sunderland.

Shortly after midday, LZ.13 once more picked up the Harwich Force which Prölss reported as a large group of enemy warships "sighted to the south." Tyrwhitt's gunners opened fire on LZ.13 and she had to climb to 6500 feet and take cover in clouds. From there Prölss did his best to compile a comprehensive report on the actual strength of the enemy, but his best was far from good. As a result, Admiral Scheer who was still ignorant of the fact that the Grand Fleet was just over the northern horizon, then asked Prölss for a more detailed account of the class of ships he was following. The airship commander was not equal to the task, but did state that by 1:00 P.M. this enemy force was now on a northwest course.

This alerted Scheer to reconsider his position, and he decided to give up the idea of bombarding Sunderland, or hoping to engage Tyrwhitt's Harwich Force which had steamed too far east. Later, the German admiral explained that he had been running on a southeast course, "hoping

to meet the British heavy units," but because of the inde-
cisive reports from the airships, he eventually concluded
that the Sunderland attack was out of the question, but at
the same time this southeasterly foray had drawn him from
the overwhelming might of Britain's Grand Fleet.

Here again was another North Sea fiasco. Prölss, the one
airship commander in a situation to direct Scheer to a position where he might have caused serious damage to the
Harwich Force, was incapable of preparing a reliable interpretation of the situation. He was not an experienced line
officer, but a reserve man who in civil life had been a fire
chief in the city of Magdeburg. By the same token, neither
Hipper nor Scheer had been able to form a sound appraisal
of the reports turned in by Mathy, Prölss, or the U-boats.
Even when Scheer received a message at 3:30 P.M. from
U-53 which was patrolling eighty miles off Sunderland,
stating that the main column of the British Grand Fleet
was steering south, when LZ.11 sighted four light cruisers,
when U-53 reported a force of ten battleships, he still either
failed or refused to believe that this was the Grand Fleet.
Instead, he feared his destroyers were running short of fuel,
and he continued on for home.

During the Grand Fleet's voyage back to its base, U-66
torpedoed the light cruiser Falmouth, and other U-boats
made similar attacks, but without success.

This, then, was the first—and the last—occasion in which
German naval airships carried out a strategic reconnaissance plan in co-operation with a major fleet operation.
The Zeppelins failed because there was no sound doctrine,
crews were not properly trained, and the officers lacked important experience. But we now know that those thirteen
dirigibles assigned to the patrol hardly could have furnished
continuous searches over the several days necessary to keep
Admiral Scheer informed of the British Fleet's position,
movements, or general battle condition.

IX

MATHY'S GALLANT END

Though the Zeppelins had failed to lead the German High Seas Fleet to a major victory, Strasser still clung to his illusions with fatalistic optimism, and continued to order his airship crews to attack Britain again and again. He sacrificed his finest and most gallant men and wasted the products of Friedrichshafen that became piles of blackened junk all over England and the North Sea.

His advocates have argued that there were reasons for this desperate stand. The High Seas Fleet had failed to break the British blockade; the U-boat, at that time, was still under restraint; along the Western Front the Germans were being held in a bloody death lock before Verdun; and since July 1, "Kitchener's Mob" had been tearing the German Army to shreds, despite its own dreadful losses. Austria was proving a worthless ally, and Romania a costly helpmate. In the face of this history Strasser can perhaps be forgiven if he believed there still was a chance that victory might be snatched from the debacle by his Zeppelin crews. He sent an appeal to Admiral Scheer, explaining his conviction that England (it always was England, never the British Isles, or the British Empire) could be overcome by airships. He believed they were capable of extensive destruction of cities, factory layouts, dockyards, harbors where war and merchant ships were lying; to say nothing of railroads. He concluded that at least twenty-two super Zeppelins were necessary to carry out this war against England.

While giving Strasser some grudging support, Scheer wondered where the airships and the crews to man them were to come from. "We shall have to wait and see," he explained.

Toward the end of July 1916 three Zeppelin raids were carried out on targets spread from Dover to Berwick in Sussex. Ground mists protected Britain, and the bombs were scattered far and wide. One boy was injured, but little property damage was inflicted. Heinrich Mathy claimed to have made two attacks on London, but British trackers proved he had flown along the Kentish coast, and when he came under fire from guns mounted at Dover, Deal, and Ramsgate, he turned tail and dropped his bombs into the sea. He explained later on that he must have been driven off course by winds above the fog level which could not be estimated. There of course was some point to his statement.

Following this, or about August 2, a new feature of defense was established when the Admiralty sent out a small seaplane carrier, *Vindex*, which bore two Bristol Scout seaplanes set up on a short flight deck. These aircraft were fine single-seater biplanes powered with 80-horsepower Gnome rotary engines, and could be considered the forerunners of the Sopwith Pup and Camel, though they were conceived in the Bristol factory. On this night in particular these aircraft, launched off *Vindex*, intercepted four Zeppelins off Lowestoft and made an attack on *LZ.17*, but could not put their bombs where they would do the most good. While the Bristol Scout pilots were unsuccessful, they were omens of what was to come.

Strasser, groaning with frustration, next queried Scheer with the idea of a major effort to be carried out in the dark period between August 20 and September 8. Obviously Scheer agreed for he permitted the transfer of *SL.8* and *SL.9*, two Schütte-Lanz airships, from the Baltic to the

17. The armament console of a Zeppelin. The bombsight is seen on the left and the releases for each bomb are shown on the tilted panel. This equipment was mounted in the control car. Note chains to rudder at the right of the picture.—LUFTSCHIFFBAU ZEPPELIN PHOTO.

18. The elevator man's position on port side of the control car. Here are shown the toggles for the gas valves, gas temperature gauge, variometer (left) and recording barograph, (right). The elevator control wheel with inclinometer and altimeter are seen at the left. — LUFTSCHIFFBAU ZEPPELIN PHOTO.

19. Some details of the Zeppelin armament. Here is shown the top forward gun platform aboard *LZ.22*. The two Maxim guns were usually wrapped in quilting to keep the water jackets from freezing. Here too, are shown two "attached type" parachutes which were provided for only a short time.—FRIEDRICH MOCH PHOTO.

20. The port after engine gondola aboard *LZ.70* which was being built at Friedrichshafen in the early summer of 1918. This shows the exhaust side of the 6-cylinder, 245 hp Maybach MB.IVa "altitude engine" and its propeller. The over-all length of the gondola was about 12½ feet.
—LUFTSCHIFFBAU ZEPPELIN PHOTO.

21. Here is a display of the bombs carried by the Zeppelins. They weighed 660 lbs., 220 lbs., 110 lbs., and 22 lbs. The incendiary bombs are at the extreme right and left of the truck. The parachute flare is seen in front of the big 660-pounder. The seamen are holding the fuses used in the explosive bombs.—FRIEDRICH MOCH PHOTO.

22. Peter Strasser with some of his commanders in front of the Officer's Club at Ahlhorn in August of 1917. Strasser had just been awarded the *Ordre Pour le Merite*. From left to right are Manger (*LZ.41*), Freudenrich (*LZ.47*), Schwonder (*LZ.50*), Prolss (*LZ.53*), Bockholt (*LZ.54*), Strasser, Gayer (*LZ.49*), Stabbert (*LZ.44*), Ehrlich (*LZ.35*), Martin Dietrich (*LZ.42*), Hollender (*LZ.46*), Dose (*LZ.51*), and Friemel, (*LZ.52*).
—FRIEDRICH MOCH PHOTO.

23. *LZ.41* and *LZ.44* arriving back to land at Ahlhorn after making an attack on England. Later *LZ.44* (lower ship) was destroyed during the "silent" raid over Britain October 19, 1917. *LZ.41* was sabotaged by her crew after the Armistice was signed.—LUFTSCHIFFBAU ZEPPELIN PHOTO.

24. All that remained after the mysterious Ahlhorn base explosion, of January 5, 1918. Five airships were destroyed, fourteen men were killed and 134 seriously injured. To this day no one knows what caused the fire and resultant explosions.—FRIEDRICH MOCH PHOTO.

North Sea force, bringing Strasser's fleet up to fourteen dirigibles.

On the night of August 24, Strasser, aboard *LZ.32*, led a fleet of thirteen airships on a raid against the south of England. Three light cruisers and a number of destroyers of the Harwich Force were sent to sea as the British had intercepted a radio warning sent out by a German station. For some reason the little seaplane carrier, *Vindex*, was not included in this surface move. Six Zeppelins claimed to have been fired on, and in fact a number of British naval vessels reported firing on the raiders, but only *LZ.13* seems to have been hit; a shell went through her Number 8 cell amidships but exploded well above the airship's upper panel. A few splinters did some minor damage to Number 9 cell, and her skipper, Kapitänleutnant Prölss, immediately dropped all his bombs and ran back to Hage. He arrived at his dock and made a safe landing.

A strong south wind hampered the raiders, and it was soon apparent most of them would be unable to attack any land targets before the 2:00 A.M. moonrise. Five of them dropped their bombs on what they claimed were outpost craft. *LZ.23*, heavy with rain, had to jettison all of her bombs and 1300 pounds of fuel, but even with this measure she landed hard and was out of action for more than three days. The rest of the formation had little better luck. Oberleutnant Kurt Frankenberg in command of *LZ.21* thought he had bombed Harwich, but his explosives fell five miles away, and he was lucky to get back, after taking a short cut across Holland. He just scraped in to a bad landing and his ship was under repair for the next six days.

Mathy in *LZ.31* and Peterson in *LZ.32* took a very roundabout course but Peterson wound up over or near Folkestone at 2:00 A.M. after mechanical and structural trouble. It was too late to chance a raid on London, so Peterson dropped his bombs on what he thought were numerous ships and naval vessels lying off Dover. He was greeted with heavy antiaircraft fire that probably accounted for the fact that his bombs fell well out to sea. With all this illumination and gunfire, an aeroplane taking off from Dover got within machine-gun range and sprayed LZ.32 with one drum of ammunition, but nothing resulted and the airship disappeared into a cloud. Peterson came down later and found himself over the island of Vlieland where Dutch gunners made life uneasy for a time, but, undamaged, LZ.32 eventually reached Nordholz safely.

Mathy took a wild chance and followed the snakelike Thames all the way to London where, since they had not been alerted in almost a year, the gunners were caught flatfooted. Mathy even evaded the searchlights, which, in turn, were canceled out by clouds and mist. By 1:30 A.M. Mathy opened up on the southeastern districts, although his report stated he had struck blocks of houses in southwestern and western parts of the city. Searchlights finally found him at 1:35 A.M., and 120 rounds of antiaircraft-gun ammunition were fired at LZ.31, so she took to a convenient cloud bank.

But it must be said that Mathy scored heavily. £130,000 damage was acknowledged which included a power station at Deptford. Nine civilians were killed and forty wounded. On the way home Mathy's ship picked up a lot of weight after running through a heavy rainstorm, and as there was no emergency ballast to jettison, LZ.31 landed hard, tore off the aft gondola, and was not airworthy until September 21.

Strong easterly winds throughout the rest of August hindered any further raids, but by September 2 Strasser staged his greatest attack. This is the raid on which Lieutenant W. Leefe Robinson shot down the Army airship SL.11. It is not clear why Strasser took this chance for the weather was far from favorable. At operating altitude the wind was strong, and as the ships neared the British coast they encountered rain and snow, and several of them iced up seriously. LZ.17 and an Army Zeppelin, L.97, turned back early.

Of the remaining Army airships, L.98 under Ernst Lehmann was the first to approach London. Once he reached

Gravesend, he came under heavy fire, and believing he was over the London docks, dumped all his bombs, rose to 13,800 feet and headed for the northeast and home, at which point Lieutenant Robinson, mentioned earlier, spotted Lehmann's ship. It scrambled into cloud cover before the young Englishman could attack.

A short time later Robinson came upon SL.11, the wooden-framed Schütte-Lanz Army airship and shot it down, details of which have been related in Chapter VII. As the flaming dirigible fell, a gigantic torch illuminating the countryside, the airships of the Naval Airship Service were feeling their way across Cambridgeshire, Norfolk, and Suffolk, and it must be assumed that the crews witnessed this tragedy, and probably sensed the blinding finality that eventually would consume them all.

The German Army Airship Service canceled all future raids over England, and, in fact, the service was disbanded within twelve months. Not so the Navy, or Strasser. They refused to admit defeat, and insult was added to injury when on the afternoon of September 16 two more Zeppelins, LZ.6 and LZ.9, both valuable training ships, were destroyed in an inflation mishap. LZ.6 went up first, and LZ.9, in the same hangar, soon caught fire, a conflagration that lasted more than two hours. Strasser thought later that rust particles in the high-pressure hydrogen storage flasks had been carried through the filling lines and set up a static electrical charge that triggered the fire. But this imaginative point was never proved.

Ignoring, or defying, the great improvement in Britain's defense measures, Strasser drew up plans for still another raid on the south of England and London. The date: September 23, 1916. Four of the latest Zeppelins, led by Mathy, and eight of the older types were selected for this memorable foray. It was hoped there would be a suitable cloud cover and a friendly wind for a change. At the last minute Mathy decided that the four new ships would make their trip via Belgium so as to keep to windward of the British metropolis. The older airships picked up a fresh southeast wind with no cloud cover, so decided to give their attention to the British Midlands.

Of this standard group, *LZ.17* with Kapitänleutnant Hermann Kraushaar made the deepest penetration and set a course for Sheffield. At 12:45 A.M. his lookout spotted a complex of glaring chimneys that he took to be blast furnaces. Kraushaar nosed into a strong southwest wind and dropped his bombs. He did not know it, but he had poured his hurried wrath on Nottingham, and as he turned away, about 1:10 A.M., he and his crew were shocked to see an airship falling in flames, a flaring nose-dive that ended only when the tangle was swallowed in a low ground mist.

The other airships of this group failed to get very far inland, and *LZ.21* was unable to get any higher than 8000 feet, and hesitating and uncertain, her skipper finally dropped all his bombs near a few Sussex villages. *LZ.22* had trouble picking up radio bearings and her commander, Martin Dietrich, believed he was in the vicinity of The Wash or Flamborough Head, and decided to make an attack on Grimsby. In fact some of his bombs did fall on the southeast section of the old fishing town. Kapitänleutnant Wilhelm Ganzel who was prowling in the vicinity of Lincoln aboard *LZ.23* reported a bright glow of fire toward the mouth of the Thames, and finally realized it was an airship falling in flames.

Of the four new super Zeppelins, airships of 1,949,600 cubic feet, 649 feet long, powered by six HSLu engines, and capable of more than sixty-two miles per hour, *LZ.30* under command of Buttlar, claimed to be the first to reach London. In fact, he reported flying up the south bank of the Thames as early as 10:35 P.M., but because of the clear visibility decided not to go too far inland, and started to release his bombs over what he believed was Gravesend. Strangely enough, British trackers could find no trace of any bombs near London or in southern England at that particular time. It is quite possible *LZ.30*'s bombs were dropped in the sea somewhere off the Norfolk coast. *LZ.14* was also in this area and was fired on by outpost vessels and coastal batteries.

Böcker, commanding LZ.33 that had been in commission only three weeks, was actually the first to reach London. Leaving the Belgian coast he first picked up the North Foreland and then steered up the Thames Estuary where destroyers opened fire at about 10:12, but Böcker held to his course and the speed of the LZ.33 caught the defenders by surprise, as they did not see her again until her German commander dropped a parachute flare over South Brentwood. Twenty minutes later he was over South Chadwell Heath where he dropped a second flare. This blinded the searchlight crews, so Böcker had no trouble in lining up with the Tower Bridge and making his bombing run across the city. He left forty-two high explosives and twenty incendiaries in his wake. Several warehouses were hit, enormous fires engulfed groups of houses; an oil depot went up as did a large lumber yard. Böcker's bombs, not all of which were finally traced, did a wicked job. Ten people were killed, twelve seriously injured, and much material damage inflicted.

Once he was rid of his bombs, Böcker forced his ship up to 13,000 feet, but by now the searchlights and batteries were alert. A direct hit was made over Bromley, the shell actually exploding inside Cell 14 near the forward engine gondola, but there was no general flare-up. Instead, the explosion severed the axial cable, fractured the main ring, and four adjacent gas cells were rent by splinters. Shell fragments spattered all through the ship, and many of the after cells were punctured.

Böcker turned and made for the sea, knowing his ship was fast losing hydrogen. Over Kelvedon another searchlight picked him out, and he dropped a tank of water ballast that from below appeared to be a smoke screen, but the Zeppelin continued to fall at about 800 feet per minute, while members of the crew worked frantically to repair the damaged cells. Then over Chelmsford a British aeroplane roared out of the glare and fired several rounds of machine-gun bullets, a few of which punctured *LZ.33*'s fuel tanks, but again luck was with them for another spell.

In this instance the pilot was Lieutenant Brandon who six months before had attacked *LZ.15*. In his official report on this occasion he stated:

> At 12.12 I saw a Zeppelin in the searchlights some distance away and made for it. Very shortly after this it escaped from the searchlights and I lost it, but I continued on and picked it up again. I went on climbing and managed with some difficulty to keep it in view, as there were no searchlights on it and my automatic pump had failed and I had to work the cocking handle of the Lewis gun. After putting on a drum of ammunition I came up behind the Zeppelin and on raising the gun I jerked it out of the mounting, the gun and the yoke falling across the nacelle. I managed to replace the gun but in the meantime I had passed under and past the Zeppelin. I turned and passed along it again from the bow, but we passed each other too quickly for me to take aim. On turning again I came up from behind and fixed a drum of ammunition. The Brock ammunition seemed to be bursting all along it but the Zepp did not catch fire. I was using Brock, Pomeroy and Sparklet (a form of tracer bullet). I turned again and put on a fresh drum and came up from behind and fired again. The gun jammed after about nine rounds. I now decided to get above the Zepp and went on climbing but there was a large bank of grey cloud all around the horizon and it was impossible to see the Zeppelin against it, after I got level with the Zeppelin. I first saw the Zeppelin at 12:13 and lost it at 12:33.

Poor Böcker, feeling harassed from all sides, put on a game show, determined to ditch his airship in the sea and sink her with all her new structural features and improvements. But his luck had run out, and *LZ.33* fell in the marshes behind Mersea Island (Little Wigborough), wrecking herself only sixty feet from a laborer's cottage. Böcker and his crew climbed out and fired signal flares into the hulk until other cells went up and destroyed everything. Then they skulked away, hoping to find a boat nearby with which to set out across the North Sea.

They were soon captured and taken to London for questioning. When interrogated by the aforementioned Major Trench, Böcker refused to supply any vital information, so with that Trench produced plans of the latest Zeppelins, a list of their secret radio call letters, and then explained that he had spent a day in Friedrichshafen gathering such material.

Two other super Zepps, *LZ.31* and *LZ.32*, under Mathy and Peterson, had stayed together all the way down the English Channel and had made their landfall at Dungeness. But instead of moving inland Peterson circled offshore for more than an hour, and it has since been assumed he was having engine trouble. Mathy, however, pressed straight on to London, carrying about five tons of bombs, but under the atmospheric conditions he could not reach a safe altitude for an attack on the city, and to lighten his craft he dropped ten 128-pound bombs somewhere near the Dungeness Lighthouse, causing no damage. By 11:30 he had crossed Tunbridge Wells and then identified the London-Eastbourne railroad tracks. Following these, and checking his position by means of parachute flares, he came over Croydon at 12:10 A.M. By this time his *LZ.31* had scrambled up to 12,500 feet.

From this point on Mathy began to drop high explosive through Streatham and Brixton, blasting small homes and shop fronts. One bomb fell on a tramcar and gutted it. Thirteen people were killed and thirty-three badly injured.

Enjoying the action, Mathy next crossed the heart of London from south to north and dropped ten more bombs along Lea Bridge Road and on Leyton, but somehow missed the center of the city completely. He claimed later that he had dropped ten 128-pound and two 660-pound bombs in the center of London, but he may have been bewildered by his own parachute flares, the British search-lights, and the glare of gunfire.

In his war log, Mathy hastily scribbled:

At 1:10 A.M., the attack of a ship (airship) on the Wool-wich area was observed. The ship was also very heavily fired on and after dropping her bombs, appeared to have reached safety when additional searchlights opened up ahead of her and, after a brief, very intense bombardment, her destruction followed. The ship fell in flames at 1:15 A.M.

The second victim of this tragic evening was Werner Peterson in *LZ.32*. After starting his move toward the capital he next drifted off considerably to the east. At 12:50 he was dropping bombs toward the Crockenhill searchlight southeast of London, and by 1:00 A.M. when he finally reached the Thames he was still twelve miles east of the city.

At a point somewhere north of the river, Peterson came out into clear air where the searchlights immediately picked him out. Ground guns opened up, and although *LZ.32* must have been at 13,000 feet a gun at Tunnel Farm may have scored two hits. With that, Peterson dumped the rest of his bomb load and turned to head for home.

At that point, unfortunately, Lieutenant Frederick Sow-rey, another pilot of Number 39 Squadron and a bosom pal of Leefe Robinson, moved into the picture.

Sowrey, aged twenty-three, was born in Gloucester, the son of a Deputy Chief Inspector of Taxes at Somerset House. He had been educated at King's College School and King's College of London University where he studied for the Indian Civil Service. At the outbreak of war Sowrey gained a commission in the Royal Fusiliers, was wounded at the Battle of Loos, January 1916, and soon made a transfer to the Royal Flying Corps where two of his brothers had already gained their brevets.

In his official report Sowrey explained that at 12:45 he had noticed an enemy airship in an easterly direction. "I at once made in this direction and maneuvered into a position underneath. The airship was well lighted by searchlights but there was not a sign of any gunfire. I could distinctly see the propellers revolving and the airship was maneuvering to avoid the searchlight beams. I fired at it. The first two drums of ammunition had apparently no effect, but the third one caused the envelope to catch on fire in several places; in the center and the front. All firing was traversing fire along the envelope. The drums were loaded with a mixture of Brock, Pomeroy and tracer ammunition. I watched the burning airship strike the ground and then proceeded to find my flares. I landed at Sutton's Farm at 1:40 A.M., 24th instant. My machine was B.E.2c 4112. After seeing the Zeppelin had caught fire, I fired a red Very light."

LZ.32 fell at Snail's Farm near Billericay, and lay burning on the ground for more than forty-five minutes. All crew members were killed, but officers of the Naval Intelligence Division searched the wreckage and found a scorched but legible copy of the latest signal book of the German Navy, something they had searched for in vain since the Battle of Jutland.

On landing back at his field, Sowrey was frozen so stiff with the cold he could scarcely speak, and for a time acted as though he had no idea what had happened, but Robinson concocted a warm drink that soon revived him, and then took him in his new motorcar to look at the smoldering wreckage of LZ.32.

The loss of LZ.32 and LZ.33 shocked even Strasser. He had dismissed the loss of the Army Schütte-Lanz SL.11, but this raid on September 23 obviously was the turning point in this lighter-than-air war against Britain. The deaths of Peterson and Böcker put an end to Strasser's great dream of aerial conquest, for he knew he would never again be able to inspire airship crews to fly against England with any sense of confidence, and equally important, he must have known that his Zeppelin giants would never again strike fear into the hearts of Englishmen.

Since air fighting at night had become another feature of the defense of London, the British pilots were not only plagued with aeroplanes that could not compete with the performances of Zeppelins, but with inefficient engines and missiles that were comic-opera productions. It was next realized that when a dirigible raider could be intercepted, the gunsights available did not fill the bill. It may appear ludicrous to argue that hitting a 600-foot-long Zeppelin with a spraying machine gun could present difficulties, but the fact remains that such was the case. It was not just a matter of hosing a great cigar-shaped form inflated with flammable gas, for, as we have seen, dozens of drums of ammunition had been poured into the raiders with no apparent result. Robinson, Sowrey, and Brandon had been all through this, and on calm reflection realized that accurate fire directed at engine nacelles, which in turn might torch the gasoline tanks, was much to be preferred.

What was needed was a precision gunsight that could be used at night, and one of the first sound steps in this direction was made by Sergeant A. E. Hutton of Number 39 Squadron. Hutton used the original bead foresight and the vee backsight, and for illumination, he bored out the base of the foresight and inserted therein a small red electric bulb that sent its glow through a small hole bored in the bead. Next, he illuminated the vee backsight which was pierced with three pinpoint holes, one in the extremity of each arm of the vee and one in the base. The power for light was provided by a 2-volt flashlight battery.

This device worked well on the B.E.2c, but later during the period of the Gotha raids when it was applied to single-seater Sopwith Pups and Camels, the muzzle glare from the Vickers guns completely blotted out the comparatively faint glow of the gunsight. To overcome this an illuminated ring sight was devised in which the outer ring was of such a circumference that when placed at a normal distance from the pilot's eye it would exactly span a Gotha at one hundred yards. It will be seen that the British were establishing the first basic principle of the computing gunsights used in World War II. Here, too, illumination was provided by small battery-powered electric bulbs, and to assist in its effectiveness, flash eliminators were fitted over the muzzle cups.

Still, another attack was scheduled, and on September 25 nine Zeppelins were assigned to a raid directed at the English Midlands, and their industrial areas, but on this occasion "caution" was ordered in case of clear weather.

The older aircraft took the North Sea crossing while *LZ.30* and *LZ.31* made for Britain via the Rhineland and Belgium. Three of the Midland raiders soon turned back, and Ganzel in *LZ.23* made three abortive approaches to the Norfolk coast, and as many times turned back, claiming engine trouble. Two months later Ganzel was transferred from airships to the light cruiser *Kolberg*.

Dietrich in command of *LZ.22* tried for Sheffield but had no luck with his radio bearings, and decided he had attacked Lincoln instead. Actually, his bombs had fallen smack into a complex of Sheffield armament factories. One incendiary fell on small houses and twenty-eight people were killed, nineteen injured.

LZ.21, forced to ignore important targets, wandered over the Midlands, and her skipper claimed afterward to have dropped several bombs on Derby, but the blackout precautions had so bewildered him his high explosive had fallen on Bolton in Lancashire, sixty miles to the northwest. *LZ.14* headed for what her commander thought was Leeds, but heavy gunfire drove him away and his bombs fell in open areas of Yorkshire.

Buttlar, aboard *LZ.30*, had a clear, starry sky with few clouds, so he ignored London and went for what he believed was Ramsgate and Margate where he reported that his heavy explosions had started several fires. Again, no bombs fell on those Kentish towns. *LZ.13* also wandered about in this area and finally dropped her bombs in the sea off Cromer.

Mathy made his bid for London, but after reaching Dungeness, realized that this was not the night for a major attack, so he ordered his helmsman to steer for Portsmouth. "None of our airships has ever been there," he commented, "and it is certain to be very interesting."

According to British trackers he started for Portsmouth, but on his approach antiaircraft guns, though handled amateurishly, unnerved him. After dropping several parachute flares to put the gunners off, Mathy turned back. Not one of his 8125 pounds of bombs was traced, and it is believed they were intentionally dumped into the sea. He then steered for home.

This strange action by Mathy puzzled the British who knew through their decoding system that it was the famous German airship commander who had approached the Portsmouth dockyards. They concluded that he had come on a naval reconnaissance mission and then jettisoned his bombs in order to gain altitude for his flight home. Closer to the truth was the fact that Mathy and his crew were by now victims of what was known as combat fatigue in World War II. They all were brooding on the events of the past weeks; their nerves were on edge; there was no cheerfulness in any of them. Mathy, himself, was no longer a bouncy inspiration. He had become more serious, and the torture of his nerves had left its lines in his face. It was only a question of time before *LZ.31* would go down, blazing and screeching, as had the others.

Inclement weather afforded a short surcease, but by October 1, Mathy's *LZ.31* and ten other Zeppelins were given another mission to raid England. Again, they ran into freshening southwest winds, and then picked up squalls and heavy clouds. A solid cloud rampart rose up over England at which point the wind veered to the northwest and brought rain, snow, and hail. Even the elements conspired against Strasser—and Heinrich Mathy. The wind strengthened, and practically all of the dirigibles were carried well south of their planned positions. Three of them found it expedient to "use caution," and returned without dropping a bomb. Buttlar, the commander of *LZ.30*, was to claim he bombed extensive installations on the south side of the Humber, when in fact he was never traced over Britain.

Five other Zeppelins floundered around over Lincolnshire and Norfolk vainly trying to find big-city targets via wireless bearings. One or two dropped bombs, hoping to arouse the antiaircraft batteries, but the gunners would not be drawn. Meanwhile, the airships were icing up, and staggering about in dull confusion. Kurt Frankenberg, aboard *LZ.21*, put in nearly ten hours seeing absolutely nothing but cloud and storm. He made a bid to reach Manchester and then Sheffield, but only picked out a few innocuous searchlight beams. Then there was a minute or so when the cloud bank opened up and he saw a Zeppelin mounted on searchlight blades, dropping bombs on London. The clouds moved in again, and then opened slowly with theatrical timing. The Zeppelin was now seen burning in the sky.

Wondering who had gone down this time, Frankenberg ran into a damp mist that plated his outer cover with ice, so much so that, although he nosed *LZ.21* up ten degrees, she began to stagger under the weight and he had to drop his bombs, one by one, as ballast. His antenna coated up with ice so his wireless set was useless. It was impossible to call some friendly station for bearings.

Robert Koch had intended to head his *LZ.24* for Manchester but cloud conditions prevented visual navigation. On taking a star sight his navigator decided they had been carried much farther south than a wireless bearing indicated, so Koch decided he might as well attack London. While flying toward the British capital he, too, saw an airship blazing and tumbling to earth "somewhere in the region northeast of the docks." In his report Koch stated he had dropped his complete bomb load on Stoke Newington and Hackney, but what he had taken to be the London district was the glare off a flying field at Hitchin thirty miles north of London. One soldier was killed, but no military damage was done. *LZ.24* then made for the coast, crossed over at Lowestoft and headed for home.

The Zeppelin that had been destroyed was Heinrich

Mathy's *LZ.31*, but he had proven his gallantry and courage to the last in ignoring Strasser's warning to use caution. More important was the phrase, "Attack London if possible according to weather conditions."

Mathy had made his landfall at Lowestoft at 9:00 P.M., and from there flew a compass course until the gleaming rails of the Great Eastern Railway were identified below as they snaked through Chelmsford. He throttled back his engines to take a wireless bearing, a point that may have played a tragic part in the upcoming drama. Had he trusted the railroad guidance he might have flown directly to London, dropped his bombs, and been away before aeroplanes of the defense force could have reached him. Instead, outer London's searchlights picked him out at 10:45, and he was forced to sheer off to the north.

Determined to elude the defense, Mathy began circling this northeastern fringe of the city while he again checked his position by wireless bearings. Just after midnight he was tracked and found to be over Hertford where he encountered a northerly wind, so he throttled his engines again, hoping to be carried south or southeast. Then, the minute he opened his engines a number of batteries below began a steady fire. Four night-flying pilots spotted him at once, and took up the chase. Mathy's lookout saw them, and Mathy jettisoned his bombs, turned sharply west and tried to climb.

We leave him at this point and pick up Second Lieutenant W. J. Tempest who had taken off from North Weald about fifteen minutes after Mathy had been spotted moving toward London. Tempest risked the heavy gunfire and flew directly across the city and then had fuel-pump trouble. His official report reads:

> As I drew up to the Zeppelin, to my relief I found that I was quite free of A.A. fire for the nearest shells were bursting quite three miles away. The Zeppelin was now nearly 12,700 feet high and mounting rapidly. I therefore started to dive at her, for, though I held a slight advantage in

speed she was climbing like a rocket and leaving me standing. I accordingly gave a tremendous pump at my petrol tank and dived straight at her, firing a burst into her as I came. I let her have another burst as I passed under her and then banking my machine over, sat under her tail, and flying along underneath her, pumped lead into her for all I was worth. I could see tracer bullets flying from her in all directions, but I was too close under her for them to concentrate on me. As I was firing I noticed her begin to go red inside like an enormous Chinese lantern and then a flame shot out of the front part of her and I realized she was on fire. She then shot up about 200 feet, paused, and came roaring straight down on me before I had time to get out of the way. I nosed-dived for all I was worth, with the Zepp tearing after me, and expected every minute to be engulfed in the flames. I put my machine into a spin and just managed to corkscrew out of the way as she shot past me, roaring like a furnace. I righted my machine and watched her hit the ground with a shower of sparks. I then proceeded to fire off dozens of green Very lights in the exuberance of my feelings.

I glanced at my watch and I saw it was about ten minutes past twelve. I then commenced to feel very sick, giddy and exhausted, and had considerable difficulty in finding my way to the ground through fog, and in landing I crashed and cut my head on my machine gun.

LZ.31 piled up in two sections in a field outside Potter's Bar, about three miles to the north of Barnet on the Great North Road. At the time it was a country village which derived its name from an ancient bar on Enfield Chase. The resting place of LZ.31 was three and a half miles to the east from Potter's Bar. The forward half of the framework piled up on a huge oak and left a grim heap of tangled wreckage of duralumin girders and burned-out gas cells. The fire, further supplied by engine fuel, spluttered and smoldered for several hours. A few villagers went out in the drizzling rain to stare at the spectacle and one small group came upon the battered body of a German officer who had apparently leaped from the burning framework. They approached slowly and found him still breathing, but he died shortly after before any medical aid arrived. On the officer's identity disc, they read by the light of the burning pyre, "*Kapit. Mathy. LZ.31.*"

The gallant Kapitänleutnant, pride of the Naval Airship Service, had made his last journey against London.

His nemesis, Lieutenant Tempest, had been dining with friends when an air-raid warning called him to Joyce Green airfield. Taking off in his B.E.2c he was to join that very exclusive band of Zeppelin killers. For his victory over *LZ.31* he was honored with the Distinguished Service Order. Tempest was twenty-six years old, and had been educated at Stonyhurst, a Roman Catholic academy in Blackburn where he had starred as a cricket player. On leaving school he entered the Merchant Navy, and then, on the outbreak of war, took a commission with the King's Own Yorkshire Light Infantry. He was wounded at Ypres and was buried in a dugout for twenty-four hours. As a consequence he was invalided out with a slight limp and rheumatic gout. But, like so many others of his breed, Tempest managed to be accepted for flight training by the Royal Flying Corps, learned to fly at one of the military schools, and took his certificate at about the same time as Leefe Robinson. And, like Robinson, was shot down over the Western Front the following year, but Tempest was killed.

As far as esprit de corps and soul were concerned, Mathy's death marked the end of the German Naval Airship Service, and Peter Strasser who lived less than two years more never really recovered from the shock. He did his best to write a letter of condolence to Mathy's young wife, but was unequal to the task. The missive was nothing more than a stereotyped note, uneven, vague, with the lugubrious lamentations of the day.

Still, the Zeppelins were sent out on the next opportunity to take part in a Fleet operation. The German Navy had hoped to batter Sunderland again, but by October 6 Admiral Scheer was ordered to send his U-boats back into the trade war, so the surface fleet had to dispense with submarine shields. An operation, sent out on October 19, sailed no farther than the eastern edge of the Dogger Bank, and there was no contact with the Royal Navy. However, at 1:30 P.M. *LZ.14* did spot a portion of Tyrwhitt's Harwich Force, but by that time Scheer had turned back for home.

All the Zeppelins did was to disclose a number of new mechanical breakdowns, and it was just as well that no major contact was made with the Grand Fleet. *LZ.21* lost a propeller. *LZ.24* had a propeller shaft bearing seize up. *LZ.17* had three engines stop, and *LZ.23*'s port elevator jammed and had to be repaired with a jury rig. *LZ.13* lost both side engines at the same time and was only able to limp back to Hage by the dawn's early light.

Tragedy struck again on November 27 when, after days of fruitless planning and stormy weather, eight Zeppelins were finally sent out to attack industrial targets in the English Midlands. The order came through while a number of airship commanders were putting on a birthday luncheon for Max Dietrich, commander of *LZ.34*, who was forty-six. The break-up of the jollification left a marked impression on several of the participants, for they all had somber presentiments.

The weather was no better than that experienced in the previous two weeks. The airships encountered great masses of cloud vapor and mist, and *LZ.35* passed within half a mile of a waterspout. *LZ.36* and *LZ.22* almost collided while moving about in cloud columns. Despite the fact that this was supposed to be a moonless winter night, there was no actual darkness, for off to the west the glow from the British industrial cities was sufficient for the crewmen to read their pocket watches. In fact, a glare to the north turned out to be the aurora borealis, all of which made the Zeppelins stand out distinctly. The airships that could get to higher altitude found strong head winds that considerably cut their speed.

Still in command of *LZ.30*, Buttlar had a crank bearing burn out shortly after take-off, and by 8:10 P.M. his starboard amidships engine quit completely, so he wisely turned back for his shed. Other dirigibles of the "Thirties" series, *LZ.34*, *LZ.35*, and *LZ.36* headed for Newcastle with the idea of continuing on and attacking targets in the Edinburgh area. The older models flew toward Flamborough Head and more southern counties. For instance, *LZ.24* had orders to bomb a benzol plant at Stockton-on-Tees.

Max Dietrich, aboard *LZ.34*, crossed the British coast near Hartlepool some time after midnight, and while flying over Hutton Henry his ship was picked out by a searchlight, and Dietrich released thirteen high-explosive bombs in retaliation. This incident impelled him to turn back for the coast where he dropped four bombs on West Hartlepool. Here sixteen heavies scored; four people were killed and eleven injured.

For some unknown reason, Dietrich continued on at 9500 feet, instead of working for altitude and safety, and after turning away from his West Hartlepool attack, his lookout reported that an aeroplane was rapidly overhauling them.

At 11:22 P.M. Second Lieutenant Ian V. Pyott of Number 36 Squadron had been sent off from an R.F.C. field at Seaton Carew. He had cruised about for almost an hour when he sighted a Zeppelin flying between Sunderland and Hartlepool that had been caught in the beam of a searchlight located at Castle Eden. The big airship seemed to be heading directly for him, and Pyott climbed to 9800 feet, at which point the Zeppelin seemed to be a few hundred feet below him. He reported later:

I flew toward the Zepp and flew at right angles to and underneath him amidships, firing as I went under. I then turned sharply east, the Zepp turning east also. We then flew on a parallel course for about five miles and I fired 71 rounds at the Zepp. I estimated his ground speed to be approximately 70 mph. I was aiming at his port quarter and noticed first a small patch become incandescent where I had seen tracers entering his envelope. I first took it for a machine gun firing at me from the Zepp, but this patch rapidly spread

and the next thing was that the whole Zepp was in flames.
I landed at 12 midnight (British Time), engine and machine
O.K. The Zeppelin which fell into the mouth of the Tees
was still burning when I landed.

And so passed Max Dietrich who had been snatched from
his birthday luncheon. He was consumed, along with his
crew, and the next day only a pattern of tangled wreckage
and scummy oil marked their grave.

But the scythe of the Grim Reaper was to swing again
before the night was over. LZ.35, under Herbert Ehrlich,
had turned back for Germany when the crew saw LZ.34
go down. Kurt Friemel in command of LZ.24 was about
fifteen miles off the coast when he saw an airship burning,
and he, too, lost interest, although he reported later he had
gone inland to bomb the coastal town of Scarborough, but
no trace of his bombs was ever found. It was much the same
with most of the others who had witnessed Dietrich's finish.

Cutting inland north of Flamborough Head, LZ.22 was
met by intense antiaircraft fire and hit severely. About 150
holes were made in her gas cells, and the Zepp became
heavy. All spare parts, extra fuel, and water ballast were
jettisoned. Her skipper, Heinrich Hollender, turned back to
sea and went down to 2000 feet, hoping to compress the gas
into the less-damaged sections of the cells. LZ.22 floundered
on, her electrical system out, and by dawn she was over
friendly territory, but was unable to get to Nordholz and
had to settle for Hage. Two tanks of fuel were dropped as
well as all parachutes (an interesting point seldom mentioned in Zeppelin operations), and everything else detachable, but LZ.22 was still well over three tons heavy, and
after fouling a fence post she slammed down hard and suffered general damage that required six days to repair.

LZ.21, commanded by Frankenberg, also failed to return
to Nordholz. She had crossed the coast at Atwich at 10:20
P.M., but was challenged by heavy antiaircraft fire, so
Frankenberg turned back to sea again and then risked another crossing farther north. LZ.21 did considerable probing

and skulking about, possibly because British aeroplanes were in the vicinity, but finally she headed for Leeds. About ten miles east of Leeds a ground gun gave considerable trouble, so Frankenberg turned and headed south and cruised between Manchester and Sheffield without seeing either city, owing to blackout precautions. He did, however, spot some hearth glare at Chesterton so dropped sixteen explosive and seven incendiary bombs that resulted in some broken windows and little else.

Frankenberg then turned east to cross the southern Midlands, but engine trouble slowed his speed, and somewhere north of Peterborough *LZ.21* spotted two aeroplanes, but making the most of a light mist her commander evaded both of them with smart maneuvering.

Another aeroplane caught up with *LZ.21* somewhere near East Dereham, but just as it moved in for an attack, its engine conked out. A short time later Frankenberg radioed he was nearing Norwich, but had a side engine that had failed.

In the meantime the naval air station at Great Yarmouth had been alerted and three planes were sent aloft to search for this dirigible, but *LZ.21* was well out to sea before these pilots caught up with her. Then began another hawk and falcon wrangle. One after another of the British planes attacked, and the last hunter, looking on as she caught fire by the stern, claimed to have seen the Zeppelin's machine gunner clamber from the top gun platform and run directly over the nose of the ship before she exploded in midair. *LZ.21* fell into the sea ten miles out from Lowestoft, and rescue craft, moving in, found a broken propeller blade, a great patch of oil and gasoline, but no survivors.

Flight Sub-Lieutenant E. L. Pulling received official credit for the destruction of *LZ.21*, but Flight Lieutenant Egbert Cadbury who fired four full drums of mixed ammunition into her, undoubtedly set her afire. He was the last pilot to make an attack and he was firing at the stern where she first began to burn, whereas the other two pilots fired only a few rounds between them. The third pilot in this foray was Lieutenant W. R. Gayner who was unfortunate in losing his engine after he first caught up with Frankenberg.

Thus it will be seen that the Royal Flying Corps, the Royal Naval Air Service, and the improved ground batteries had taken the measure of the Zeppelins. While 1916 saw twenty-two major Zeppelin raids, there were only seven in 1917, and in 1918 only four, one of which never crossed the British coastline.

Strasser, who had been aboard LZ.22 commanded by Hollender, was forced to admit defeat—at least as far as any further raids on the important targets in Britain were concerned. He stated that machine guns were of no value in the defense of dirigibles because the aeroplanes were superior in speed, yet over the following fortnight he laid up three early type Zepps, LZ.22, LZ.23, and LZ.24 to have machine-gun platforms built into their tails. He did admit, however, that his Zeppelins could hope to attack England only by using the best of cloud cover, and that in the future he would order all raids to be made under those conditions. There was a period of experimentation with camouflage paint, and some consideration for mounting a searchlight on the top platform to assist in finding attacking planes—all pathetic moves in a desperate situation.

Another raid was attempted on December 28, 1916, in which six Zeppelins took part, including SL.12, an almost obsolete Schütte-Lanz airship that had been commissioned only a month or so before. This attack on Britain was recalled early, owing to adverse wind conditions, and SL.12, under Kapitänleutnant Waldemar Kölle, was flown in to be put down at Ahlhorn, but in the attempt the wooden-framework dirigible smashed against a gasometer and ripped open her bow. This left the nose so crumpled that Kölle, refusing to risk a turn into the freshening wind, tried to put her down outside the area of the field. There she was presumably pegged down, but during the night the wind increased and SL.12 was battered to complete wreckage.

But there was more destruction. On that same day in December two of the Tondern-based ships went up in flames. *LZ.16* and *LZ.24* had been assigned a patrol to protect a number of minesweepers off the western and northern edges of the German Bight. *LZ.24* returned early to beat a rising wind, and landed safely near her shed, but as she was being walked in, the after tackle snapped and *LZ.24* swung around hard, breaking her back across the heavy framework of the shed entrance. She caught fire immediately, and the conflagration spread to *LZ.17* berthed on the north side of the hangar. Both dirigibles were a total loss.

Within a few weeks the Chief of the General Staff proposed disbanding the Army Airship Service, but Strasser still believed the Navy Airship Service could bring Britain to her knees.

X

SAFETY IN HEIGHT

The original vigor and vital spirit of the German Naval Airship Service had been completely drained by the close of 1916. The great Mathy, hero of the popular Berlin press, was gone, and four more of the nine original Zeppelin commanders were dead or captured. The London defenses had spread northward, and alternate targets, once in areas safe for airships, were becoming increasingly difficult to locate.

In the last program of attacks against Britain, it had become clear, even to the redoubtable Strasser, that his Naval dirigibles could no longer bomb England without suffering heavy losses. Officials of the higher echelons debated whether a continuance of the attacks would justify the results. But Strasser still pleaded with Admiral Scheer, begging his patience, and pointing out that it was not only the direct material damage that was important, but rather the general result of these aerial onslaughts upon England's insularity that was otherwise undisturbed by the war. Taking the psychological viewpoint, Strasser argued that the disruption of transportation, the dread of airships overhead by the British working classes, and the necessity of assigning considerable armament and military personnel to the defense, were sound reasons for continuing the attacks.

It might be pertinent at this point to add that Strasser, who was to be awarded the post of Leader of Airships, did not lead every attack, and that he was considered to be a Jonah whenever he adopted one of the raiding airships as his flagship, for nine times out of ten, as the saying goes, that Zeppelin was immediately plagued with engine trouble, mechanical failures, or encountered impossible weather. As a result Strasser seldom saw the hostile shores of Great Britain.

But Strasser had a sound point when he indicated that the threat of the Zeppelins compelled the British to set up a formidable Home Defence organization that diverted men, guns, and aircraft from other military fronts. For instance, by the end of 1916 no less than 17,341 officers and men were retained in Great Britain for antiaircraft defense. There were twelve Royal Flying Corps squadrons, comprising some 200 officers, 2000 men, and 110 aeroplanes. The antiaircraft guns were manned by 12,000 officers and men who might have been more profitably employed in France.

Thus, it was agreed that the Zeppelin raids should be continued, if only for their nuisance value, although Strasser was still convinced his airships could seriously damage London. The fact remains, however, that Britain's capital was bombed only once more by an airship.

Though the heavier-than-air exponents were coming into their own at last, and their first twin-engined Gotha bombers were being test-flown and shown to be capable of flying a loaded weight of 25,318 pounds, they still could not reach vital targets in the British Midlands or the north of England, even by flying from Belgian bases, so Strasser pointed out that naval Zeppelins would still be needed to "harass if not destroy."

However, the Naval Airship Service could not afford to lose one or two airships on every raid. It was obvious that at that rate Strasser's service would soon be extinct. The most rational answer was that the performance of the dirigibles had to be improved. The German Aviation Division first proposed that greater speed might be obtained by streamlining the engine gondolas and fitting each with two Maybach HSLu power plants that would be geared to a single propeller. This was at least a great improvement on previous arrangements, and the Zeppelin Company devised two general adaptations utilizing this new twin-engine gondola that was to be incorporated into a seven-engine dirigible of 2,090,000 cubic feet capacity. The main hull was to be 682 feet long, and the dirigible was expected to move at 65½ miles per hour.

Still another design was for an eight-engine airship of 2,239,000 cubic feet, and 718 feet in length. It was hoped that this model would be capable of approaching 75 miles per hour, but problems in the production of the twin-engine drive delayed the building of these new models, and Strasser, frantic with apprehension, suddenly decided on another solution—to aim for a much higher ceiling and dispense with high speed.

This new proposal came out of a suggestion made by Adolf Schultz who had been a machinist's mate aboard LZ.33, and who through a prisoner-exchange system, had been sent from England to Switzerland. There, aided by the German Naval Attaché in Berne, he had a letter forwarded in which he recommended in part:

In order to be able to continue effective air attacks without suffering such severe losses, the airships must be able to go to at least 20,000 feet where they will be able to escape aeroplane attack . . . To reach this altitude will require a great decrease in weight. Two motors could be removed, specifically the two side engines from the after gondola . . . For controlling the ship it would be immaterial whether the commander's position is in the forward or after car in place of the two superfluous engines, and many long control cables could be dispensed with and the transmissions of orders greatly simplified. The forward gondola would be merely a small engine car . . . In order to keep the ship in the air in case of dire emergencies all four gondolas should be droppable, so that one could keep going with the two midline, the two side gondolas, or with a midships or two side gondolas.

Strasser, of course, could not bow to Schultz's sound reasoning, but indicated later that he did consider having side gondolas that could be jettisoned, and in a letter to his Admiralty he argued that airships of the present "Thirty" type might be improved so that they could reach an altitude of 16,500 feet. To do this, he suggested that much weight could be eliminated by substituting the streamlined two-engine gondola with the single propeller for the ungainly three-engine after car. There also was some discussion as to whether the whole framework could be lightened.

After considerable technical consultation a test model was made of *LZ.44* in which the two-engine gondola was substituted for the three-engine gondola that employed one rear and two side propellers. Fuel capacity was reduced to a thirty-hour range instead of a thirty-six-hour supply. All machine guns were dispensed with and a new arrangement of bomb releases limited the bomb-carrying capacity. All hull girders were lightened, and there was a complete elimination of the crew's quarters and conveniences.

These and other modifications were incorporated into several Zeppelins, and as a result *LZ.35*, carrying a useful load of 15,600 pounds, climbed to 16,100 feet. *LZ.36* reached 16,400 feet. *LZ.39* stopped her engines at 16,400 feet and continued to rise statically until the level of 17,-700 feet was reached. *LZ.40* climbed to 17,100 feet. All well and good, but at these altitudes the temperature dropped to 18–22 degrees below zero. Ballast water froze despite the antifreeze glycerin, so Strasser proposed sand in bags for ballast. Beyond this, these short stays at high altitude disclosed no other defects. A few of the men spoke of slight dizziness and mild palpitations, but whiffs of oxygen seemed to remedy the conditions.

Late in February 1917 Martin Dietrich, with Strasser aboard, took the new *LZ.42* aloft for a height test. He left

Nordholz, and three hours later, after dropping twenty-three tons of water-glycerin ballast, he climbed to 19,700 feet. LZ.42 was carrying over 16,000 pounds of useful load, including 4400 pounds of water in lieu of bombs. Dietrich stated later that he thought he could have reached 21,000 feet.

This experimentation went on day after day, and by April 1917 LZ.44 appeared with the streamlined gondola, twin engines, and a single propeller. During the summer this new gondola arrangement was fitted to all available Zeppelins. LZ.46 was commissioned with streamlined, amidships power cars, and a small, light control car was built into LZ.45 that made her lighter than LZ.46 by 2430 pounds. Then, on August 1, 1917, LZ.53, with a major change in her hull frames that produced a useful lift of 89,523 pounds, reached an altitude of 20,700 feet on her first raid attempt. But this class was built too lightly to withstand full-speed maneuvers at low altitude, so it was relegated to the North Sea force until almost a year later.

Other general refinements included the painting of the underside of the hull, gondolas, and elevators black, and to reduce skin friction the entire outer envelope was tightly doped instead of being left porous on top to permit the escape of valved hydrogen. This led to some unexpected accidents, as no provision had been made for equalizing air pressure within the huge hull. Later on, to counter the removal of the machine guns, Strasser encouraged the development of the Becker 20-millimeter machine cannon, but these were not available until the summer of 1918.

This development of high-altitude dirigibles made obsolete the main complement of British anti-Zeppelin aircraft. The B.E.2c, the B.E.12, and the redoubtable F.E.2b pusher that was being replaced on the Western Front by the Bristol Fighter, were not capable of such ceilings, and though a number of single-seater fighters might have met the new Zeppelin challenge, they could not be spared from the front-line combat zones. It was not until well into 1918 that aircraft with comparable performance could be spared to battle the new Zeppelin menace. Also, this black-painted raider was difficult to pick out by searchlight, and once more the ground gunners felt frustrated and helpless.

But it was not all beer and skittles for the Zeppelin forces, as they soon discovered that this high-altitude protection was bought at serious cost. Not only were the men hampered by the cold and the thin air conditions, but the service meteorologists were unequal to the task of providing accurate weather reports for the airship men who risked these tremendous heights. For instance, their most western weather station was only 235 miles from the Hamburg Observatory, and they could not predict the strength of winds above 15,000 feet. Although German U-boats were frequently cruising in the Atlantic well west of the British Isles, no one thought of using them as weather stations.

The high-altitude levels also provided new problems for the navigators. All important or dense clouds lay below, rather than above the airships, and it was difficult from these heights to identify features of the landscape even when they were not shielded by cloud layers. Whenever the navigators tried to use radio triangulation to determine their positions, they found the air cluttered with the appeals of other airship men; so much so the British had no trouble in using the same system to learn where the Zeppelins were.

But it was the frailty of man that posed the greatest problem. The medical profession of the military services was very capable when it came to wounds, surgery, tropical diseases, and sanitation, but the German Navy doctors were stymied with the problems of high-altitude flying, or the effects of low-oxygen tension on air-crew physiology. They discovered that while the human body can compensate for some decrease in oxygen tension, the symptoms of "altitude sickness" made themselves felt above 12,000 feet. These developments could be controlled only by continuously breathing oxygen from cylinders, and because of this it was difficult to provide the crews with any nourishment on long, high-altitude flights. It was also learned that the only food that was agreeable at low temperatures was chocolate. Although the men were advised to eat as little as possible, it was appreciated that long, high-altitude flights under such conditions could be very exhausting for the crews. As an example, on the night of August 7, 1917, *LZ.49*'s elevator man, who had an undetected heart ailment, dropped dead in the control car during a high-altitude trial flight.

Furnishing oxygen raised several problems. At first it was issued in individual bottles, but there were complaints that it tasted strongly of oil that caused nausea. These bottles were replaced later with heavy metal containers of liquid air. This was more palatable, gave a feeling of unusual alertness, and seemed to eliminate all fatigue.

As it was most difficult to provide artificial heating in the airships, the penetrating cold could be countered only with extra clothing, and eventually regulation uniforms were replaced with fur-lined flying suits, and helmets under which layers of newspapers were wadded. Some attempts were made to develop high-altitude Maybach engines, but nothing much was accomplished until late in November 1917.

Believing he had at last developed airships, crews, and oxygen systems to dare the British defenses again, Strasser requested late in February 1917 a total of thirty dirigibles, twenty-four for the North Sea, and six for the Baltic. With Germany's determination to push the unrestricted U-boat warfare, a number of Zeppelins were sent out over the North Sea to report on Allied merchant traffic in the blockade area around the British Isles. In reply, the British so intensified their minelaying in the German Bight, the German minesweepers could only try to keep certain channels clear that led to the open sea. All this required hour-by-hour air reconnaissance, and the available airships spent many long hours on such ventures.

LZ.36, the Zeppelin that had been specially lightened for the high-altitude raids, was sent out from Nordholz on a

scouting mission. She was commanded by Kapitänleutnant Georg Eichler, and during the night, February 6, she
showed a disposition to be stern heavy and Cell 7 over the
rear gondola seemed to be losing gas. Flying out of trim,
with her nose up about 17 degrees, Eichler was forced to
drop much ballast aft, pump fuel forward, and have five
bombs hauled from the after bomb bay to a space in the
nose.

At dawn of the following morning, Eichler had to descend through a layer of fog that the Nordholz station reported to be within 65 feet of the ground. This created a
landing problem as the ship was 6000 pounds light, and
moving in with her nose down at an angle of 5 degrees.
LZ.36 bore into the fog at 1600 feet, and by the time she
had descended to 800 feet, she encountered a temperature
change that caused the airship to be extra nose-heavy, and
she began to drop at speed, so Eichler ordered all engines
at high speed to provide pressure for the elevators, but this
did not prevent them from breaking through the fog where
they found they were nosing down at the ice-covered estuary of the Weser River. All precautions were taken, and
much ballast dropped, but the control car smashed hard on
the ice throwing one man out. The airship then rebounded
and shot up to 3300 feet, and with the control car struts
broken, and the threat of having the car fall clear, Eichler
valved some gas and landed on the ice again.

He then ordered the control crew to take over the emergency rudder and elevator controls that were in the aft
gondola, and again LZ.36 lifted and moved ESE in bright
sunshine above the fog. It was well that the control crew
had moved aft, as the forward control car finally wrenched
itself free and fell into the sea.

Below, the fog held, and Eichler could not find the Nordholz kite-balloon marker. He had lost all his charts and
radio equipment when the forward car fell, so he floundered
about until he came upon the upper peaks of a mountain
chain looming above the clouds. With the loss of the gondola, and the lifting gas heated by the outside temperature

of 27 degrees, the crippled *LZ.36* was now 5500 pounds light. Eichler did the best he could by valving more gas, and setting his crew members where they could handle the individual maneuvering wires. He finally got his craft down to 750 feet, or under the cloud layer, and circled about until he found the railroad tracks running between Verden and Celle, some ninety miles SSE of Nordholz.

All went fairly well until the ship suddenly became stern heavy. They jettisoned what remaining ballast they had, but she continued to drop fast. The rear gondola was dragged through some treetops and then hooked into a string of high-tension lines, contributing to *LZ.36*'s finish. She crashed on the surface of the Aller River where a high wind took over and drove the hulk across the ice where she broke up on the river bank.

Strasser, who had been promoted to Leader of Airships, was convinced that his new high-altitude ships were ready for their first test against Britain. On March 16, 1917, he ordered Viktor Schütz, now Commander of the Naval Airship Division, to plot a raid out of Nordholz. Strasser went on the raid and observed from the control car of *LZ.42*, skippered by Martin Dietrich. Zeppelins *LZ.35*, *LZ.39*, *LZ.40*, and *LZ.41* were also assigned to the mission that proved to be a very expensive experiment.

The lightened ships carried bomb loads of 4000 pounds, which was somewhat less than the explosive weight hauled in the latter part of 1916. Again, adverse weather conditions that could not be predicted by the German weather stations, plagued the airship captains. And to make matters worse, the British had learned to jam the various radio wavelengths used by the German Navy, and for about five hours the airship captains received only fragments of the advisory messages. Owing to an unexpected northwest wind all of the raiders were carried south of their dead-reckoning positions, and as a final curse the Bruges radio-bearing station went off the air at the height of the raid.

Robert Koch, aboard *LZ.39*, apparently crossed the British coast at Margate but moved southwest over Kent, and went out to sea again, but finally selected St. Leonards, near Hastings. He dropped two bombs in the town and damaged two houses. Two more dropped short and fell into the sea. By 3:55 A.M. Koch had flown to the French coast and recognized Dieppe, but the prevailing gale took him almost to Paris. Realizing he was approaching the City of Light he headed into the wind and tried to reach the safety of the German front line.

What happened from this point is mere conjecture, but shortly after Koch passed Beauvais he must have lost some engine power for by 6:00 A.M. *LZ.39* was drifting southeast, and by 6:40 she next appeared in the early dawn over Compiègne. There she hung aimlessly while French antiaircraft guns shelled her until a direct hit set her on fire. *LZ.39* gushed flame and fell earthward, dragging a greasy pall of smoke across the rosy sky. A violent explosion ripped the framework apart and a number of crewmen were seen falling from the wreckage. The twin hulks of smoke and flame fell on opposite sides of a garden wall of a house outside the town. The German people did not know of this loss until the next day when the radio station of the Eiffel Tower put out a complete wireless report of the episode.

Other ships of this formation were also driven over France, and many of us remember the plaintive appeals being made by the airship radio operators as they begged for information, bearings, and advice. We who were serving on the Western Front at the time were told of these tragic situations, and it was clear that the day of the Zeppelin could be over.

Herbert Erhlich in *LZ.35* and Erich Sommerfeldt in *LZ.40* both reported that they had bombed London; in fact Sommerfeldt stated he had seen blue lights of an aeroplane over the city, and well he might have, for there were sixteen Royal Flying Corps aircraft aloft that evening. British trackers reported *LZ.35*, *LZ.40*, *LZ.41* following Koch's *LZ.39* across the eastern corner of Kent where they apparently did their bombing, for what few were dropped fell in the open country causing little damage.

LZ.35 hit the French coast somewhere near Calais, and managed to cross the British trenches north of Ypres. Setting course for Ahlhorn, Ehrlich was amazed to find himself at 6:00 A.M. at least one hundred miles south of his base, or between Münster and Hamm. Three hours later he received a directive from Viktor Schütze at Nordholz, explaining that no drop in the wind was expected, and that *LZ.35* should try to reach Friedrichshafen or Mannheim. This was an impossibility for Ehrlich had only enough fuel to stay in the air until 1:00 P.M., so he tried to make Hannover, but the violent northwest wind carried him almost to Kassel. Frantic, and bewildered by more messages, all predicting dire weather conditions, he next headed for Dresden where he finally arrived at 1:30 after running on two engines and a fifty miles-per-hour tail wind. Then, while trying to dock in a hangar a forty miles-per-hour wind took charge and slammed the airship about. Just as she was entering the hangar door a sharp gust hoisted her tail, slammed it down again and broke *LZ.35* in two. It required three months to put her back into shape and return her to Ahlhorn.

LZ.40 was luckier, but her skipper, Sommerfeldt had a hair-raising experience. He managed to get across the English Channel and identify the French coast near Wissant. By 4:20 A.M. a rising moon saw *LZ.40* high over the Western Front, and by 9.00 A.M. Sommerfeldt had managed to reach Euskirchen near Bonn. He had also received Schütze's message but because he had used up much of his fuel he knew it was impossible to reach any south German base that could accommodate his ship. He tried for Ahlhorn and arrived over that field with but one engine working, and as his *LZ.40* was taken over by the ground crew the last engine quit cold for lack of fuel. *LZ.40* had been in the air for twenty-six hours.

LZ.41 found Boulogne and managed to get to German territory by 4:00 A.M., and crossed the trenches near Cambrai. Her skipper, Kuno Manger, realizing he was running short of fuel, also headed for Ahlhorn and arrived there just as the ground crew was attending to *LZ.40*, so *LZ.41* drifted off into the fog with only two engines operating. Manger was unable to nose into his hangar until 3:53 P.M., having been in the air for twenty-seven hours.

Strasser aboard *LZ.42* lived up to his Jonah role, and so hexed the airship she never did reach England. Her skipper, Martin Dietrich, had planned to cross the coast near Orfordness, and head for London from there. Dietrich caught the freshening northwest wind and immediately steered a more northerly course and made for Lowestoft. At this point the radio-bearing system broke down, and *LZ.42* was next tracked over a point south of the Ostend lighthouse. From here Dietrich steered due north, but only four engines were working with the result that the ship was actually drifting southward stern first. At 12:47 Dietrich decided to try for Nordholz, and after a wearying search that was blinded by fog, and with all fuel tanks low, he finally landed at Jüterborg at 4:04 P.M. with less than one hour's fuel on board.

When carefully assessed, the damage inflicted amounted to £163 and the 79 bombs dropped killed no one, but there was some general complaint in Britain that none of the Zeppelins had been brought down in England, although it was realized that the aircraft employed were foiled by the improved performance of the modified dirigibles. It was revealed later that *LZ.35* had reached 18,400 feet, *LZ.40* had climbed to 19,000 feet, and *LZ.41* had risen to 17,100 feet. Strasser was pleased with the over-all performance and began plotting new ventures.

When the spring weather was propitious for long-distance scouting and training patrols, two of the new airships were sent out after dawn on May 1, 1917. *LZ.43* was to spot shipping off the Firth of Forth, and *LZ.45* was assigned to the area off Aberdeen. The latter encountered nothing of importance and returned safely at 8:15 P.M. *LZ.43* reported the wreck of a Norwegian sailing vessel near the Dogger

Bank South Lightship, and after cruising about for several hours came upon nothing of interest, so her commander, Hermann Kraushaar, after sending out several radio messages—mainly to see if he could draw out any Royal Navy vessels—spent the rest of his cruising time checking his radio-bearing instruments, and returned to Ahlhorn at 9:27 P.M.

Again on May 4, a number of Zeppelins were sent out to provide cover for the German minesweepers. Kraushaar, once more aboard LZ.43, found good visibility off Terschelling and decided to venture farther. Somewhere off the Dogger Bank he came upon some light cruisers steaming at high speed near a sailing vessel. Kraushaar went up to 13,000 feet and reported his find, and when a number of additional cruisers joined the maneuvers, he decided to try some high-altitude bombing. He dropped three 110-pound bombs and claimed to have started what appeared to be smoke and fires aboard one ship that continued to burn until the vessel was out of sight. The British later credited Kraushaar with a series of determined bombing attacks, but stated no hits were scored, although the destroyer *Dublin* did bring in several splinters from bombs that had burst on the water. This was one of the few occasions when a Zeppelin actually made an attack on an enemy warship.

Kraushaar increased his stature as an airship captain on May 23 when Strasser sent out six of his dirigibles to make an attack on London and the south of England. The weather was not too kindly and from some accounts Kraushaar's LZ.43 was the only Zepp to get anywhere near London. There were strong south to southwest winds that threatened to prevent any of the airships from reaching London until just before dawn.

Shortly after leaving Ahlhorn Kraushaar had engine trouble when an exhaust valve of the forward engine burned out, so the cylinder was "cut out," probably meaning the ignition was switched off, and the engine continued to run at 1200 revolutions per minute, until finally switched off on landing. Held below 10,000 feet, LZ.43 came within sight of the lights of Sheerness by 2:00 A.M., and with that Kraushaar decided to head for London.

He later reported dropping bombs on the Thames dock areas from a height of 19,000–20,000 feet, and stated that while making his run out he could see bursts among the dock lights.

Here again is a situation where the Zeppelin commander was confused as to his actual position. British trackers had LZ.43 crossing the Suffolk coast between Felixstowe and Orfordness, and the bombs that Kraushaar thought had dropped on the London docks were aimed, instead, at open areas between East Wrentham and Great Ryburgh, killing one man and damaging a few cottages. With that, LZ.43, probably finding she was being carried well to the north, descended to 1600 feet, and by crabbing across a SSW wind managed to make some progress toward home. Then, to add to Kraushaar's several problems, a message was received from Nordholz warning that the airship base at Wittmund was experiencing thunderstorms, and that thunderstorms were approaching Nordholz and Tondern, but that Ahlhorn was clear. Kraushaar headed for Ahlhorn, and after nearly twenty-three hours of flying evaded two thunder squalls and put down at his home base.

LZ.44, aboard which Strasser rode as an observer, was also fortunate to return safely. She made only a brief appearance over England at 2:23 A.M., but retired a few minutes later without dropping a bomb. According to Franz Stabbert, LZ.44's commander, he crossed the coast at Harwich where searchlights flashed and guns roared but no damage was suffered. Two engines came to a halt, however, but it was agreed to try for London on the three remaining engines as weather and visibility seemed favorable. But on making the turn another engine failed and the ship began to lose height, so the attempt to reach London was abandoned, and all available bombs were dropped over Harwich when the last two engines gave up the ghost. The ship began to drop again, and fuel tanks, ballast water, spare parts, and ship's equipment were tossed overboard,

enabling her skipper to hold her at 12,800 feet. She had
been up to 18,700 feet, but now she was nothing more
than a free balloon drifting between Harwich and Lowestoft, and this condition was endured for nearly an hour
until one engine was finally put in order. With this limited
power the ship suddenly nosed up to 21,000 feet, a condition set up first by mis-trimming, and then the lack of
ballast to re-trim the dirigible. She floundered on, as two
more engines were repaired, but running only at half speed.
By 11:28 A.M. *LZ.23* took off from Tondern to act as escort,
make radio contact, and direct surface ships to wherever
LZ.44 might have to land on the water. However, by 5:10
P.M. Stabbert had limped past Helgoland and put down
at Nordholz at 6:00 P.M. It is said that Strasser on this
occasion loudly bellowed his rage on again proving to be
a Jonah, for the service-wide superstition seemed to be fast
becoming a proven fact.

It would appear that Martin Dietrich aboard *LZ.42* made
the best approach to London, daring hail squalls and St.
Elmo's fire that lit up the interior of the hull like some
ghostly stage setting. After midnight a solid cloud layer
blotted off all view of the ground, so he dropped several
bombs to bait the defenses below. The ruse worked, and
about twenty searchlights slashed back and forth. Dietrich
decided he was over Sheerness, but on taking bearings on
the incendiaries he had dropped *LZ.42* was shown to be
making no way against a strong head wind. While thus de-
tained, Dietrich dropped the rest of his bomb load but did
not know where they had fallen because of the cloud cover.
British-tracker reports have it that *LZ.42* crossed the English coast south of the Naze and flew inland as far as
Braintree. Turning south *LZ.42* then crossed Norfolk and
went out to sea again near Sheringham. The bombs thought
to have been dropped on Sheerness were actually distributed between Mildenhall and East Dereham (Suffolk and
Norfolk), inflicting no damage.

Dietrich had his troubles fighting his way back to the
base. He first ran into a veritable buttress of black thunder

clouds that towered up to 23,000 feet, and had no choice but to chance flying through them. Taking the precaution of reeling in his antenna, and knowing his pressure height was 19,400 feet, he guided *LZ.42* into the inky inferno at the 16,400-foot level. Hail immediately pounded the outer envelope that was as tight as a drum, and then at 4:45 A.M. a flash of lightning struck and charged the metal framework so heavily it was dangerous to make contact with any of the duralumin. In fact, a machinist's mate in the port amidships car suffered a severe shock that knocked him off his stool. All kinds of strange smells were reported, including the inevitable ozone so familiar at all areas of electric power stations. Terror-stricken, the crewmen either huddled in the gondolas or crawled along the interior cat-walks, bewildered by the glare, afraid to touch anything with their hands.

Some semblance of discipline was restored, but within ten minutes another lightning bolt charged the framework, actually striking near the upper lookout's nest, bouncing along the envelope to break up around the fin and rudder. A sailmaker who was carrying out an inspection along the keel was fascinated by the glare that filtered through the translucent cells and the taut outer cover. He continued his patrol and was flattened on the catwalk by a third, but less effective bolt, that struck well forward. A careful examination made later at the Nordholz base revealed six holes in the envelope near the bow, some as large as the commander's cap. Two bracing wires had been burned through, and a bullet-sized hole had been "drilled" through a Duralumin girder. The port after propeller also showed some traces of fire.

A brand-new airship, *LZ.47* under command of Kapitän-leutnant Richard Wolff, went on this raid (May 23, 1917) hoping to use it as a final altitude trial, as bad weather over Germany had forbidden any form of height test since her commissioning early in May. Wolff also encountered the bad weather and cloud cover, but thought he had crossed the British coastline and had spent at least two hours cruising at well over 18,000 feet, but British records show no trace of *LZ.47* anywhere over the land. *LZ.40* and *LZ.45* probably crossed East Anglia on a friendly wind, and both skippers claimed to have bombed Norwich, but only three bombs, dropped in their time brackets, were ever traced.

The results of this raid included one man killed, none injured and £599 damage inflicted. When the German Naval Staff made its formal report to the Kaiser, Wilhelm stated, "In spite of this success, I am of the opinion that the day of the airship is past for attacks on London. They should be used as scouts for the High Seas Fleet and for strategic reconnaissance, not for bombing raids on London." In response to this the Chief of the Naval Staff made the repeated argument that a large number of troops, guns, and aeroplanes would be released for service on the Western Front if the airships ceased their attacks, and so the Kaiser was persuaded to permit the raids to continue, but only "when the circumstances seem favorable."

This raid had repeated the problems of high altitude on men and machinery, and it was found that men could not move about, climb ladders from the gondolas to the interior framework, or carry out strenuous work without becoming so exhausted they were useless for long periods of time, often for the rest of the raid. Flying for more than four hours at a time at levels above 16,000 feet often brought on headaches, nausea, and abdominal discomforts. Men who were expected to carry heavy cans of gasoline forward, or who pumped fuel by hand, or had to move distances along the tilted gangways when carrying out re-trim duties, were often so fatigued they had to be put away in hammocks. It was obvious that men in this condition could not be relied on, and the ship's safety was seriously endangered. It was also revealed that the men who resorted to oxygen bottles only when they began to feel exhausted, discovered it was too late.

These high-altitude problems were multiplied by the low

temperatures; oil lines snapped under the sub-zero conditions, radiator water evaporated rapidly, and it was necessary to carry reserve coolant in containers slung near the
gondolas. This supply was often used to top off all radiators
before starting up for the attack-altitude. This also eliminated the original central supply of water, since the men
were often fatigued after hauling this coolant to the engine
gondolas.

Taking into consideration these various high-altitude
problems, it was agreed that only one raid would be staged
during each attack period, and on June 16 Strasser ordered
a force of his dirigibles to attack southern England and
London. Why he risked this period is an indication of his
senseless frenzy, for Klaus Hirsch had warned they would
have nights of only three or four hours of semidarkness
during midsummer. But by now Strasser was a stubborn
fanatic who would hear of no addition in Britain's defenses,
nor take into consideration the laws of the earth's inclina-
tion, and he often insisted that his airship captains imagined seeing British aeroplanes in the sky. He apparently
had influenced his deputy, Viktor Schütze, to adopt the
same blind attitude.

In this Greek tragedy Schütze was selected to lead the
raid, and was given *LZ.48* as his flagship, though the dirigible was actually under the command of Franz Georg
Eichler, whom we left a few pages back when he crashed
his *LZ.36* on the ice of the Aller River. *LZ.48*, one of the
first to be daubed underneath with a coat of black paint,
was walked out of her hangar at Nordholz while the Division Band struck up *The Admiral of the Air* march, but the
skeptics and the superstitious exchanged glances and elbow
nudges when the head of the base drum split across its full
diameter; and Eichler's crew suddenly remembered this
would be their thirteenth raid.

Those dread souls who see tokens and feel presentiments
were treated next to the spectacle of *LZ.46* and *LZ.47* giving
trouble as they were walked out of their sheds owing to
high cross winds. Later on *LZ.44* and *LZ.45* had a full

schedule of engine trouble and both had to limp home across Holland, so only *LZ.42* and *LZ.48* actually reached England.

It was 8:30 P.M. when Dietrich in *LZ.42* saw the British coast and what he took to be Southwold, but he did not head inland immediately. He stood off because of the light and thunderstorms that appeared over the eastern countryside. Shortly after 11:30 P.M. Schütze aboard *LZ.48* radioed that the weather was good for a raid on London, and advised that the attack and departure course be set between east and north.

Dietrich, however, had planned to move inland somewhere between Dover and Dungeness on his track for London, and then by midnight when he thought he was approaching the lights of Dover he found that the SSE wind had strengthened to twenty-seven miles an hour, and he now could see definite thunderstorms off to the west. So he decided to make a short attack on Dover, and following that to go on to London if conditions warranted, but it was not until 2:10 A.M. that he could get into a position where he thought he was doing any good around Dover. When he dropped his first bomb more than a dozen searchlights opened up, antiaircraft guns barked, and an aeroplane was seen some distance below the airship. Several searchlights caught *LZ.42* but could not hold her because of the black undercoating. Dietrich dropped one 660-pound bomb that set up a gigantic explosion below, indicating that a munitions dump had gone up. This fire lasted for more than an hour, and by that time it was impossible to risk a strike on London.

From British newspaper reports Dietrich learned later that though he thought he had bombed both Dover and Deal, he had really struck at Ramsgate about twenty-five miles north of Dover, and somewhat less from Deal. One of his bombs did score roundly, having struck a naval ammunition depot wrecking the naval base. Damage was listed at £29,000. Three civilians were killed, fourteen injured. Only two servicemen were wounded in the ammunition blast. Another point on which Dietrich had been ignorant was that three British aeroplanes had tried to intercept him as he started for his base. A seaplane flying at 11,000 feet off Lowestoft encountered *LZ.42,* but as Dietrich was moving at a 14,800-foot level the pilot in the seaplane had no chance at all.

While *LZ.42* was running clear of this menace, Flight Lieutenant Egbert Cadbury of the R.N.A.S., who was flying a Sopwith Pup out of Great Yarmouth, also took up the chase, but he was too late and too low. An H.12 flying boat from the Yarmouth base chased Dietrich to within ten miles north of Amelund with no better luck, and *LZ.42* returned safely to Nordholz, completing a flight of more than nineteen hours, most of them at an altitude well over 13,000 feet.

LZ.48 under Eichler, with Schütze as raid commander, was first spotted about forty miles northeast of Harwich shortly after 11:30 P.M. The starboard engine quit completely, and the forward engine was running in fits and starts, so Eichler stayed well out to sea until some of the trouble could be corrected—or until 2:00 A.M. The intense cold affected all navigation instruments and Eichler could only determine his position with difficulty and decided there was no chance of getting to London. It was agreed to bomb Harwich instead, and the turn for Nordholz before dawn caught up with them.

LZ.48 apparently crossed the coastline near Orfordness at 3:10 A.M. and approached Harwich from the north. Eichler believed that his bombs had saturated the British naval base "from 18,400 feet in the face of heavy gunfire," but they fell in some open fields five miles north of Harwich. By that time his magnetic compass froze.

The night of June 16–17 was exceptionally clear, and from the ground the Zeppelin could be clearly seen moving across the starlit backdrop. Once he had off-loaded his bombs, Eichler called wireless stations in the German Bight requesting bearings. He was advised to go down to 13,000 feet, a tragic order as matters turned out. During all this

delay several aeroplanes had taken off from local flying
fields. The pilot of one of them was Lieutenant L. P. Watkins of Number 37 Squadron who found the big dirigible
just inside the coastline and heading north. He was fortunate in that Eichler had apparently slowed down to use his
radio for transmissions and reception. Lieutenant Watkins's
report filed afterward read:

> I climbed to 8,000 feet over the aerodrome, then struck off
> in the direction of Harwich, still climbing, when at 11,000
> feet over Harwich I saw the A.A. guns firing and several
> searchlights pointing toward the same spot. A minute later
> I observed the Zeppelin about 2,000 feet above me. After
> climbing about 500 feet I fired one drum into its tail, but
> it took no effect. I then decided to wait until I was at close
> range before firing another drum; then I climbed steadily
> until I reached 13,200 feet and was then about 500 feet
> under the Zeppelin. I fired three short bursts of about seven
> rounds and then the rest of the drum. The Zeppelin burst
> into flames at the tail, the fire running along both sides;
> the whole Zeppelin caught fire and fell burning.

Martin Dietrich, aboard *LZ.42*, was at least seventy miles
away when *LZ.48* went down in flames, but he and his
whole crew witnessed the tragedy, and he wrote in his log:

> At 3:35, two points abaft the port beam, a red ball of fire
> suddenly appeared, which quickly grew bigger and in fall-
> ing showed the shape of a Zeppelin airship. The burning
> ship was at the same altitude as LZ.42, therefore between
> 13,000–14,800 feet. Some 1,600 feet higher a plane was
> clearly visible, which twice fired a white light.

The flame-torched *LZ.48* fell in a field at Holly Tree Farm
near Theberton (near Aldeburgh), and as the hulk continued to burn the lovely midsummer dawn was breaking
across the Suffolk countryside. Schütze and Eichler and
twelve of the crew were killed, either by jumping or by being burned to death.

Amazingly, three members of *LZ.48*'s crew survived—a modern miracle—owing perhaps to the fact that the bow structure remained intact, and it must be presumed that the main framework fell slowly. The executive officer, Leutnant Otto Mieth, survived with two broken legs. Machinist's Mate Heinrich Ellerkamm who had been in charge of the starboard amidships gondola escaped with only superficial burns, but Machinist's Mate Hermann van Stockum died two days later of internal injuries.

Many years later Heinrich Ellerkamm in talking reminiscently with Dr. Douglas H. Robinson, the true Boswell of the German Naval Airship Service, recalled that his life had been miraculously saved twice. He had been a regular crew member of Loewe's ill-fated *LZ.19*, but prior to her last flight he had given up his post to a friend who wished to earn the customary Iron Cross for making a raid.

Ellerkamm always believed it was the frozen compass that betrayed them and sent *LZ.48* off on a northern course when she could have flown due east and been well away from any British aeroplanes. He added: "I still think it was that radio message, telling us to go down to 13,000 feet, explaining that we would find a tail wind at that level, that started our trouble. The English must have intercepted that message."

Ellerkamm was under the impression that they were well out to sea a few minutes prior to Watkins's attack. He was checking fuel for his engine, and then told his helper to take over. He climbed the metal ladder from the gondola to the hull, and as he swung in space there was a faint gleam of the coming dawn to the east. He then suddenly heard a machine gun chattering, and looking below while he still swung from the ladder, he spotted the British aeroplane.

Ellerkamm scrambled up the last few rungs and reached the lateral gangway inside the hull, and because the airship was below pressure height he could look aft, and it was then he spotted a burst of flaming bullets hissing through the after cells. He stood transfixed with horror, and to some extent, fascinated.

"This I knew must be the end!" he explained. "Any one of those bullets could set our hydrogen on fire. There was, in fact, an explosion—not loud—but a dull 'whoof!' just like when you put a match to a gas-range burner. There was a burst of flame. Then another dull explosion."

The German machinist saw one gas cell after another take fire, and he scrambled to climb high into the curved girders. Flames billowed and danced against the upper envelope, and the heat almost overcame him. The fur collar of his flight jacket caught fire and he tried to beat it out with his gloves.

By that time the weight of the heavy two-engined gondola aft was pulling down the stern section, putting the framework into an almost vertical position with the bow up. Ellerkamm hanging there watched the great gouts of flame stream past him, but as the cells and outer envelope were devoured, the slipstream draft carried the flame from him, and he seriously considered taking Schütze's routine advice and jumping, which was "better than burning to death in blazing wreckage on the ground."

At this point the miracle occurred. Still debating whether to jump or not, Ellerkamm suddenly sensed a mad chorus of sound—the smashing of metal against the ground when the burned-out stern struck and the rest of the hull collapsed beneath him. He was snatched from his frail perch and next found himself on the ground, gasping for breath. More framework toppled around him and the fuel, oil, and water tanks, bursting on impact, sloshed their contents over him. Burning fuel spread in all directions, and then began churning toward him like a mad sea. It was this new dread that forced Ellerkamm to his hands and knees to scramble through the tangle of wreckage. All around him were red-hot girders, and the heat bored through his heavy flying coat. He hung on to consciousness, and with his bare hands forced some of the hot girders apart. He had no sense of pain until some time later. He managed to break out of this Dantesque prison and fall full length on the cool wet grass.

He fought to keep his reason, and then realized that a number of farm horses, frightened by the gigantic torch that had been hurled into their pasture, were galloping in all directions, their tails and manes flowing like creatures in a classical frieze. At the same time he again caught the roar of an aeroplane engine, and looking up saw a British plane circling over the funeral pyre of LZ.48. He believed the pilot waved to him, for it was almost full daylight.

"I wanted to rest there and collect my senses, but by now the fire was roaring at my back," Ellerkamm remembered. "I crawled away a little and then tried to look about and take some stock. Korvettenkapitän Schütze had jumped as he always said he would. He was dead, and his legs had gone into the ground up to his knees."

Some English people appeared and helped him drag Leutnant Mieth out of the wreckage of the radio cabin in the control car. One of them took Ellerkamm to his home where he collapsed for a time. When he came to he asked to see Mieth, but this was refused. In all probability the injured Leutnant had been taken to a hospital nearby.

Later consideration indicated that Ellerkamm survived with so few injuries because his gondola was 300 feet from the tail cone, and considering the position during the fall, the tail structure broke the force of the impact, and the bow that remained intact did not completely trap the machinist.

This loss was the most devastating blow Strasser suffered. He not only lost his valued deputy, but a brand-new airship and most experienced crew. When Dietrich sent his message telling of the destruction of LZ.48, Strasser went out to the field to get the details first hand. He climbed aboard LZ.42 the minute she touched down and imperiously demanded to know what had happened. He could not be reconciled to the fact that a British aeroplane had trapped LZ.48.

"Impossible!" he raged. "The English have no real defense against our 'height climbers.' "

Martin Dietrich did his best to explain that he had really seen an aeroplane above the burning airship. With that, Strasser climbed down again, only partly convinced, but dejected nevertheless. He went to his quarters and refused to be disturbed. He would see no one, or answer the telephone.

Then, a few days later, he suddenly appeared, fairly cheerful, and invited all his airship commanders to a small party—which was unusual—and he was encouraged when one or two of his chief officers assured him that with the new height climbers they would be able to outwit the British pilots. "It means we'll have to use our oxygen," they explained.

Strasser was so inspired with this, he immediately wrote a note to Admiral Scheer in which he repeated his belief in the Zeppelins, and revealed that he dreaded having the British laugh at him if the raids were called off. He pounded at the old factor that the raids still caused tremendous expense to the British, and that they had always "deliberately minimized the effects of the attacks," and had shown such jubilation whenever a German airship was destroyed. On the face of this, the attacks should be continued.

There is no record of what Admiral Scheer remarked in return.

XI

THE FLYING BOAT MENACE

In the late spring of 1917 the British anti-Zeppelin crusade took a bizarre turn when a new type of aircraft and airman picked up the gauntlet. While the land planes of the Royal Flying Corps were being modified and improved to compete with the increased speed and performance capabilities of the dirigibles, while the Royal Navy was making some progress in their development of what we know today as an aircraft carrier, the Royal Naval Air Service provided a new menace in the form—of all things—a "giant" flying boat that carried a crew of four and mounted several machine guns in very efficient turrets. In other words, the R.N.A.S. at last had an aircraft that could carry the offensive deep into the enemy's area.

The development of this flying boat furnishes an interesting story. A few months prior to the outbreak of the war, Lieutenant John Cyril Porte, an airman of the British Navy, planned to make a flight across the Atlantic Ocean, and designed a seaplane he considered to be capable of making the long crossing. His effort, both sporting and scientific, was backed by Rodman Wanamaker, scion of John Wanamaker the department store tycoon. As a result Porte's flying boat, by now named *America*, was built by Glenn Curtiss at Hammondsport, New York, and was powered by two

25. An aerial view of the famous revolving hangar at Nordholz. The administrative buildings and the radio station are to be seen at the upper portion of the photograph.—FRIEDRICH MOCH PHOTO.

26. The short-run deck mounted on a Navy barge and the Sopwith Camel flown by Lieutenant Culley. The officer in the foreground is Commander C. R. Samson, legendary hero of the Royal Naval Air Service.—WHITEHOUSE PHOTO.

27. The German Zeppelin *LZ.53* which was shot down by Lieutenant S. D. Culley who had taken off aboard a Sopwith Camel, mounted on a lighter towed by a British destroyer. This was the first intercept and kill by a deck-launched aircraft.—IMPERIAL WAR MUSEUM PHOTO.

27a. Another view of *LZ.53*, the last dirigible to be destroyed by British forces, is shown being walked into the building shed at Friedrichshafen. This gives some idea of the size of these late wartime Zeppelins.—LUFTSCHIFFBAU ZEPPELIN PHOTO.

28. Fregattenkapitan Peter Strasser, leader of Airships of the German Naval Airship Division posing with his *Ordre Pour le Merite* ribbon around his neck outside the Officers' Club of the Ahlhorn station.—FRIEDRICH MOCH PHOTO.

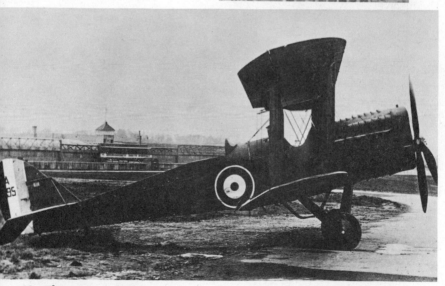

29. The type of D.H.4 two-seater employed by the British Home Defense forces to intercept and destroy German Zeppelins. It was aboard this type of plane that Cadbury and Leckie brought down *LZ.70* and ended Peter Strasser's career.—DE HAVILLAND PHOTO.

30. The Felixstown type flying boat employed by the Royal Naval Air Service to track down and destroy Zeppelins. In spite of their bulk and vintage, these aircraft performed their tasks well.—ROLLS-ROYCE PHOTO.

31. These black-painted F.E. 2b pushers, first used as two-seater fighters on the Western Front, were later employed as Zeppelin fighters, flying from British bases. They also served with rare distinction with General Hugh Trenchard's famous Independent Air Force.—DE HAVILLAND PHOTO.

90-horsepower Curtiss engines. After a number of successful
flights over Lake Keuka in July 1914, the final preparations
to make the attempt were well under way when the German Army stormed into Belgium.

Lieutenant Porte was recalled to England and almost immediately placed in charge of the R.N.A.S. station at Felixstowe, and commissioned to build a number of flying boats
along the lines of the Curtiss-built *America* but incorporating many features to fit the military program. Porte immediately went to work but it was early in 1917 before this
particular type was ready for war patrols. Part of the delay
was due to the fact that the young British naval man had
to devote some time to the development of smaller types
that became known as *Baby* seaplanes. He also produced,
in co-operation with the Short brothers, the even more famous "F" type flying boats, particularly the F3, a twin-
engined, four-place machine that was powered with two
Rolls-Royce engines of 400-horsepower each, and which are
known in some histories as the H.12. Other versions of the
original *America* evolved into the famed "NC" boats of the
United States Navy, one of which, the NC-4, was the first
aeroplane to cross the Atlantic.

A number of these H.12-type flying boats (as we shall
call them in this chapter), had a new and quite unexpected
role in the continued war against the Zeppelins. Much of
this resulted from the British Navy's lack of a practical
lighter-than-air craft, and, to some extent, the Air Staff's
annoyance with the enemy's ability to protect German
minesweepers and submarines with Zeppelin reconnaissance, for the dirigibles generally could spot British surface
vessels whenever they moved into the German Bight—particularly in good weather.

To counter this the British planned a form of naval aviation attack that either would destroy the gasbags in their
hangars or meet them on more even terms at the lower
levels used by the Zeppelins when carrying out naval reconnaissance. This required wheeled aircraft that could be
flown off flight decks, or hydroplanes that could be put

over the side from mother ships to attack the airships as they flew their escort patrols over the minesweepers or U-boats. But what appeared to be a more practical proposal was the development of long-range flying boats—aircraft that could reach out across the North Sea, bomb the Zeppelin hangars, and still be able to protect themselves against land-based enemy aircraft. It will be seen that all the later problems of strategic aviation were being encountered, one by one.

The Germans did not believe their enemies had such a naval aircraft, although they themselves were developing the twin-engined Gotha that was to bomb London from the Gontrode base in Belgium. They were smug in their belief that the British had nothing that could fly out to the German Bight and return, and they were to eat crow for their complacency. For months they had quietly enjoyed Britain's vain effort to bring floatplanes into the Bight, a feature they thought had been given up two years before.

But something new was being developed. In the early months of 1917 the Grand Fleet took Sopwith Pup land-plane-fighters to sea aboard cross-Channel steamers, *Manxman, Pegasus,* and *Nairana* fitted with short flying-off decks mounted forward. The aircraft were launched successfully, but no Zeppelins were sighted, and no outstanding success achieved. In March of that year the Aircraft Committee of the Royal Navy recommended that the *Furious,* a light battle cruiser, be converted into an aircraft carrier, and the result came as close to the design of the modern concept of a flattop as one could expect to find in those early days. *Furious* had a 228-foot-long flight deck that was built over the stern half of the hull. She also had a variation of the offset bridge, and her speed of thirty knots permitted planes to be flown off, but the problem of flying back on was not solved until August 3, 1917, when Squadron Commander E. H. Dunning, flying a Sopwith Pup, made the first true deck landing. This was accomplished by skidding to a stop, rather than relying on any built-in arrester gear. But two days later, in trying to repeat the performance, a wheel tire burst, the Pup rolled over the side, and Dunning was lost. After this accident further study was made of an elementary arrester gear, and a rope-net buffer was erected to protect the bridge.

Furious was later placed in service with this deck modification. She accommodated five Pups, and it was agreed that for the time being they would take off from the flight deck, but would not attempt a landing on, but "ditch" in the sea nearby. Added to this flight fleet was one vessel in each light cruiser squadron that was equipped to carry a Pup on a short platform mounted over the forward guns. HMS *Yarmouth,* the first light cruiser so equipped, was to achieve a memorable victory.

The Germans contributed to their own downfall by careless use of their radio facilities, not realizing how well the British Admiralty's radio intelligence service was improving. It was routine for the Zeppelins to give an initial signal whenever they left their bases for a raid, but when on Naval reconnaissance missions they not only signaled their departure, but keyed off an advice with every change of course. They made bold requests for bearings, made uncoded reports on the position of ships, and carelessly gave out local weather conditions. In fact, while LZ.22 was in an exposed area off Terschelling, she sent off nine definite radio signals during a thirteen-and-one-half-hour patrol. Each of these messages enabled the British to fix her position accurately. Augmenting this hour-by-hour coverage of Zeppelin movements, they developed a coded position chart for all air stations, and each dirigible as it unwittingly announced its departure was plotted as "Annie," "Betty," or "Clara," in alphabetical order, just as today we designate the movement of threatening hurricanes. It was the development of this tracing system that brought about the destruction of LZ.22 by a British flying boat crew on their first aerial foray into the Bight.

On the morning of May 14, after being frustrated for more than a week by foul weather, Strasser ordered LZ.23

to fly a defensive patrol to the north. *LZ.22*, berthed in the ex-Army hangar at Wittmundhaven, was sent to the western sector. Admiralty monitors caught *LZ.22*'s take-off report, and guessing that she was heading for the area north and south off Terschelling, alerted the Great Yarmouth air station, and ordered a flying boat out to intercept her.

At 4:30 A.M. the H.12 flying boat Number 8666, manned by Flight Lieutenant C. J. Galpin and Flight Lieutenant Robert Leckie, Chief Petty Officer V. F. Whatling, and Air Mechanic O. R. Laycock, was airborne, carrying three Lewis guns and drums of explosive and incendiary ammunition as well as four 100-pound bombs. Leckie who had been born in Glasgow, later became Air Marshal of the Royal Canadian Air Force and served with distinction during World War II.

The take-off with 265 gallons of gasoline and her full complement was uneventful, but once she was eighty miles from her base the crew observed radio silence to cover her approach. Galpin first sighted *LZ.22* when she was about fifteen miles away, and fortunately flying at a very low level. The flying boat was passing the Terschelling Light vessel at about 5000 feet and cruising at 60 knots. Galpin, who was at the wheel, increased speed and climbed to 6000 feet, after jettisoning three of her four bombs. At this time Leckie took over the controls, Whatling went aft to man the rear gun, and Galpin moved up into the nose cockpit where he settled behind a double-Lewis clamped on a Scarff mounting.

They watched the Zeppelin turn north and then northeast, showing her full broadside. By this time Number 8666 was about two miles astern, and by nosing down to 5000 feet increased her speed to 75 knots. Up to this point there was no indication the Zeppelin lookouts had spotted the British flying boat, but when Leckie moved in to within half a mile, *LZ.22* seemed to raise her nose and put on increased speed. Leckie dived steeper and reached 90 knots and came up slightly astern at 3800 feet where he leveled off at 75 knots. They soon overhauled the Zeppelin and crossed under the starboard quarter about twenty feet below the gondolas.

Galpin opened fire at fifty yards range and watched his incendiaries enter the envelope on the starboard quarter. After a few rounds the port gun jammed, but the other continued to fire until it had consumed almost a full drum when it jammed too. Galpin took immediate action to clear his weapons, and when about one hundred feet from the Zeppelin Leckie put the flying boat into a tight, banked turn. It was then that Galpin saw what appeared to be a slight glow inside the outer envelope. A few seconds later when they could study her from the other side, LZ.22 had seemed to become tail-heavy, and obviously was struggling to climb at a 45-degree angle. The lower half of the envelope was now on fire, and five or six seconds later she was being consumed and falling vertically by the tail. Whatling, who was observing from the rear hatch, saw the number "22" painted under the nose before that part of the envelope was destroyed.

Galpin also saw two crew members leap out, one from the gun position near the tail fin, and one from the after gondola. As the doomed Zeppelin reached the 1000-foot level, four towering columns of water shot up from the sea, indicating that bombs or engines had fallen from the gondolas. Within forty-five seconds the gaunt skeleton of LZ.22 nosed into the water like a giant shell, sending up a pillar of brown smoke and leaving a pattern of black ash on the surface. The pillar of smoke rose to a height of 1500 feet and held there like a brown granite monolithic shaft. Number 8666 then set course for home with only a few bullet holes in her wings.

An interesting feature of this attack and victory is that the Zeppelin commander apparently had no time to radio he was being attacked by a British flying boat, and that Leckie and Galpin had managed to conceal their presence. Strasser did not know what had brought on this tragedy, or that his airships might be attacked again by this improbable weapon.

Erich Sommerfeldt, skipper of *LZ.40*, was the first German commander to meet one of these H.12 flying boats, and
live to tell the tale. While returning from the raid made on
the evening of May 23–24, he was intercepted by the same
Number 8666 piloted by Flight Lieutenant Galpin. The flying boat had been sent off from Yarmouth early that morning, and had immediately headed out for Terschelling but
failed to sight anything. Galpin returned, flying at 1200 feet
because of low visibility. Then, at 6:38 A.M. a German dirigible nosed out of the clouds at the 1600-foot level.

On spotting the flying boat Sommerfeldt dropped two
white flares, probably requesting a recognition signal, but
Galpin dropped his bombs instead, and nosed up toward the
dirigible. *LZ.40* was then put into a sharp climbing turn and
when she had reached 3000 feet Galpin had gained on the
airship, and was only 300 yards astern. Sommerfeldt released a smoke screen, and aided by that reached a nearby
bank of clouds. Galpin decided not to risk following, but
fired off half a drum of Brock, Pomeroy, and tracer bullets with no observable effect.

Sommerfeldt turned in a report on this encounter and
admitted he had received twelve bullet holes, but could not
bring himself to concede that the flying boat had flown from
British soil; it must have been launched from an enemy vessel below. He was to encounter Number 8666 once more
within two weeks.

While making a patrol west of Terschelling on June 5,
LZ.40 was again attacked by the Leckie-Galpin duo who
were aboard the same H.12 flying boat. The airship was first
observed six miles away about 2000 feet below their level,
and off to the northeast. The Britishers went down to 4000
feet but the Zeppelin disappeared in a low layer of mist.
About 8:10 A.M. they picked her up again, now flying east
by north, and at the same level as the flying boat. *LZ.40*'s
signalman fired a white light and Leckie replied with a
white Very signal but continued the pursuit for half an
hour. In that time *LZ.40* had been taken up to 10,500 feet,
but Number 8666 was almost directly under her. At one

time the British crew opened fire from 600 yards with the
two forward guns, and in the next twenty minutes triggered
off at least ten drums of Brock, Pomeroy, and Buckingham
ammunition, but because of the range it is possible that the
incendiary effect of the rounds was nullified; at any rate
LZ.40 escaped again.

Amazingly, Sommerfeldt persisted in believing this aircraft had been put overboard from a seaplane carrier, and
as such was to be treated with contempt. This is all the
more remarkable as Sommerfeldt had had five hours of ex-
traordinary visibility but had seen no enemy vessel that
could have brought the flying boat into his area.

June 14, 1917, was another fateful day in the history of
Zeppelin operations when Strasser sent off two of his latest
airships, *LZ.46* and *LZ.48* with orders to patrol the U-boat
blockade seas, and to pay special attention to traffic in the
Dogger Bank area and along the western portion of a line
through Lindesnes-St. Abb's Head, Scotland, and Farne Islands off Northumberland. *LZ.48* was given a particular mission to scout between Kristiansand, Norway, and the Firth
of Forth. Airships *LZ.23*, *LZ.42*, and *LZ.43* were assigned
to routine patrol duties.

These last three Zeppelins took off about 2:00 A.M. to
cover German minesweepers working forty miles north of
Terschelling, and *LZ.43* was assigned to the exposed western sector from where her commander Kraushaar reported
by radio at 6:36 A.M. that he was on station near the lightship and was starting his patrol. Unknown to Kraushaar,
the British Admiralty had been operating their search network and had located two airships over the German Bight,
and as the first one monitored appeared to be heading west,
an H.12, Number 8677, flying boat took off from Felixstowe
with Flight Sub-Lieutenants B. D. Hobbs and R. F. L.
Dickey, Air Mechanic H. M. Davies, a wireless operator,
and Air Mechanic A. W. Goody, an engineer.

Number 8677 was airborne at 5:15 (British time) and by
7:30 was near Vlieland off the Dutch coast. Their patrol

was carried out under a prearranged system that because of its efficiency was known as the Spider Web. At 7:58 they were off Ameland Island from where they changed course for Felixstowe. By 8:40 A.M. they were again off Vlieland, flying at 500 feet when they saw a Zeppelin about five miles off their starboard bow. The airship was flying at the 1500-foot level and heading north.

The British crew put on top speed and went in for an attack, climbing to 2000 feet as they closed the gap. Hobbs was piloting the flying boat while Dickey manned the single gun in the bow. Davies took over the amidship weapon, and Goody manned the stern turret that bore two guns.

Hobbs put Number 8677 into a sharp dive, moving at 100 knots, and in time they could identify the airship as LZ.43, marked on her bow and tail. She also bore a Maltese (Iron) Cross on her bow. Davies in the amidship turret opened fire with tracer ammunition, and Dickey followed suit with Brock and Pomeroy, and then as the flying boat passed over the dirigible two more bursts were fired and LZ.43 burst into flames. Hobbs cut his engines and went into a sharp turn as they watched the airship falling enveloped completely in flames. On the way down three men fell or jumped from the gondolas. The smoke and flame were observed for some time after the blackened wreckage hit the water. Setting course for Felixstowe Number 8677 arrived back at 11:15 A.M.

LZ.43 had been in service for about three months, and as the British Admiralty issued only a short concise statement concerning the victory of Number 8677, all the German Naval Airship Service knew was that LZ.43 failed to acknowledge the weather map radioed from Nordholz that morning, and only when a report turned in by Heinrich Hollender of LZ.46 was studied did Strasser have any idea what new menace was threatening his service.

Hollender had arrived off Dogger Bank and found a strong SSE wind, so obeying orders he moved to cover the southern sector of the blockade area, instead of heading for the Firth of Forth. He, also, could not know that his moves had been traced in London, and that H.12 Number 8660 flying boat with the staunch team of Galpin and Leckie, had been sent out to intercept him. At 8:18 *LZ.46* was near the Hook of Holland, and at 9:08 A.M. the British flying boat had reached the Noord Hinder Light and was turning north to weave the Spider Web. A few minutes later they spotted *LZ.46* some fifteen miles to the east, and heading west at an altitude of about 10,500 feet.

Leckie was at the wheel, and he turned and climbed to meet the Zeppelin. Hollender spotted his adversary and immediately dumped considerable water ballast and went up to 15,000 feet. He then turned NNE and cleared off. Leckie decided to hang on and by 8:45 (his time) had climbed to 12,500 feet and was in a position directly below the big gasbag. Galpin fired four drums of Brock, Pomeroy, and Buckingham, and thought some of his tracers were perforating the envelope, but, again, the phosphorous core must have burned out before contact was made with the gas cells. He also thought a number of his explosive bullets scored, but they afforded no satisfaction. In reply, Hollender's gunners fired a short burst of tracer at the flying boat, but scored no hits. At 9:15 Leckie decided he was wasting time and ammunition, so broke off the action.

Hollender reported he had been attacked by an English seaplane, a biplane with two occupants and one machine gun that fired from the stern. This was the best his lookouts could make of the twin-engined flying boat that carried a crew of four and had three gun positions. With this vague interpretation of his adversary, it is understandable that Strasser presumed that this was the same British aeroplane that had destroyed *LZ.43*, and he issued a new order setting up special precautions and new minimum altitudes for all airships patrolling off Terschelling.

The success of Britain's new flying boats weaving their Spider Web across the German Bight added new terrors to the Zeppelin crews, for now each simple scouting flight had become as dangerous as a major raid on London. The added height brought all the altitude problems, and made more difficult the requirements for reliable reconnaissance. The airshipmen were to learn that the long-range flying boats seriously restricted the range of fleet scouting.

Another point, somewhat personal, arises at this juncture. It would be interesting to learn who of these four-man flying boat crews was given credit for the destruction of these dirigibles. Unquestionably, in many instances, the credit went to the pilot, a standard used in most British two-seater fighter squadrons on the Western Front. Who, for instance, actually shot down *LZ.43?* Air Mechanic Davies or Sub-Lieutenant Dickey? The author spent many months as a noncommissioned aerial gunner with a two-seater fighter squadron on the Western Front, and it has always been difficult to learn whether all my "kills" were credited to me, to my pilot, or to the squadron score in general. Who would have been given credit for *LZ.48*, had she been shot down? Galpin, or one of the NCO gunners? And how could they tell? Also, how would the score value of a Zeppelin compare to shooting down a single Fokker D-VII?

Ah, but we mustn't confuse the long-standing "ace" situation.

Galpin, Leckie and Co., a very profitable flight organization, was sent off again on the morning of July 26 after monitored radio signals indicated that three Zeppelins had been ordered to patrol the German Bight. The airships concerned were *LZ.45*, assigned to the north, *LZ.44* to the middle, and *LZ.46* for the west. In the vicinity of Texel, Leckie headed farther east to use the islands as a camouflage, and at 9:10 A.M. his crew sighted a Zeppelin (*LZ.46*) flying at 10,000 feet some fifteen miles to the north. Number 8666 was at the same altitude and when the Zepp turned westward the flying boat was approaching on the airship's port beam, and from all indications the dirigible commander was unaware of the plane's presence. Leckie had the sun behind him, and it wasn't until he was within a mile of *LZ.46* that he noticed any reaction. Ballast went overboard and the airship began to climb fast and did not ease off until she had reached 12,000 feet when she turned northeast and headed for home.

Galpin fired several drums of explosive and incendiary ammunition from the 11,500-foot level but with no effect. When the flying boat appeared to be directly below, the Zeppelin released two bombs and then opened up with a machine gun. Some bullet holes were found in the center section of the top plane, just missing the built-in gravity tank.

Maintaining their position, Leckie and Galpin flew the web until 10:00 A.M. when they observed another Zeppelin about ten miles away and moving at 8000 feet. They worked to within three miles of this airship when she too put up her nose, released ballast and soared to 15,000 feet, and turned east. Galpin decided this one had been warned by *LZ.46*, so he gave up the hopeless chase and returned home.

Hollender reported that he had had several unhappy moments, particularly when Number 8666 was firing long bursts of incendiary ammunition, and had feared his ship's destruction was certain. Only his ability to get a 2960-feet-per-minute rate of climb enabled him to evade the twin-engined nemesis. *LZ.44*, which had indeed been warned by Hollender, turned to a northeast course before the wind. Then in response to a series of radio messages, two squadrons of seaplane fighters were sent out of Borkum, and land-based fighters from Wilhelmshaven. Four of these planes did furnish escort for *LZ.44*, but were not there in time to intercept Number 8666.

In recording this aeroplane co-operation, it might be well to report that on the morning of August 21, *LZ.23* took off from Tondern to make a routine patrol. At 5:40 A.M. her commander, Oberleutnant Bernhard Dinter, reported sighting four British *Aurora* class light cruisers and fifteen destroyers thirty miles west of Bovbjerg. The cruisers were the 3rd Light Cruiser Squadron of the Grand Fleet making a periodic sweep off the coast of Jutland.

This foray showed that something new had been added,

for HMS *Yarmouth* was carrying a Sopwith Pup on a platform mounted over the forward guns. While the unsuspect-
ing Dinter stalked the British warships, Flight Sub-Lieutenant B. A. Smart took off to make an attack. It should be
noted that in this instance the standard roundels, usually
shown on the wings and fuselage, had been daubed out
with gray paint. Lieutenant Smart got off safely at 6:40
A.M. and went after the Zeppelin which at that time was
about ten to fifteen miles away. He climbed steadily at 55
knots until he reached 9000 feet, keeping the airship in sight
most of the time. He then nosed down until his air speed
touched 100 knots, for the Zeppelin was well below him.

He managed to get to a position 1500 feet above the
dirigible, or at an altitude of 7000 feet. Moving to a location
directly astern, and in such a spot where none of the
gondola guns could be trained on him, he dived at 45 degrees at a speed of 130 knots. Spotting a top gun platform
he then began to zigzag until he was well within range.

His first burst fired from 150–200 yards was a trifle high,
so he nose-dived, leveled off, and fired continuously until
he was within twenty yards of the tail and rudders. A
tongue of flame burst out and Smart turned only just in
time to avoid crashing into the Zeppelin. He cleared and
flew around until the flaming hulk smashed into the sea.
He then flew on to join the surface ships, ditched ahead of
a destroyer, and was picked up safely, but only his plane's
engine and one of his machine guns was salvaged. From the
British viewpoint, however, it was better than a fair exchange. One Sopwith Pup for a new Zeppelin and her crew.

XII

BALTIC OPERATIONS

Intermittent references have been made to Zeppelin operations in the Baltic and along the Russian front, and it would seem well at this point to provide some details. Historians have not given much time or space to these actions, possibly because of the nature of the patrols, the lack of drama, compared to the raids and actions carried out across the North Sea, and quite possibly because the missions and incidents were not diligently recorded at the time. At any rate, the popular histories published shortly after the war afforded little space to the careers of the airshipmen who served their time in keeping a watch on the inert Russian Navy.

But interestingly enough, it was on the Baltic Front that the German Naval Airship Division suffered its first wartime loss on January 25, 1915, when *PL.19* (a small Parseval type) went down while attempting to carry out a varied-duty mission over the Baltic.

PL.19 was a small pressure airship capable of handling a useful load of only 7300 pounds, and on her arrival at the scene of operations she was selected to raid the Russian naval base at Libau (Liepāja), 125 miles to the north; taking on as a sideline a foundry, some rolling mills, an oil refinery, storage tanks, Navy Yard barracks and machine shops, and the railroad bridge over the river on the main line to Vilna and Riga. On the way there and back her commander, an Oberleutnant Meier who was assisted by a Dr. Rötzell, a "volunteer airship pilot," was asked to search for Russian minefields off Libau and Memel (Klaipèda). How such an airship and its scratch crew could be expected to carry out such a fantastic mission is beyond normal understanding.

Twice Meier and Rötzell tried to get off, but were held on the ground by the weather. Then, on January 15, with a full crew of seven, and carrying seven 110-pound bombs, *PL.19* headed north over the Baltic where she immediately ran into low clouds and severe icing conditions. Neither Meier or Dr. Rötzell had encountered such a situation before, and when chunks of ice were slung from the propellers and through the envelope Dr. Rötzell thought it was congealed oil from the gear casing. Meier was just as bewildered by the coating of hoarfrost that accumulated all over the airship.

These conditions soon forced the 650-foot-long Parseval down low and damp gas had to be valved, after which the seat of an automatic valve iced up and hydrogen leaked out at a dangerous rate. The ship had taken off at 3:20 A.M., and by 8:45 A.M. had reached the vicinity of Libau that could be seen through a hole in the clouds.

Meier brought his ship as close as he could, and tried from 1500 feet to bomb what looked like a factory. His first 110-pounder failed to explode, so he dropped the rest, and shot up into the clouds again with no idea of what might have happened below. He ventured back through the cloud layer and came under heavy fire from a Russian battery, but, according to Meier's log, no damage was done and he turned away and steered for the open sea.

Once in the clear, the crew of *PL.19*, believing they had struck a telling blow, suddenly heard a terrific crash overhead. Then the starboard propeller halted and the engine stalled. It was discovered that a gear case had broken up, unmeshing the gears, and *PL.19*, still heavy with ice, began to lose height, threatening to nose into the sea. The crew jettisoned everything available and held her at the 1000-foot level, but then the port engine stopped, simply because the airship was tilted at a sharp angle and the gravity fuel line could not get gasoline to the carburetors. This loss of power cut off the blowers that maintained the ballonets and the main envelope buckled amidships.

Meier and Rötzell did their best, but it was not enough, and at 9:40 A.M. *PL.19* piled up in the sea seven miles offshore. They hoped they might be rescued by a German vessel, but no such succor was in sight, and by noon two Russian minesweepers chugged up and started firing at the hulk with machine guns. Meier had no choice but to surrender. He and his crew were taken aboard, after which the Russians set their airship afire and left her blazing on the water.

This setback discouraged further airship operations in that area until mid-July 1915 when *LZ.5* was sent to take part in the German assault on Riga, but before she could assume any role in that campaign she was lost during a daylight raid on Dünamünde (Daugavgriva), a harbor and fortress at the mouth of the Dvina River on the Gulf of Riga. She was replaced by a Schütte-Lanz, *SL.4*, that made a number of short reconnaissance flights for the German Fleet's attempt to break into the Gulf of Riga that August, but after this plan failed the Baltic airship service became a secondary arm to which Strasser shipped most of his Schütte-Lanz dirigibles, airships he heartily despised.

By the middle of 1915 Admiral Prince Henry, a brother of the Kaiser and commander-in-chief in the Baltic, became interested in dirigibles and thought they could make a vital raid on the then Russian capital, St. Petersburg, although the small airships assigned to the Baltic could not fly that far. But in August 1916 the Kaiser thought the bombing of St. Petersburg would cause the Russian Army to surrender immediately. Finally Strasser was convinced that with the long winter nights such a raid might be carried out, and eventually the plan, known as Operation Iron

Cross, was slated for November 29, 1916, but nothing much was accomplished until mid-December by which time *LZ.35* and *LZ.38* were flown east from Ahlhorn to be accommodated in available sheds built at Wainoden, Courland (Kurland), formerly Russian territory. It was less than four hundred miles from this temporary base to St. Petersburg, now Leningrad.

A few short forays were made, mainly to "dry out" the airships, while waiting for favorable weather, but by December 26, 1916, the two big Zeppelins left during the early dusk with more than three tons of bombs and fuel for a twenty-four-hour flight, and began another saga of wartime airship raiding.

LZ.35, commanded by Herbert Ehrlich, logged a dreadful flight. He found himself over Libau at 5:00 P.M. and he hoped to fly on to Winau and make the Finnish Gulf. Ninety minutes later he tried climbing through a 3000-foot cloud layer and came out at 8200 feet where his ship iced up fast. A layer of frozen snow, collecting on the tail section, put *LZ.35* into a nose-up position that had to be compensated for by hurried ballast shifting. At 7:00 she was in the clear under a bright star-sprinkled sky, but it was bitterly cold and a northwest wind was blowing at 45 miles per hour. The port engine failed and froze up after an oil line broke, which made the battle with the wind all the more difficult, and engine trouble increased as the cold congealed the oil in the feed lines. The mechanics had to ladle the semi-solid lubricant out of the tanks and supply it to the engines by hand.

About 1:00 A.M. Ehrlich spotted a number of lights that he thought were Baltic Port (Paldiski), but had to give up any thought of an attack there knowing it would be dawn before he could reach the target against that wind. Turning southwest, he moved along the coast buffeted by heavy snow squalls. When he was at 1300 feet he found that the wind had veered into the SSE and was still blowing at 45 miles per hour. His troubles compounded when the starboard outrigger propeller shaft broke, and there were times when Ehrlich's airship was standing still. As the time approached 5:00 A.M. he risked going down to 500 feet where he found a more favorable wind and conditions that might permit him to start up the port after engine without serious damage to the bearings. Under all these hazards he finally brought LZ.35 in and landed at 9:10 A.M., having been in the air for nearly seventeen hours.

LZ.38 was under command of Martin Dietrich who had much the same experience. On taking off, he climbed through two layers of heavy cloud and came out in the clear at 9200 feet. Continuing up to 10,200 feet he found the temperature down to 8 degrees below zero, and his crew suffered severely in their inadequate clothing. The compass froze, and the oil lines soon clogged with congealed lubricant, and the mechanics had to drag 90-pound oil containers along the greasy catwalk, down ice-coated ladders to get oil to the engines. This improvisation in turn provided too much oil, and one by one the spark plugs fouled and had to be changed and cleaned, time after time.

By 9:00 P.M. Dietrich turned to the north, hoping to bomb military installations on Oesel Island, better known as Sarema, in the east Baltic Sea, but a display of the aurora borealis was so bright he wondered if he should take the risk. At 1:22 A.M. he thought he was near the port of Arendsburg on Oesel, but he could not see through the heavy cloud layer, so he abandoned the whole thing at 2:21 A.M. and turned SSW. At that time, too, the starboard amidships engine ran unevenly and caused some damage to the reduction gears.

All during this time Dietrich had been relying on radio bearings, and believed the prevailing wind had come from the southwest. Uncertain and plagued with so many hazards, he hovered above the clouds until dawn. At 4:45 A.M. his starboard after engine went out with the freezing of its radiator while plugs were being changed, so at 7:00 A.M. Dietrich went down to 1000 feet and steered for the coast through a driving snowstorm. A layer of ice accumulated almost immediately, and fragments were breaking off and being batted through the outer cover and gas cells from the blades of the propellers. The ship became heavy with the loss of lifting gas and she was also stern heavy. This continued for some minutes until at last LZ.38 wallowed down toward the water.

Dietrich ordered many of the bombs jettisoned, and 880 pounds of fuel was dropped overboard, actions that halted the descent just as the rear section was dragging across the waters of the Baltic. Still weighted down by a pile of snow on the stabilizers, LZ.38 was 15 degrees out of trim. The engines had to be stopped, the men had to rush ballast forward to keep her from nosing up into the clouds, the remaining 1200 pounds of bombs had to be man-hauled along the catwalks to the nose of the ship, and the fuel redistributed by hand pumping. Dietrich finally brought LZ.38 in this condition back to the coast near Libau, and at 10:00 A.M. she was still struggling south through thick snow with her crewmen hardly able to see the ground. More bombs were dropped off, the reserve fuel went overboard, and she just staggered on. Knowing there was a good chance he could be driven out to sea, Dietrich finally decided to put her down on land, and when an evergreen forest came into sight he dropped the 6600-pound heavy ship into the trees without the loss of a single life. A few men were sent off to get aid while the rest of the crew tried to tie LZ.38 down safely. The strong wind repeatedly wrenched the great frame about and she eventually broke her back in the middle. The whole hulk finally collapsed in the snow.

This forced landing had fortunately been made at Seemuppen, Courland, formerly Russian territory, but now in the hands of the Germans.

Strasser was disgusted with this Baltic interlude and evaded sending a new airship to replace LZ.38, and then induced the Naval Staff to return Ehrlich's LZ.35 to the

North Sea Fleet. No further attempts were made to bomb St. Petersburg, and what airship missions were made in the Baltic area were routine reconnaissance flights, chiefly to combat boredom.

When the Baltic detachment of the Naval Airship Division was called on in September and October of 1917 to support the German Army's major move on the islands of Dago, Oesel, and Moon, a new Zeppelin problem arose when it was discovered that the available hydrogen-producing plants could not keep up with the enormous expenditure of gas needed to keep the six ships employed by the Baltic force in the air, and by this time the 2,000,000-cubic foot capacity Schütte-Lanz ship, the SL.20, had been sent east.

There was a mild furor over the gas situation, and eventually the problem was partly solved by having a number of railroad gas-tank cars rushed to the Baltic Command. Several of the available dirigibles could then put on a show of sorts, but though the German Army's only amphibious operation of that war was a success, their real support was furnished by the German Navy warships that had little scouting help from the airships. Inclement weather prevented their covering the actual landing on Oesel, and shortly after this doubtful operation the Baltic detachment was disbanded.

Kapitänleutnant Johann von Lossnitzer, commander of L.120 of the Baltic detachment, wrote an impassioned appreciation of the airship, claiming that the High Seas Fleet would be unable to operate without the high-level scouting of Zeppelins and argued further that it was Germany's responsibility to develop this weapon to its utmost. Strasser was delighted with this report and made Lossnitzer his adjutant. Nine months later he signed the Prussian nobleman's death warrant when he gave him command of Germany's newest and finest airship, the LZ.70.

The entrance of the United States into the war on the side of the Allies had immediate repercussions in the German High Command, particularly when American politicians boasted that Made-in-America warplanes would darken the European skies by 1918—boasts that were never even remotely fulfilled. However, General Erich Ludendorff, then First Quartermaster General, put forward his "Amerika-Programm" that featured a greatly expanded aeroplane production, and to attempt this vast quantities of aluminum and rubber would be needed. This meant a drastic cut in the Zeppelin program. Until the summer of 1917 the German Navy had been receiving an average of two new Zeppelins every month. By the time Ludendorff was through, this production had been cut to one half a ship every month. This meant that Strasser might be limited to Naval scouting patrols with a fleet of eighteen airships and replacements of one half an airship per month.

Of course Strasser had no intention of being confined to such a minor role in the war, and by late summer of 1917 was drawing up new plans to vent his wrath on the British. On August 21, flying in *LZ.46*, one of the high-altitude ships, he led an eight-Zeppelin raid, but only one of these airships reached England. *LZ.41* cruised over the Hull area, and her bombs destroyed a chapel and injured one civilian. The others, running true to form, justified the time expended by penning fictitious reports, claiming attacks on Grimsby, Lincoln, and Louth in Lincolnshire. This raid did provide one disturbing feature. The British Observer Corps admitted that it was impossible to spot the one Zeppelin that crossed the coast because of the altitude at which it had been flown—20,000 feet. It was also admitted that the raiders had nothing to fear from the night-flying fighters as none then in Home Defence service could reach such a ceiling.

But this viewpoint is not clear, as the Bristol Fighter had a ceiling of 20,000 feet. The D.H.4, then available to Home Defence, was capable of 22,000 feet when powered with the Rolls-Royce Eagle engine, and between 18,000 and 19,500 feet with alternate power plants. Various types of the S.E.5, a single-seater, were capable of ceilings of 17,000 to 20,000, and the Sopwith Triplane could be taken up to 20,500 feet in about twenty minutes.

But the Germans had their troubles, too, for they had not yet conquered all the hazards of high-altitude flying. As stated before, instruments froze, rudder cables went slack and slipped off their pulleys, and the compressed oxygen equipment for breathing was far from satisfactory. The oxygen situation was most serious at times as some of the crew could not adapt to it, some were nauseated, while others moved about completely helpless and most apathetic toward their vital duties.

As related in a previous chapter, the compressed oxygen was replaced by liquid air, and once this situation seemed to be under control, Strasser lined up another raid for September 12 but stormy weather kept his ships in their sheds. Finally, by September 24 he decided to take advantage of a weather report that promised some hope of success, so nine airships were sent out to attack England—middle or north.

This raid was little better than the previous one, for only Ehrlich aboard war-weary LZ.35 made much of a penetration. He tried to hit Sheffield but a head wind forced him to give up that idea, so he turned south and went after what looked like a battery of blast furnaces. These lights were a steel works and a colliery north of Rotherham, but Ehrlich became confused and dropped his bombs in a line, succeeding in breaking only a few windows and knocking down a wall. What the other raiders accomplished is difficult to assess, but the total damage totted up by the British came to only £2210.

But persistent as ever, Strasser, on the morning of October 19, 1917, put in calls to Nordholz, Tondern, Ahlhorn, and Wittmundhaven bases, ordering thirteen Zeppelins to rendezvous for an attack on middle England, particularly in the Sheffield, Manchester, and Liverpool areas. The aircraft concerned were LZ.42, LZ.51, LZ.53, LZ.45, LZ.54, LZ.41, LZ.44, LZ.46, LZ.47, LZ.50, LZ.55, LZ.49, and LZ.52.

Once more Strasser planned blindly with little knowledge

of actual weather conditions, relying mainly on what weather maps could be provided by his Meteorological Station at Ostend. He did not know that a deep depression over Iceland was moving inexorably toward the British Isles and bringing north to northeast winds of gale force. In fact, just before his airships left, Strasser radioed their captains, "The weather conditions are good; go right into the interior, and good luck!"

LZ.42 and LZ.51 were lucky. They were held in their Nordholz shed by a strong cross wind, but by 1:54 P.M., October 19, the eleven others were airborne and heading for a historic disaster.

Once they were over the eastern section of the North Sea the airship commanders found a flat calm, particularly in the vicinity of Norderney Light. They did encounter several thunderstorms but skirted them safely. Some ships reported light southwest winds over the German Bight, but because of the temperatures—15 degrees Fahrenheit—at 11,500 feet, LZ.52 jettisoned all water ballast without antifreeze, and continued west at 13,000 feet. Another encouraging weather report came from Strasser at Ahlhorn: "Weather especially favorable for Central England. Winds, German Bight, west to southwest. To westward, moderate west to northwest currents up to high altitude."

But airships that had flown to 16,000 feet were already finding far different conditions. The wind had veered to the north and was freshening. Kapitänleutnant von Buttlar aboard LZ.54 soon abandoned the plan to attack Sheffield or Manchester. He claimed afterward that he had crossed inland south of the Humber and that he had dropped his bombs on Derby and Nottingham. By 3:35 A.M. he was returning and was in sight of Den Helder. Buttlar had actually crossed the Norfolk coast near Happisburgh and his bombs on "Derby and Nottingham" fell in open fields near Colchester and Ipswich. He never knew how lucky he was, for a B.E.2c out of Yarmouth almost caught up with him, but after trailing him some twenty miles out to sea the pilot had to give up and return.

By 7:00 P.M. *LZ.46,* under Hollender, was at 19,400 feet and steering NNW by compass, but actually flying southward past The Wash, so strong were the north winds at that altitude. Hollender then decided to attack Norwich and claimed to have dropped 4900 pounds of bombs on that city, but they too fell near Happisburgh doing no damage. Hollender fought his way out and had to cross over Holland, and on coming down through the clouds found himself over the Ruhr industrial area where German antiaircraft fire sent him back into the clouds. He was most fortunate to reach Ahlhorn by 1:00 P.M. the next day.

Kapitänleutnant Michael von Freudenreich in command of *LZ.47* was also making his way home across Dutch territory after an abortive attempt to raid Scarborough. This officer had a dreadful night, being carried south past Sheffield, or so he thought, but never in a position to bomb anything of importance. As had Buttlar and Hollender, he bombed all sorts of areas in the belief he was battering important industrial cities, all the while trying to figure where he was. One radio bearing had him over Ostend, so he went down to 3300 feet and avoided the gale and was able to proceed northeast until 3:30 A.M. when both after engines quit for lack of fuel. The forward engine went out next with a broken radiator pipe when he was drifting over Dutch territory and came under Dutch rifle fire. He got the engines going again, and scrambled along the Frisian Islands, finally landing at Ahlhorn at 12:40 P.M. with only ninety gallons of fuel in his tanks.

This was the general pattern of the raid. Some airships did roam far inland and had to make their way home across France. For instance, *LZ.41,* skippered by Hauptmann Kuno Manger, struggled to 9500 feet while crossing the North Sea, but by 6:30 P.M. had to nose up to 15 degrees into the wind to make any headway over Britain. He went inland over Spurn Head at 7:45 P.M. and by that time had climbed to 16,400 feet and started for Manchester. To make any headway westerly he had to steer northwest, and then NNW, but even then *LZ.41* was carried in a south-westerly direction. When Manger thought he was over Sheffield by 10:00 P.M., he was actually over Derby, thirty-seven miles southward.

Realizing the wind was increasing, Manger decided, nevertheless, to try for Sheffield, and by 11:45 thought he had reached Manchester. He was on the outskirts of Birmingham, however, and was fortunate in accidently selecting the Austin Motor Works, located at Longbridge, where he caused some damage.

By this time he felt the strength of the northerly gale, and did his best to get away, and still hold a safe course for home. Steering ENE the 45-per-mile-hour wind drove him southward so that *LZ.41* left England at a point just north of Dover. Once out over the English Channel Manger brought her down to 8500 feet, but thinking some warships were firing at him, he took her back to 16,400 feet. Still trying his northeasterly course he next found himself being driven stern first on a southeasterly direction over northern France, and by 5:50 A.M. was floundering over the Western Front at La Bassée. Knowing that he could come under aeroplane attack, Manger radioed the Flanders naval station to send out a plane to escort him through this dangerous area. A two-seater was provided and Manger managed to cross the line and head for Brussels. He brought his craft down to 3300 feet, made a turn to the north at Aachen, and finally nosed into Ahlhorn at 3:08 P.M. but damaged his forward gondola with a hard landing. He had been in the air more than 26½ hours.

LZ.53, under Kapitänleutnant Prölss flew an aimless course all over Britain and was so uncertain in his wanderings he did not draw up a chart to go with his flight report. He thought he had bombed Birmingham when he had actually dropped his contribution near Herne Bay on the south shore of the Thames Estuary. Later, when he thought he was over London, he was tracked over Arras on the British front in France. He was lucky to pick up reliable radio bearings and eventually make a safe landing at Nord-holz.

The other airships, battered and harassed by various forms of engine trouble, experienced many of Prölss' vicissitudes and were driven across France. LZ.52, under Oberleutnant Kurt Friemel, went inland at Theddlethorpe south of The Wash, headed for Sheffield through a layer of mist, failed to reach Sheffield, so turned east to bomb Norwich, or in fact any southeast coastal town. Shortly after 10:00 he was over Northampton, but a short time later found himself close to what he took to be the eastern defenses of London where he said guns opened up and searchlights probed, so he dropped all of his bombs. Twenty-six of them were traced near Hertford and Waltham Marshes, but they inflicted little damage.

As Friemel passed east of London he was pursued by a Royal Flying Corps B.E.2c, but the pilot could not gain enough altitude to make an attack. Meanwhile LZ.52 headed across the Channel and went inland at Boulogne, passing over the Allied trenches at Saint-Dié southeast of Verdun. Descending to 3300 feet Friemel saw he was over Worms, and so decided to head for Ahlhorn, instead of trying for his home base at Wittmundhaven.

Airships LZ.55 and LZ.47 made vain attempts to attack "important cities," but spent most of the night battling the northerly gale. They staggered into the outer London defense areas, dodged the searchlights and evaded the gunfire until they had delivered their bombs, and then anxiously turned for home. Kurt Flemming, aboard LZ.55 was leaving Hastings at 11:20 P.M. At 3:30 A.M. his forward engine failed, and then both after engines quit with burned-out exhaust valves. The radio generator went with these engines, silencing the main transmitter, and the battery-operated set could not reach any German station. So Flemming started emergency measures and prepared to jettison any loose equipment. At 4:00 A.M. guns below LZ.55 were firing leading her skipper to believe he was over Dover when in fact he was drifting along the Western Front between Reims and Saint-Quentin. As dawn arrived, Flemming went up to 19,700 feet at which point his port amidships engine failed. At 8:40 A.M. the lookout spotted two planes, although they were well to the north and at a low altitude, Flemming took LZ.55 to 24,000 feet, at that time a record for any airship.

By 10:45 A.M. Flemming was completely lost. He thought he was over Aachen when he was over Darmstadt 125 miles ESE of Aachen. From here he steered NNE by his compass, hoping to be over Ahlhorn in a short while. At 2:40 P.M. he went down through heavy clouds, fully expecting to see the town of Hamm, but instead found a broad stretch of woodlands, and heavy rain squalls. One of his officers using binoculars saw a small railroad station and read the name "*Immelborn*" which indicated they were over Thuringia, 200 miles southeast of their base. Knowing he had fuel for about two hours' flight, Flemming decided to make an emergency landing. LZ.55 was brought down hard at 6:16 P.M. in a clearing near Tiefenort on the Werra River. There was considerable damage; the forward and aft gondolas were torn away, propellers were smashed, and the main framework bent and broken. The crew had completely dismantled the airship by October 31.

The aforementioned dirigibles, though suffering damage in the unpredicted storm, were fortunate, for there were far grimmer results before the night was over. Franz Stabbert in LZ.44 never returned. As mentioned before, Stabbert, when aboard LZ.20, escaped with his life about eighteen months previously, but on this occasion his number was up.

From all accounts LZ.44 crossed over The Wash at 8:30 P.M. and headed for Bedford and bombed an engineering works with no spectacular success. He then turned southeast and at 10:40 P.M. dropped ten bombs, one a 660-pounder that fell near Leighton Buzzard. From there Stabbert headed for, and passed east of London, and by 12:30 A.M. was out to sea near Folkestone. At this point he was very close to LZ.52 as both airships were being blown southeast across France, but the dawn found *LZ.44* forty miles inside the Allied line.

Stabbert must have realized his plight, but he tried to break through and reach his own area. As he approached the trenches French seventy-fives opened up and Stabbert took his ship from 12,000 to 19,000 feet, but at 7:45 A.M. an incendiary shell scored a direct hit. *LZ.44* caught fire and went down, nose first, enveloped in flames.

LZ.49 and *LZ.50* were hopelessly adrift, and their crews exhausted. They may have been following *LZ.44*, as both airships were close behind when Stabbert's ship went down. Kapitänleutnant Hans-Karl Gayer in *LZ.49* had waited out at sea in total darkness with one engine out of commission, and had crossed the British coastline at Norfolk where he claimed later to have bombed two batteries, two flying fields, and a railroad station. *LZ.49*'s bombs were actually dumped in farm areas west of Norwich where they killed a few barnyard animals and damaged some sheds. Then two more engines failed, mainly because the mechanics were air-sick and could not service their charges. At 10:20 Gayer left The Naze, circled over the Kentish coast and headed out over the Channel from Folkestone, and by 12:40 A.M. was over Cape Gris Nez, but thought he was over the Dutch coast. Flying with only two engines in operation, *LZ.49*'s crew saw Stabbert's airship and followed it until Stabbert's ship went down in flames.

Thinking that *LZ.44* had been shot down by Dutch anti-aircraft guns, Gayer turned back toward the west and then went down to 6500 feet to try to pick up a reliable identification point. *LZ.49* was then suddenly attacked by five Nieuport Scouts of N.152 Escadrille, a French squadron known as the Crocodiles because of their insignia. The Nieuports carried only tracer and regular ammunition, so failed to torch the Zeppelin, but their attack was enough to convince Gayer he had no chance of getting home, so he brought his airship down in the woods on the bank of a river near Bourbonne-les-Bains. Once down, the exhausted crew crawled out of their gondolas and tried vainly to set fire to their airship, but had no luck, and soon all of them were disarmed and taken prisoner.

It has been said that *LZ.49*, before being dismantled and stowed away, was carefully examined and a complete set of plans drawn that were distributed to all Allied powers, and, furthermore, America's first rigid airship, *Shenandoah*, was designed on basic plans of *LZ.49*.

A few hours later another Zeppelin fell near Bourbonne-les-Bains. This was *LZ.50*, commanded by Kapitänleutnant Roderich Schwonder. This dirigible first lost an engine over the North Sea on the way out, and another quit over England, so the radio was useless. After his release from a French prison cell, Schwonder said he thought he had bombed Grimsby and Hull, but because of the gunfire encountered decided later he must have been over London. The truth was *LZ.50* had been tracked over Norfolk where it turned back and went out over the sea and cruised about north of Harwich. No one knows where his bombs fell, but he was next picked up at 9:50 P.M. southeast over France. Schwonder was still uncertain where he was. At one time he crossed the front-line trenches and wandered into German-held territory near Valenciennes, but made no effort to head for home. Instead, *LZ.50* must have drifted back into French territory somewhere near Reims, from where she turned west until she reached Provins at 3:50 A.M. and then cruised about over Lorraine. At 6:00 A.M. Schwonder, peering through a hole in the cloud cover, decided he was over Holland, but he saw *LZ.44* going down in flames. He immediately reversed his course and flew west for two hours in broad daylight. From this time on Schwonder's chart is unbelievable, for he seems to have flown in all directions, until he saw a strange-looking railroad car and a cafe called Cafe du Centre, and knew he was in trouble. After a vain effort to fly eastward with his three remaining engines, he realized his task was hopeless, and on seeing another Zeppelin draped across woodlands below, Schwonder decided to destroy his ship by "diving her vertically into the ground from 6500 feet to crumple her bow." Schwonder may have tried that. He did fly LZ.50 at high speed into the ground, but not from the vertical. The control car was ripped away, and several men leaped from the other gondolas. Schwonder was knocked out by the engine telegraphs and came to in time to see LZ.50 drifting off several hundred feet in the air. His crew vainly fired signal pistol cartridges at the hulk to put it to flames, but the battered airship suddenly nosed up to 45 degrees and disappeared carrying four of the unfortunate crew with her. For the rest of the day the German derelict sailed south with the wind while numerous French airmen vainly tried to reach her and pot the cells with incendiary ammunition. LZ.50 was last seen heading out to sea at Fréjus at 6:30 P.M. It is presumed she finally went to her finish somewhere in the Mediterranean, but Schwonder and fifteen of his crew were safe, and of course were interned in a French prison camp.

Kapitänleutnant Waldemar Kölle took LZ.45 on a wild sightseeing tour as his contribution to the raid, and from all accounts his flight included everything from Denmark to the Riviera by way of London and Paris, within twenty hours.

Intending to strike at Sheffield, Kölle soon identified the unpredicted gale. His LZ.45 was blown southward with the other airships. There was considerable cloud cover and no fixed points could be discerned. Bearings could not be obtained, and he apparently drifted about seeking an area he might identify as British industrial works. Kölle spotted searchlights, and saw guns fired, so dropped a few bombs that fell on Northampton where a woman and two children were killed. Kölle explained afterward that he was certain he had bombed Oxford, and with that decided to head for London, but could find none of the general glare, gunfire, or searchlight beams. So by 11:30 P.M. his navigator sensed that they had been driven far south by the gale, and with that Kölle dropped a number of his bombs, most of which fell in the northwest sector of London, and in fact accounted for the most damage of the whole raid.

Batteries on the outskirts of the city opened up, and this gunfire assured Kölle that he was dead over the center of the city. He dropped more bombs, and a 660-pounder fell in Camberwell and another near Piccadilly Circus where it blew out the windows of several well-known shops, and killed seven people. Other 660-pounders demolished a number of small houses in Hither Green where fourteen people were killed and nine injured.

Knowing exactly where he was, Kölle next tried to work his way eastward, and was doing so well he might have reached home safely, had he not had an unfortunate encounter with Second Lieutenant T. B. Pritchard who was aloft in a B.E.2c over the Medway. The R.F.C. pilot had reached 13,000 feet when he spotted *LZ.45,* and he started firing at the dirigible that seemed to be about 2000 feet higher. The Zeppelin nosed up hard and tried to run south before the gale.

Kölle then had engine trouble. Plugs had fouled, and weary, frozen-fingered mechanics could not clean them in time to keep the radiators from freezing. Their joy in having scored so well against London, was replaced by dread and anxiety. The cold was intense at their altitude. In fact, they were so high the earth below was scarcely visible, and it was difficult to learn whether they were moving over water or small cloud formations. From all sections of the airship came reports of frostbite, airsickness, and weariness that left men leaning immobile against the fuel tanks. As the hours went by these conditions worsened, the gale drove the airship past Amiens, Compiègne, and Auxerre. With the dawn the forward engine stalled with loss of fuel, caused by a leak the fuel tender had missed. He was flat out with airsickness.

Kölle thought for a time that he was over Germany, but when he went down to make certain, French antiaircraft guns opened fire and forced him to a safer altitude. He crossed Lyons in broad daylight, but the enemy guns could not touch him, and he made good time across the mountainous country to the south. He was heading toward Switzerland when a third engine failed, owing to a frozen radiator.

Harried by the gale and with the power of but two engines, LZ.45 drifted south, and then it was learned that she had fuel for only one more hour of flight. Kölle then crossed Sisteron at 11:00 A.M. and headed for the shallow bed of the Bueche River, intending to force-land. All went well until he made his first approach when an eddy forced the airship against a rock that tore off the port amidships gondola. LZ.45 rose, drifted down the valley and became stranded on an island in the middle of the river. Kölle ordered his crew out and told them to start firing signal cartridges into the hulk which soon went up in a great burst of flame. The men then waded the stream and surrendered to French soldiers who were guarding German prisoners engaged in agricultural work. While they were being lined up, the crew of LZ.45 saw Schwonder's LZ.50 drifting overhead to her eventual grave in the Mediterranean.

There is no reliable record of how Strasser received this disaster, but the effect on the whole airship personnel must have been staggering. It is quite possible that had the Leader of Airships gone on this raid he might have recognized early the danger of the development of the northeast gale, and ordered his ships home before any damage could have been done. But whether Strasser was ready to admit defeat is debatable.

On the other side of the picture, officials responsible for the defense of Britain were the first to see they had been lucky and that next time, with more favorable weather, the Zeppelin captains might score with impunity. What could ground guns do to airships flying at 19,000 feet? What could the available aeroplanes do under these circumstances? During this so-called "Silent Raid" in which the guns around London were supposed to have been muzzled so as to provide no guidance for the Zepps, no less than seventy-three pilots were sent aloft, but not one was equipped with an aeroplane that could reach the heights of the new Zeppelins. All that had saved London that night was an unpredicted gale, and the extreme conditions suffered by the airshipmen at those altitudes.

XIII

DISASTER ENGULFS STRASSER

Early in 1917 a memorable effort was made to bring military supplies to General Paul von Lettow-Vorbeck who, with a few white troops and some natives, was still holding out against the British in German East Africa. After considerable planning it was agreed that the Naval Airship Service might attempt to fly medicines and munitions to this tiny East African force; a flight that could improve the prestige of the whole German Navy.

From an airship base at Yanboli, Bulgaria, the southernmost point in the territory still held by the Central Powers, the distance to Mahenge in Von Lettow-Vorbeck's area was 3600 miles. To cover this distance an airship would require a still-air range of 4350 miles, and moving at forty miles per hour, under four engines, she possibly could make the trip in 108 hours, or 4½ days. The proposed cargo would weigh sixteen tons, and would require a craft of 2,365,000 cubic feet capacity. For a time it was hoped a special ship could be built for this flight, but as the East African situation worsened, it was decided to take LZ.57, lengthen her to take two more 15-meter gas cells, and put her in charge of a less experienced captain who could be spared from the more vital operations across the North Sea. Kapitänleutnant

Ludwig Bockholt was selected, and the whole venture worked out under the code name "China Matter."

By September 26 LZ.57 had been modified for the flight and in fact had made her first test flight. In this configuration—743 feet long and carrying 2,418,700 cubic feet of hydrogen—she was at that time the largest airship ever built, but LZ.57 proved to be difficult to handle. She was underpowered, and more trial flights were made. She was then flown from the Zeppelin factory to Jüterborg, fifty miles south of Berlin, where she was fully loaded with eighty-five cases of medical supplies. On October 7, 1917, Bockholt decided to make his final full-speed trial, and ordered the airship out of her shed for that purpose, ignoring the warnings of an approaching low-pressure area. He thought he could take off, do a two-hour test flight and be back in his shed before the storm broke.

He failed to make it. LZ.57 was wrecked, the airship caught fire and with it went the cargo of precious medical supplies destined for Von Lettow-Vorbeck's East African force. Bockholt took full blame for the disaster, but was soon given command of LZ.59 that was remodeled and assigned to the East African flight. She was ready late in October, and fighting against time, Bockholt had her fueled and loaded with fifteen tons of military cargo and set off for Yanboli.

After an air journey of twenty-eight hours LZ.59 arrived at the Bulgarian airfield at noon on November 4. Eleven days later Bockholt made his first attempt to continue on to Africa, but he ran into an inversion condition and had to drop so much ballast there was no possibility of continuing. He tried again November 16 and was halfway across Asia Minor when he ran into a severe thunderstorm and once more had to jettison valuable ballast and turn back.

By this time the East African force was being harried and attacked while gradually falling back before superior troops that were well equipped. The month lost after the breakup of LZ.57 was the measure of defeat or victory. Back at Yanboli LZ.59 was loaded with 20,200 pounds of ballast and

48,000 pounds of gasoline, bringing the cargo weight to 98,900 pounds in excess of the crew and their provisions. On the morning of November 21 the airship was walked out of its shed, and in cloudy, freezing weather, started once more on her mission of rescue.

She made good time southward, crossed Adrianople (Edirne) in European Turkey, steered for the Sea of Marmara, reached Asia Minor and followed a railroad into Smyrna (Izmir). The course continued from the Turkish coast for Lipsos Strait and then on to the island of Crete where Bockholt encountered black clouds and thunderstorms. The ship was decorated with St. Elmo's fire, but weathered this and came out with the North African coastline ahead. During the electrical storm Bockholt had wound in his wireless aerial and so had failed to receive important messages from Berlin that explained the British had scored a final victory over Von Lettow-Vorbeck. The German Naval Staff announced that it no longer could be responsible for the mission, and ordered Yanboli to recall LZ.59. The officials at Yanboli did their best, but could not make contact with Bockholt, and suggested he be called from Nauen in eastern Germany where there was a powerful radio station. The operators tried all through the night of November 21 to get through to LZ.59, but had no success, and Bockholt continued on ignorant of the general situation he had set out to relieve.

He crossed the African coastline near Mersa Matrûh and faced the wastes of the Libyan Desert where heat turbulence from the dunes below made many an experienced crewman violently airsick. The big airship bored on, crossed the Dakhla Oasis, the journey a tribute to Bockholt's navigation over the trackless desert. One engine went out when a reduction-gear housing cracked, and the loss of this plant eliminated the prospects of radio transmission, although wireless messages could be received.

Finally, shortly after noon of November 23, the Nauen radio station made contact with Bockholt and ordered him to break off the operation, and return to Yanboli. At that time LZ.59 was 125 miles due west of Khartoum.

That order set up an anticlimax. The men who had endured the gaseous effect from canned food, preserved ham and sausages, midday temperatures of 82 degrees and 14 above zero at night, lost all interest in their own safety. The four engines had to be turned on and off to conserve fuel, and to keep them from breaking up. They encountered thunderstorms once more, but LZ.59 somehow returned to Yanboli after having been in the air for 95 hours, or nearly four days. She had covered 4200 miles and still nosed into her shed with 19,900 pounds of fuel, enough to have kept her in the air for another 64 hours. Whatever his luck, it must be admitted that Ludwig Bockholt contributed much to the cult of the airship, and the science of lighter-than-air navigation.

But no one had expected LZ.59 to return after she had reached Von Lettow-Vorbeck, and now that she was safely down in Bulgaria no one knew exactly what to do with her. Another African flight was out of the question, but there was a plan to have her carry arms to the beleagured Turkish Army of Enver Pasha in Yemen, Arabia. Nothing came of that, and someone thought LZ.59 might be used for mine-searching flights off Constantinople, but weather conditions in that area forbad any detailed operations.

After a few abortive attempts to carry out a number of pointless patrols, a few bomb-dropping forays, and reconnaissance flights, LZ.59 took off from Yanboli for the last time. Bockholt planned to attack the British naval base at Malta, and he proceeded across the Balkans to the Strait of Otranto, but what happened on this trip will never be known.

On the evening of April 7 a German submarine, UB-53, saw an airship following in its wake. The skipper, an Oberleutnant Sprenger, reported that he watched her fly at about 700 feet, so close in fact the details of the gondolas could be seen clearly. A few minutes later, Sprenger noted two bursts of fire in the air, and shortly after a gigantic flame enveloped the airship and it finally nosed down and fell into the water. No claims were made by either the British or the Italians, so it was presumed LZ.59 had suffered an accident, and had set up her own destruction.

Trouble and disaster were stalking Peter Strasser to his doom. He had lost five out of eleven Zeppelins during his last raid on England, despite the fact his new craft were capable of remarkable altitude performances. But he knew that though he could get his aircraft to 20,000 feet, the Maybach HSLu engines were not capable of maintaining their rated power at these levels, and were unable to drive the dirigibles against the powerful gales of the sub-stratosphere.

For months now, some effort was made to produce a suitable high-altitude engine that would meet these new conditions. The Maybach MB IVa engine was provided with oversize cylinders, aluminum pistons, and an improved compression ratio. It was hoped these engines would turn out 142 horsepower at levels over 19,000 feet.

When LZ.58 was equipped with a set of these new Maybachs Strasser was charged with fresh optimism, as this airship not only put on sixty-seven miles an hour at sea level, but at 19,700 feet could still produce a speed of sixty miles an hour. He then appealed to Admiral Scheer to have all new airships furnished with these power plants. It was agreed eventually that the next ten Zeppelins would be so equipped, and many of the older dirigibles would be powered with the new MB IVa engines.

While all this was taking place the German direction-finding equipment that played false with many airship captains, was modified and improved. Two new stations were set up at Cleve and Tondern that were to transmit directional signals on a regular schedule fifteen minutes before and after each hour. An airship navigator could determine his bearing from each station by using his own radio receiver and the long trailing antenna, but with no special equipment except a stop watch and Great Circle charts.

The British could no longer track the Zeppelins, as the ships would not be making requests for bearings. The system could still be used if the airship's transmitter was out of order.

With these general improvements Strasser planned to renew his raids on England, although for the time being he was forced to limit his forays to important naval reconnaissance. Daily patrols were made over the German Bight all through December of 1917, and then the New Year brought in a series of storms and periods of bad weather that kept the airships in their sheds, but this inaction only gave Strasser time to plot new raids on Britain in the next favorable period of the moon. As he waited he had his crews and ground personnel check the airships, engines, and gondolas and have them in readiness for future raids.

It was on January 5, 1918, during one of these periods of ground activity that conditions were set up that brought on a new disaster. Maintenance men were all over the airships, electric cables that fed hand lamps ran in every direction through apertures and openings. Men swabbed out the bottoms of gondolas, mechanics scraped and painted. Everything was checked, tightened, adjusted, and prepared for the next raid. Shed I at Ahlhorn housed LZ.51, and LZ.47 was on the other side of the hangar. LZ.58 lay in Shed II, and LZ.46 was in Shed III where she had been lying idle since December 21. Only in Shed IV that housed SL.20 was there any particular activity after the noon-hour roll call. The big Schütte-Lanz was having several breaks in her Ring 4 repaired.

Strasser was in his office talking over routine matters with Arnold Schütze when both men, looking out a window saw a large bright flame shoot up and break through the roof of Shed I. Schütze gasped, and before he could make for the door he saw his own Shed II go up. This was bewildering for these two sheds were two hundred yards apart. Then there were two heavy explosions, and Sheds III and IV collapsed with a roar. Within five minutes four hangars and five airships had been reduced to piles of flaming wreckage.

For a few minutes it was thought that an air raid had started the conflagration, but there were no aircraft in sight. No one knew how it started, but it was generally agreed later that a frayed light cable may have ignited a small pool of gasoline in the aft gondola of LZ.51 and that resulting explosions hurled pieces of metal sky high to drop down on the other sheds, triggering more explosions. There was some talk of sabotage, but this was never proved. All that was known was that this new disaster cost the Naval Airship Division ten men dead, thirty badly injured, and 104 slightly injured. Four civilian workmen were killed in the Schütte-Lanz hangar, and Kapitänleutnant Hollender suffered a broken leg, and never flew again.

With the coming of spring Strasser gathered what he had left, and continued his planning. A few minor raids were made against England, but with no startling results logged. Nuisance raids were frequent, but no real damage inflicted. During the night of April 4 Lieutenant C. H. Noble-Campbell of Number 38 Squadron flying a black-painted F.E.2b pusher, encountered LZ.62 in the Coventry-Birmingham area, and chased the airship for a full half hour, finally managing to get within firing distance. But instead of his destroying the Zeppelin, the British pilot was shot in the head by a German gunner in a gondola, and he had to make a fast return to his base at Coventry. This was the first and only time an attacking pilot was wounded in combat with a Zeppelin.

While Strasser continued to peck away at his old enemy, the Royal Navy was stepping up its minelaying operations in the German Bight. Eleven destroyers were added to the minefields in the south, while a British-American force was setting up a tremendous belt across the northern outlet to the North Sea to bar the U-boats from the Atlantic Ocean. The newly modified HMS *Furious,* equipped with a true flight deck, had joined the minelaying fleet working in the northern and eastern portions of the Bight. At the same time the Harwich Force was completing a plan whereby light cruisers would tow high-speed lighters, each carrying a large flying boat. The aircraft, usually F.2a boats, would be floated off and then take off from the surface of the sea.

On May 10, 1918, LZ.62 left Nordholz to patrol the north and after passing over some German surface craft, moved into a tower of cumulus cloud, and a few minutes later the seamen below heard a tremendous explosion, and LZ.62 came down in flames, and apparently broken in two.

This disaster has provided an argument that has not subsided for half a century. Strasser thought LZ.62 ran into a heavy electrical charge that either ignited some fuel or exploded a bomb. On the other hand the British gave full credit to Captain T. C. Pattinson (sometimes spelled Pattison) and Captain A. H. Munday who were in this area flying a twin-engined Felixstowe F.2a flying boat. The Admiralty monitoring station in Whitehall had picked up several airship wireless signals out of the Helgoland area and by 1:08 P.M. of that same day decided that a Zeppelin was heading west. The Royal Naval Air Service station at Killingholm was advised and the flying boat sent off to intercept.

This particular aircraft had a Porte type hull of great seaworthiness. It could stay in the air for 9½ hours, and the pilot could throw it about like a two-seater fighter of the period. It was powered by two Rolls-Royce 350-horsepower Eagle engines, and carried up to seven Lewis guns, mounted at four cockpit positions, and usually two 250-pound bombs set in racks below the lower wings.

Besides Pattinson and Munday there were a radio man and an engineer aboard, but as they were noncommissioned their names have not been given in any of the reports. According to Munday, they were about fifty miles NNW of Borkum Reef Lightship when they discovered a Zeppelin about one mile away. The F.2a was flying at 6000 feet and the airship was thought to be about 2000 feet higher.

As the flying boat approached, the Zeppelin dropped bombs and ballast and started to climb but the flying boat continued to pursue and finally opened fire with its forward and amidships guns.

The engagement took the flying boat to 11,000 feet and though the Zeppelin had reached 12,500 feet the British crew kept firing drums of explosive and tracer bullets until the propeller of the port engine of the Zeppelin came to a slow stop, and the airship turned hard to port. The firing continued and explosive bullets bounced into the gondolas and envelope. There was considerable smoke and the Zeppelin went off crabwise toward Holstein. Pattinson and Munday believed they had started the big dirigible on the way to its finish.

On the strength of this most British records claim that Pattinson and Munday were responsible for the destruction of LZ.62. It is, however, doubtful that the flying boat could reach the 11,000-foot level, for reliable data on the F.2a limits her ceiling to 9000 feet. According to German archives, the British flying boat had attacked LZ.56, not LZ.62. This statement was made by Kapitänleutnant Walter Zaechmar in command of LZ.56, who related he first sighted the flying boat when they were at least seven miles apart. Then, when Pattinson made a move toward the airship, Zaechmar took his dirigible up to 21,700 feet while the enemy plane continued to circle below in an attempt to climb after it. He declared that at no time was the flying boat at anything better than a 16,400-foot level, a statement the more bewildering as we are sure the F.2a had no such capability. Zaechmar also stated that if any shots were fired by Munday or Pattinson, none was noticed by the Zeppelin's crew.

But none of this helps explain the loss of LZ.62, and the years have done little to unscramble the confusion.

Routine patrols across the German Bight and occasional ventures into the U-boat blockade area off the British coast, went on through June and July. The flying boats, though carrying out valuable antisubmarine patrols were unable to compete with the high-altitude probes by the airshipmen, and while some shipboard aviation was made from the deck of the *Furious*, the men flying the single-seater aircraft were not successful in intercepting the enemy dirigibles.

There was no other future for the British but to plan to destroy the Zeppelins in their sheds before they could take to the air to carry out Strasser's plans. The hangars at Tondern just south of the border of Denmark were first selected for such an effort, for the airships operating from this base were in an excellent position to keep watch on the movements of Great Britain's Grand Fleet.

The first carrier strike in history against a land target was set for the summer of 1918, and late in June two flights of Sopwith Camel single-seaters were placed aboard *Furious*, and the pilots trained for such a raid. On June 29, this primitive carrier together with the 1st Light Cruiser Squadron and some accompanying destroyers, moved to a position off the Danish coast, but a series of unfavorable days forced an abandonment of the plan although no Zeppelins were in the air at the time.

On July 17 the same surface force moved out of Rosyth, and by next morning was steaming toward the Lyngvig light, but again inclement weather, including severe thunderstorms, forced another postponement. Then, early in the morning of July 19, *Furious* had moved to a position off the Schleswig coast from where she launched two flights of Camels (actually seven planes), each carrying two 50-pound bombs. Six of these aircraft reached Tondern and two Zeppelins were destroyed. The seventh aeroplane was trapped by bad weather and had to land in Denmark.

This early morning attack caught the Germans by complete surprise. At 4:32 A.M. a sentry at Scherrebeck, a village southeast of the Tondern base, reported three unidentified planes approaching, but before any steps could be made to prepare the defense, three Camels were diving on the sheds, their major target being what was known as the double-dock Toska hangar on the north which at the time housed *LZ.54* and *LZ.60*. A smaller shed accommodated the base captive balloon, while a third was being dismantled.

Boring in from 100 feet the Camels dropped three bombs on the Toska shed, and almost immediately the two big airships were in flames, and devouring the double hangar as well. One bomb hit the captive balloon shed, but no large damage was done beyond a few splinters in the base balloon. The three Camels then roared away at low level and finally climbed into some cloud cover. A few minutes later three more Camels appeared and boldly attacked the captive balloon shed. Two bombs went through the roof and set fire to the balloon inside, and four others fell on outside equipment. One hit a gas truck carrying hydrogen flasks, but none of them exploded. These three Camels also escaped before any ground fire could be organized. (The base had once been protected by five Albatros D-III fighters, but they had been withdrawn for use on a more active front, and it is possible British intelligence had learned of this.) It was reported later that although two airships, LZ.54 and LZ.60 had been totally destroyed, they had burned slowly, and the double hangar was damaged only slightly.

Only Captains W. F. Dickson and B. A. Smart of the seven pilots managed to return to *Furious,* but owing to the faulty design of the flight deck and high turbulence around the funnel and superstructure, it was impossible to hold the Camels on the landing deck. They had to ditch and be picked up by a destroyer. Because of bad weather four other pilots had to land in Denmark, and a fifth fell into the sea and was drowned.

The loss of LZ.54 and LZ.60 was another shocker to Strasser, but he refused to be daunted, and stated that the development of a new type of airship would quickly erase the setback. He remained secure in his faith in the Zeppelin and scoffed at any suggestion of doom. He was devoted to his airships, and to some extent to his men, but he made excessive demands on everyone under his command. Like Adolf Hitler, he was a bachelor, and the service was his whole life. Had he lived he could have become a flame-torched dictator, capable of leading the whole German nation to its doom. No one knew him completely, for no one could break through the physical hardness that seemed almost inhuman, and no one could understand how he could so completely repress his feelings.

Misfortune followed misfortune in the German Naval Airship Service, and Peter Strasser moved on to his fate, but he faced his fortune like a man, and died making one last effort aboard what was probably the finest airship produced during the war.

By August 1, 1918, about three months before the Germans made a plea for an armistice, they had been forced to call a halt in their aeroplane raids by Gothas. The tocsin of defeat began its deliberate beat with the failure of the March 1918 Push that was followed by the total breakup of the drive on Paris, now known as the Second Battle of the Marne; and the terrific defeat inflicted by the British before Amiens on August 8, which is still remembered as the "black day of the German Army."

But Strasser still refused to heed the writing in the sky, and argued that he now had his *LZ.70*, the first of a new type and believed to be the last word in high-altitude airships capable of attacking London. As noted previously, the Silent Raid of October 19, 1917, had seen the loss of nearly half of the airships taking part when they were swept up and taken over by a high-altitude gale that had driven them across France. This debacle had clearly shown the necessity for a larger airship with greater power for high speed and a high-altitude performance.

By mid-December of 1917 the German Admiralty had ordered four new airships that actually were only lengthened versions of the "Thirties," and could provide space for gas cells of 2,190,000-cubic-foot capacity.

Less than three months after the order was signed, *LZ.70* was completed, and made her first trial flight at Wilhelmshaven on July 1, 1918. Unquestionably, this was a beautiful airship with long, slender classic lines, and to add to this impression her control car and engine gondolas were comparatively streamlined and slung in closer to the main frame. Her useful load under standard conditions totaled 97,130 pounds of ballast, gasoline, oil, crew, and bombs. On raids against Britain this type was to carry a bomb load of well over 10,000 pounds.

The outstanding feature of *LZ.70*, beyond the fact that she held sixteen gas cells carrying 2,195,800 cubic feet of hydrogen, was her power output provided by seven engines, whereas earlier models carried but five. The new power plants were 245-horsepower, super-compressed Maybach MB IVa "altitude engines" that produced a total of 1715 horsepower. Placing one engine aft of the control car and two in a large center-line gondola aft was standard procedure in the "Thirties," but the remaining four engines were mounted in wing gondolas hung in pairs amidships. These additional power eggs were only twelve feet, five inches long; five feet, nine inches high; and about four feet wide. The engines measured six feet, two inches in length, so it can be seen there was not much room for the machinists assigned to the maintenance of these engines. It was impossible for them to stand upright. To save weight short exhaust stacks were installed, but they were far from efficient, and spewed showers of sparks and flame that could be seen from long distances.

There were other drawbacks to the *LZ.70* type airship among which were the gondola shutters that were designed to direct cold air to the engines, a feature that made conditions almost unbearable. The machinists were soon complaining of rheumatic pains after long flights. Several routine reconnaissance flights were made over the North Sea to work in the machinery and furnish crew-training. On one occasion an experimental bombing attack was made on the Harwich Force, but with no appreciable results.

LZ.70 was placed under the command of Kapitänleutnant von Lossnitzer, who it will be recalled had made an impassioned report on the strategic value of Zeppelins after his short period with the Baltic Airship Division. He was, in truth, an inexperienced Zeppelin captain for he had never flown against England, but on the strength of his eight "war flights" in the Baltic area he was selected by Strasser to command *LZ.70*, the finest airship in the service. This was another prime example of Strasser's favoritism. He always selected a man with a title rather than a commoner, regardless of relative experience or past performance. However, after selecting Lossnitzer to fly *LZ.70*, and lead the next raid on England, slated for August 5, Strasser willingly went along with him, although his superiors were not convinced the new airship was ready for a major attack. But Strasser insisted she was equipped with a brace of Becker 20-millimeter cannon that would easily outrange the British .303 machine guns, and so was capable of holding off any enemy aircraft.

British historians with a psychological turn of mind have felt that Strasser, knowing his war was lost, decided to embark on this hopeless, suicidal quest as a "worthy" ending to his career. Closer to the truth may be that the Leader of Airships, always overconfident of the capabilities of the dirigible, was blinded by the size and equipment of the new *LZ.70*, while still scorning the improvement of the British defenses. Also, he had not made a raid on England since April 12, 1918. His last was to be flown on August 5–6. There is no truth to one statement put out from Germany that Strasser had not planned to go on this raid, but had impulsively gone aboard Lossnitzer's ship at the last minute. Those who knew him well are positive he intended to take full command, and not send the inexperienced Lossnitzer off alone on such a task, his first raid on England.

London was not to be attacked unless Strasser so ordered, and the formation, headed by *LZ.70*, was made up of *LZ.53*, *LZ.63*, and *LZ.65* out of Nordholz. *LZ.56*, berthed at Wittmundhaven, was ordered to take off at 3:00 P.M. and join the others over the North Sea. Why this take-off was made is still a mystery, for the temperature on the ground at Nordholz was 75 degrees, the humidity was 85 per cent, and the barometer read 29.77 inches, conditions that made many wonder why Strasser took off at all. All the airships had to jettison much water ballast to make up for the loss in lift created by the atmospheric conditions.

All went well, however, and the assembly was completed by 3:12 P.M., but shortly after adverse weather created several flight problems. Flying at 16,400 feet over the North Sea when all crews were on the oxygen system, they found the usual low cloud cover below. The fresh winds, expected at high altitudes, failed to materialize, in fact the westerly wind decreased as they continued to climb higher. By 6:30 P.M. all the airships, now fairly close together, were within sixty miles of the English coast but it was still broad daylight. High temperature caused Kapitänleutnant Walter Dose in LZ.65 to drop even more ballast and some unfused bombs in his frantic effort to reach 17,700 feet, but the formation moved on and by 9:00 P.M. Strasser radioed a final order to attack "according to plan" from Karl 727 (a secret map designation). However, since all the airships had been tracked through this area pinpoint two hours before, it has been concluded that Strasser was already lost, or had been relying on faulty radio bearings.

Even worse, it was this short radio message that betrayed Strasser to his enemies, although LZ.53, LZ.65, and LZ.70 had all been spotted by coastguards stationed at the Leman Tail Lightship thirty miles north of Happisburgh on the Norfolk coast. At the time LZ.70 was in the lead, but after considering the telltale exhaust stacks of Lossnitzer's ship, both Dose and Prölss decided not to follow their beloved leader. They were wise and realistic, for within forty minutes of the call from the Leman Tail Light, activity at the Great Yarmouth air station went into high gear. Thirteen aeroplanes were in the air and ten of them formed a pattern inland to greet the invaders. Three flew out to sea to make an initial intercept before the Zeppelins could reach the English coast.

Leading this trio was Major Egbert Cadbury who had already downed LZ.21 almost two years before. With him was Captain Robert Leckie, the same Scot-Canadian who had shot down LZ.22 early in 1917. They were aboard a De

Havilland DH.4 two-seater bomber that, according to some historians, was capable of 136 miles per hour, and able to climb to 22,000 feet. Cadbury was the pilot and Leckie flew as gunner-observer. There is an interesting story concerning this arrangement, for it seems that when the call came through both Cadbury and Leckie made a dash for the one DH.4 left, and the Englishman, son of the famous cocoa and chocolate manufacturer, beat Leckie to the pilot's seat by a stride, and so these two Zeppelin aces were selected by fate for this memorable mission.

In the scramble at the Great Yarmouth station Lieutenant R. E. Keys and Private A. T. Harman had taken off first, having grabbed one of the two DH.4s. Cadbury and Leckie tore into the picture next, and believing, or perhaps hoping, that the report of Zeppelins indicated a major operation by the German High Seas Fleet, Cadbury decided to keep the two 100-pound bombs that were already in the racks under the wings. Next in order came Captain C. S. Iron and Sergeant Wills, flying a lower-powered aircraft, a DH.9, a real dog of an aeroplane. Captain B. S. Jardine and Lieutenant E. R. Munday, also in a "Nine" were the last to leave the station.

As Cadbury climbed into the clouds three German raiders were seen in the fading twilight, approaching the coast of England. He pulled the bomb plugs, and worked to gain much-needed height. By 10:20 P.M. Cadbury was up to 16,400 feet and found himself head-on near the lead Zeppelin. Leckie had no air sights on his gun and his first burst of five rounds passed to port of the airship, but the tracers continued to sparkle long after they had passed the dirigible. He fired again, and this time the Pomeroy was seen to blow a great hole in the fabric and the airship seemed to catch fire instantly. The flames ran along the side of the Zepp consuming the envelope in one great gulp. Within a few seconds LZ.70—for it was Lossnitzer's command bearing Peter Strasser—was falling through a large cloud layer. A few shots had been fired by the Becker cannon but they went wide of their mark.

The two airships flying behind LZ.70 saw their leader go down in flames, and they dumped ballast fast and turned away. Cadbury stayed upstairs and climbed after what proved to be LZ.65. Leckie fired a few rounds and thought he saw a glow from the amidships gondola, but that had been caused when a mechanic raised the blackout curtain before extinguishing the interior light. Then Leckie's gun jammed and LZ.65 scuttled off, eventually getting home. In vain Cadbury tried to hoik his nose high to get off a few shots from his fixed Vickers gun, but was unsuccessful. By this time Leckie who had scrambled aboard without gloves or flying coat was very cold and uncomfortable, so they decided to return, satisfied with their bag. They were fortunate in finding an aerodrome open at Sedgeford where they landed and discovered to their horror that one of the bombs they thought they had jettisoned was still hung up in the rack. Had it been jolted out when they landed both airmen and their machine would have been blown to atoms.

On sober reflection in later years Cadbury felt there would have been no great importance in destroying LZ.65 or LZ.53. "We might have killed 150 more gallant men, but that would not have brought the close of the war any nearer. The loss of LZ.70 must have been a great shock and should have clearly demonstrated the hopelessness of sending Zeppelins to attack England."

It was true. The other airships had seen LZ.70 go down, and they dropped their bombs through the clouds, none of them falling on land although the commander of LZ.65 claimed to have attacked King's Lynn, and LZ.53's skipper swore he had dropped explosives on Boston.

In Germany Strasser's handling of the raid was criticized severely, and he was especially berated for undue recklessness in allowing his fleet to approach the English coast at slow speed, at a comparatively early hour, and at a low altitude.

Whether Strasser knew where he was, or whether he thought he was flying into good Zeppelin weather will always be debated. Unquestionably, he used poor judgment in continuing his approach when he could clearly see he had no hope of approaching England without suitable cloud cover.

The wreckage of *LZ.70* piled up among the shallow sand banks off the Lincolnshire coast, actually falling close to the Hull trawler *Amethyst,* near which some of the Zepp's bombs had exploded. She went down like a "great golden cigar" and left a wide pool of gasoline on the water that burned for nearly an hour. Almost instantly a group of British intelligence officers were on hand to salvage signal books, cipher keys, and codes from the wreck, and for the next twenty-four hours British trawlers dragged wires beneath the wreckage and brought to the surface most of the important structure of the airship, including girders, gondolas, engines, propellers, gas cells, and outer cover. One tail fin was so complete it gave the British Admiralty and naval architects some idea of the novel cantilever section that eliminated drag-producing external bracing.

Several bodies of the crew, including that of Fregatten-kapitän Peter Strasser were recovered, and in his uniform pockets were found several "Secret" documents and a Summary of Operations of the North Sea Airships, all of which were of great interest to Admiralty intelligence. A dispatch case full of important papers was also salvaged.

Most of the bodies were finally recovered and buried at sea by Royal Naval burial parties, but one, that of an unknown airshipman still lies in Weybourne Cemetery near the village of Holt on the northern coast of Norfolk. It is believed to be that of Kurt Kruger, executive officer of *LZ.70.*

And thus a burned wreck of Germany's latest and finest airship was the tomb of Strasser's dream of conquering England by air power, and with his death came the conclusion of a fantastic history and the end of the Zeppelin as a military weapon.

Strasser's subordinates tried to carry on, but there was no service enthusiasm left. All airships were kept in their shed for nearly a week, and then, so as to forget the dismal past, routine scouting ventures were drawn up. On August 10, *LZ.52* and *LZ.63* were sent off. On the next day *LZ.56* lifted off from Wittmundhaven at 2:13 A.M. to make a patrol to the north, and *LZ.53* left Nordholz at 2:40 A.M. to make a scouting assignment from Terschelling to the Dogger Bank South Lightship.

Again disaster took a bloody hand.

On the evening of August 10, 1918, a British destroyer, HMS *Redoubt*, left her moorings at Harwich, towing an ungainly contrivance called a lighter. Actually it was simply a creaky old raft mounted on the gunwales of a bargelike hull. A Sopwith Camel biplane was perched on this precarious platform and taken out to sea. A young Anglo-Canadian-American, Stuart D. Culley, sat in the cockpit hoping this general collection of gadgets would enable him to clamber off this spray-sodden deck to attack a Zeppelin reported to be heading across the North Sea.

Surprisingly, this fantastic experiment worked, and the naval historians of the day recorded the first successful shipborne fighter interception. The enemy Zeppelin was destroyed, but more important, the marriage of the aeroplane and the surface vessel was consummated. Unlimited range was provided for the aircraft, and the firepower of the surface fleet was greatly increased. The fact that the first aeroplane had to land on the water near its mother destroyer was not important. The problem of retrieving carrierborne aircraft was eventually solved.

This incident has long been dismissed and forgotten. At the time only a few sage minds realized that the aeroplane had become a long-range naval weapon, that the dreadnought was no longer Mistress of the Seas, and that an amazing vessel, to be known as an aircraft carrier, would evolve from this historic experiment.

As we have noted, a few Zeppelins had been destroyed by aircraft, but in many cases the contact had been made more through good luck than the capabilities of the plane or the pilot. The great problem lay in the limited range of contemporary aircraft, as well as their inability to match the airship in gaining altitude. To counter these enemy advantages, Commander Sir Reginald Tyrwhitt of the British Harwich Force submitted the idea of improvising a form of launching platform from which fighter aircraft could be flown at the most favorable time.

Commander Charles Rumney Samson of the Royal Naval Air Service was the first to be approached with this idea. Having learned that naval flying boats had been hauled about the North Sea on lighters so as to extend their range of action, Samson agreed that a small, light, high-powered aircraft could be launched from a towed platform. The Sopwith Camel was chosen because at the time it was powered with a 150-horsepower Bentley rotary engine of high efficiency which could climb to 20,000 feet in approximately twenty minutes while carrying a full load of fuel, two machine guns, and four 20-pound fragmentation bombs. Her top speed was 115 miles per hour.

As was to be expected of such a flamboyant character, Commander Samson decided to make the off-the-lighter experiments himself. In his first attempt he removed the wheels from the Camel and substituted a set of skids that were designed to slide along a pair of shallow troughs built into the deck of the lighter. The aeroplane got off successfully in its first trial, but the Camel was too delicate of control for this ham-fisted exhibitionist, and she quickly spun into the sea. The aircraft was wrecked, but, as usual, the energetic one bobbed to the surface little the worse for the experiment. A short consultation with his staff convinced Samson that armored cars were more in his line, and that someone who had had deck-flying experience might handle the experiment more successfully.

To give him his former service rank, Sub-Flight Lieutenant Stuart D. Culley was born in Nebraska in 1895, the son of a Canadian mother and an English father. In 1916 he enlisted in Canada and was accepted by the Royal Naval Air Service, but on completing his flight training in England, he was transferred from the light cruiser *Cassandra* to the shore base at Great Yarmouth. Up till then his deck flying had been aboard early and most primitive carrier decks built over the hulls of converted cruisers or liners. In these operations Sopwith Pups were launched successfully, but no true deck landings had been carried out. The planes either landed on the surface of the sea, to be fished out, or were ordered to return to a nearby land base. In a few instances the landing gear was jettisoned to make these water landings less hazardous. Culley had had some experience in taking off from these seagoing platforms, but flying a powerful and very tricky aircraft off a platform only fifty-eight feet long and sixteen feet wide was something else.

Culley approached the experiment with an open mind, but wanted no part of the slide-and-trough contrivance Samson had designed; instead he retained the conventional wheeled undercarriage. A destroyer was to tow the lighter at thirty knots, and at the appropriate moment one of the lighter's crew would start the engine by swinging the prop. To offset any chance of his being blown overboard and sucked into the airscrew, the mechanic was lashed to the lighter deck by a safety belt and a cord that permitted him just sufficient reach to carry out his task. As soon as the Bentley was started, the mechanic pulled himself back with the safety line, unshackled the cordage and darted to the shelter of the lighter's deck. The aeroplane itself was launched by a conventional bomb-release gear operated from the pilot's cockpit. Steel cables were attached to the ends of the wheels' axle and run over simple claw pieces that allowed the plane to move forward freely at any time, but until Culley pulled the release toggle there could be no upward or backward movement. Amazingly enough, this impractical arrangement worked perfectly.

On August 1, 1918, Culley made his first trial off Great Yarmouth. The towing destroyer was HMS *Redoubt*, and the lighter was worked up to about thirty-six knots before Culley released the Camel and was airborne with scarcely any run over the deck. Once in the air he turned away and eventually landed safely at his shore base.

It was then agreed that a modification in the plane's armament might be worthwhile, and the two Vickers .303 guns mounted to fire through the propeller were discarded and a pair of lighter Lewis guns mounted on suitable brackets and placed on the upper side of the top wing. In this arrangement they could not be lowered to change the ammunition drums, and as each drum carried only ninety-seven rounds, Culley went into action with a total of only 194 bullets. Why this change was made, depriving the pilot of 1000 rounds provided by the Vickers fixed guns has never been clarified.

Nine days later, August 10, Commander Tyrwhitt, aboard the light cruiser *Curacoa*, took the whole Harwich Force of four light cruisers and thirteen destroyers out to sea to make an offensive sweep in the southeastern sector of the North Sea. *Redoubt* again hauled the lighter and its Camel fighter. Other destroyers towed lighters on which reconnaissance flying boats had been set up, and the cruisers of the force were burdened with CMBs (coastal motorboats) that were to attack German minesweepers operating off the Dutch coast.

At dawn on August 11 the CMBs were put overboard twenty-five miles northwest of Vlieland, and an attempt was made to launch the flying boats, but there was not enough wind to get them into the air. They had to be reloaded aboard their lighters and were finally returned to the harbor. As a result the six CMBs that were to have been escorted by the flying boats made their attacks off Terschelling but were intercepted by German seaplanes. Three of the CMBs were sunk in the action that followed, and the remainder limped back to safety areas along the Dutch coast.

While this air-surface action was taking place, Samson, Culley, and the lighter crew left the destroyer's deck and prepared to launch the Camel. It was reasoned that the Germans would investigate the activity of Tyrwhitt's force, and at 8:00 A.M. the Admiralty had monitored a signal that indicated a Zeppelin was cruising over the Helgoland

Bight. Thus alerted, every man in the force searched the sky, but Culley was the first to spot a great silver cigar cruising at about 10,000 feet. It was LZ.53, commanded by Kapitänleutnant Prölss, which had flown out of Nordholz early that morning to investigate this impudent intrusion by the Tyrwhitt flotilla.

Lieutenant Culley jumped into the cockpit of the Camel, and *Redoubt* worked up speed. A handsome young man was keeping a rendezvous with destiny, and a new factor of naval warfare was to be introduced. When the speed of the lighter had reached thirty knots, Culley checked his engine and gave Samson the conventional "thumbs-up" signal. At 8:41 A.M. the Camel leaped into the air after a run of less than five feet. Culley climbed straight over the stacks of *Redoubt,* saw the whole flotilla spread out before him, and for the first time probably realized he was the leading actor in this drama. Possibly no airman played to such a breathless audience, but when he looked up again, the Zeppelin was nowhere in sight.

Culley begged and pleaded for better luck, and within a minute or two the silver airship reappeared, and from that instant on, the young Canadian never took his eyes off the glinting gasbag. At 5000 feet she appeared to have changed very little—a disturbing thing—and the Camel pilot realized the enemy ship was climbing fast. He remembered that the Zeppelins of this "50" category were noted for their ability to gain height rapidly, but he stuck to his task, keeping a discreet distance. At 15,000 feet the controls of the Sopwith began to mush out and become sluggish. The Bentley gave one disturbing cough but soon picked up her rotary rhythm. Culley forced her up to 18,000 feet at which time he was positive the Zeppelin had altered course and was heading out to sea.

"I hoped she would try to scurry back to Germany," Culley said afterward. "I knew I would never head her off if she steered farther out to sea."

He continued to stalk the airship, but his hopes were dying, when suddenly the light changed and the silver raider appeared to be heading directly toward him. He figured, as near as he could, that she was a few hundred feet above his present level and approaching at a relative speed of 150 knots (meaning a combination of their two speeds), and he had to consider Samson's admonition to attack only from above.

"You must dive on her," his chief had ordered. "You must avoid any position behind or below the tail. Dive on her from above and then race past, just along her beam, to avoid any flames. If you fail in this method, dive on her from behind the port quarter. You perhaps will come under heavy fire so don't expend all your ammunition in the first attack. They are not likely to use the gun mounted on the top of the main frame, and you'll be able to get in closer by going in from above."

From Culley's position, and judging the speed at which the Zeppelin approached, it was immediately obvious that an attack from above and behind was out of the question. In a matter of seconds the great bulk of the Zeppelin loomed ahead. Culley could see the forward control car and the outboard gondolas, their propellers flailing like broadswords. For a short time he was spellbound by the gigantic spectacle, but as his eyes searched for any crew activity, his hand instinctively drew back on the stick, the nose of the puny biplane came up and she almost stalled.

Culley recalled later, "I can hardly remember doing all that and I only came to when I realized I was actually attacking that great thing. One gun operated beautifully and fired the complete drum without a slip-up, the other jammed after pooping off half a dozen rounds. By then I sensed I was about to stall out so I leveled off and raced along under the massive belly of the craft and then I saw something either fall or jump from a slit in the framework and disappear below."

(The object was the only survivor from LZ.53, and his parachute descent from about 19,000 feet must have been a record for those days. The man was seen later and picked up by a German destroyer.)

The instant Culley's guns stopped firing, and as the Camel faltered in her stall, she nosed down about 2000 feet before Culley could ease her out. During this time he lost sight of his target, but when he leveled off again and stared up he saw to his consternation that the Zeppelin was cruising along as though nothing had happened. He turned to make an adjustment to his throttle trying to regain the lost altitude, when a glint above caught his eye. At three widely separated points gushes of yellow flame slashed from the envelope and within a minute practically all of the airship, except the tail section, was enveloped. The giant conflagration burned itself out in a few seconds, leaving a blackened skeleton floundering in the sky. A flag fluttered pathetically from a rudder post as LZ.53 started her final dive. Culley saw the airship writhe and break her back before she hit the water. The clock on his instrument panel showed it was 9:41 A.M. Exactly one hour before he had become airborne from the bobbing lighter.

He had scored his "kill," but now a new problem arose. Valor and training had been devoted to the destruction of an enemy raider; now it was time to consider the possibility of a safe return. He knew there would be a number of German seaplanes in this area and they would have firepower, whereas one of his guns was empty, the other jammed. It was here that discretion replaced the spirit of valor. He opened the throttle wide, went into a fairly steep dive and headed for the area parallel to the coast of the Netherlands.

In a hurried arrangement, made just before he had bounced off the lighter, it was agreed that one of Tyrwhitt's ships would rendezvous with him in the vicinity of the Texel Lightship, but whether this plan could be carried out was mainly a matter of luck. So considering everything, Culley studied a small-scale map he had brought with him and tried to locate some outstanding landmark, hoping to find the Texel Light. While he was thus engaged his engine cut out and he knew he had used up the fuel in his main tank while struggling to get to the level of the Zeppelin.

He switched over to a small reserve tank and throttled back, holding just enough power to remain airborne.

He probed his way through a light coverlet of offshore mist and thought he could identify a couple of Dutch fishing vessels, but once he had eased down into the clear he was overjoyed to see they were British destroyers, and another look told him that the whole Harwich Force was in the vicinity.

Now he could pick and choose, but he selected the *Redoubt* which had towed his lighter, for he noted that they had stopped and were transferring the lighter's crew and lowering a whale boat. Culley put the Camel down so skillfully it was soon hoisted out of the water with little damage and placed back aboard the lighter. Some time later it was patched up and placed on exhibition in the Imperial War Museum in London, where it remains to this day.

Culley was awarded the Distinguished Service Order, although many men who were closely involved thought he should have been honored with Great Britain's highest military decoration, the Victoria Cross. The whole undertaking was an excellent example of the efficient co-operation between the Royal Navy and the then infant Royal Air Force, but one wonders how many men in either service realized at the time the full significance of that first successful air interception by a shipborne fighter aircraft.

The Zeppelins of the German Naval Airship Service never attempted to raid England, or fly scouting missions again.

BIBLIOGRAPHY

Cameron, James, *1914*, Rinehart & Company, 1959.

Churchill, Winston S., *The World Crisis, 1911–1918*, Thornton Butterworth, Ltd., 1923.

Dudley, Ernest, *Monsters of the Purple Twilight*, George G. Harrap, Co., 1960.

Duke and Lanchberry, *The Saga of Flight*, John Day Company, 1945.

Ellis, Frank H., *Canada's Flying Heritage*, University of Toronto Press, 1954.

Falls, Cyril, *The Great War*, Capricorn Books, 1959.

Golding, Harry, *The Wonder Book of Aircraft*, Ward, Lock & Co., Ltd., 1919.

Jackson, A. J., *De Havilland Aircraft*, Putnam & Company, London, 1962.

Jane, Fred T., *All the World's Aircraft*, Sampson Low, Marston and Co., 1919.

Joubert, Sir Philip, *Birds and Fishes*, Hutchinson, 1960.

Kemp, P. K., *Fleet Air Arm*, Herbert Jenkins, 1954.

Kerr and Granville, *The R.N.V.R.*, George G. Harrap, Co., 1957.

Lewis, Peter, *British Aircraft, 1809–1914*, Putnam & Company, London, 1962.

Monk and Winter, *Great Exploits in the Air*, Blackie and Son, Ltd., 1932.

Nielson, Thor, *The Zeppelin Story*, Allan Wingate, 1955.

Poolman, Kenneth, *Zeppelins Over England*, Evans Brothers, Ltd., 1960.

Pudney, John, *The Camel Fighter*, Hamish Hamilton, 1964.

Roberts, Leslie, *There Shall Be Wings*, Clarke, Irwin & Company, 1959.

Robinson, Douglas, *The Zeppelin in Combat*, Foulis & Company, 1962.

Saunders, Hilary St. George, *Per Ardua*, Oxford University Press, 1945.

Slessor, Sir John, *The Central Blue*, Cassell & Company, Ltd., 1956.

Smith, Sir John, *The Story of the Victoria Cross*, Frederick Muller, Co., 1956.

Sutton, H. T., *Raiders Approach!*, Gale & Polden, Ltd., 1956.

Thetford, Owen, *British Naval Aircraft Since 1912*, Putnam & Company, London, 1962.

Thetford, Owen, *Aircraft of the 1914–1918 War*, Harborough Publishing Company, 1954.

Vaeth, J. Gordon, *Graf Zeppelin*, Harper & Brothers, 1958.

INDEX

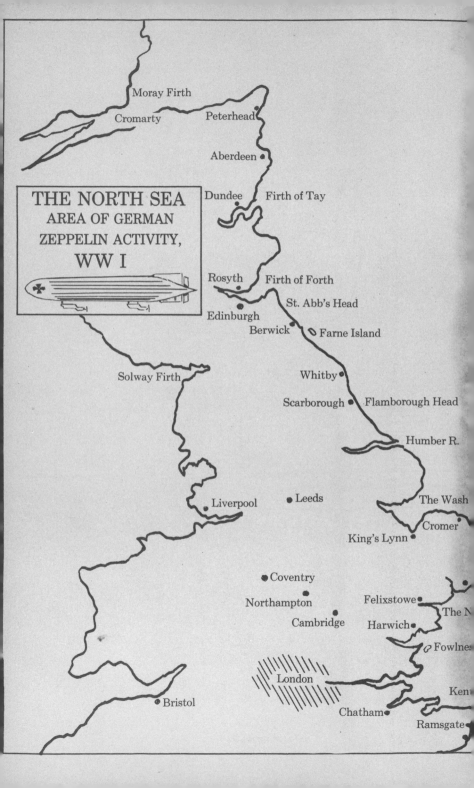

THE NORTH SEA
AREA OF GERMAN
ZEPPELIN ACTIVITY,
WW I

Moray Firth
Cromarty
Peterhead
Aberdeen
Dundee
Firth of Tay
Rosyth
Firth of Forth
St. Abb's Head
Edinburgh
Berwick
Farne Island
Solway Firth
Whitby
Scarborough
Flamborough Head
Humber R.
Leeds
Liverpool
The Wash
Cromer
King's Lynn
Coventry
Felixstowe
Northampton
The N
Cambridge
Harwich
Fowlnes
London
Ken
Bristol
Chatham
Ramsgate